SUBJECTS OF EXPERIENCE

CAMBRIDGE STUDIES IN PHILOSOPHY

General editor ERNEST SOSA

Advisory editors

JONATHAN DANCY   University of Keele
GILBERT HARMAN   Princeton University
FRANK JACKSON   Australian National University
WILLIAM G. LYCAN   University of North Carolina, Chapel Hill
SYDNEY SHOEMAKER   Cornell University
JUDITH J. THOMSON   Massachusetts Institute of Technology

RECENT TITLES

Subjects of experience

E. J. LOWE

University of Durham

Published by the Press Syndicate of the University of Cambridge
The Pitt Building, Trumpington Street, Cambridge CB2 1RP
40 West 20th Street, New York, NY 10011-4211, USA
10 Stamford Road, Oakleigh, Melbourne 3166, Australia

First published 1996

A catalogue record for this book is available from the British Library

Library of Congress cataloguing in publication data

Lowe, E. Jonathan
Subjects of experience / E. Jonathan Lowe.
p. cm.
Includes index.
ISBN 0 521 47503 1 (hardback)
1. Agent (Philosophy) 2. Self (Philosophy) 3. Subject
(Philosophy) I. Title.
BD450. L65 1995
126–dc20   95-15748 CIP

ISBN 0 521 47503 1 (hardback)

Transferred to digital printing 2003

Contents

Preface

The overall message of this book is the inadequacy of physicalism, even in its mildest non-reductionist guises, as a basis for a scientifically and philosophically acceptable account of human beings, as subjects of experience, thought and action. The book is organized in the following way. Chapter 1 is mainly a matter of scene-setting. Then, in chapter 2, I defend a substantival theory of the self as an enduring and irreducible entity, essentially a self-conscious subject of thought and experience and source of intentional action. This theory is unashamedly committed to a dualism of self and body, though emphatically *not* one along traditional 'Cartesian' lines, for I do not represent the self as being an essentially immaterial thing existing in some mysterious union with physical substance. Chapter 3 takes up the physicalist challenge to any robust form of psychophysical dualism and attempts to show how an attribution of independent causal powers to the mental states of human subjects is not only consistent with a naturalistic and scientific world-view, but also a great deal more plausible than various physicalist alternatives, whether reductionist, non-reductionist or eliminativist. Finally, chapters 4, 5, 6 and 7 examine in more detail the nature of the central capacities of the self – for perception, action, thought and self-knowledge – and once again the underlying theme is that a naturalistic approach can and must accord an indispensable and independent explanatory role to the conscious states, both experiential and volitional, of human subjects.

Some of the book's material has appeared in earlier versions elsewhere. In particular, I am grateful to the editors and publishers concerned for permission to reproduce here material from the following papers of mine: 'Real Selves: Persons as a Substantial Kind', in David Cockburn (ed.), *Human Beings* (Cambridge: Cambridge University Press, 1991), pp. 87-107; 'Substance and Selfhood', *Philosophy* 66 (1991), pp. 81-99; 'The Problem of Psychophysical Causation', *Australasian Journal of Philosophy* 70 (1992), pp. 263-76; 'Experience and its Objects', in Tim Crane (ed.), *The Contents of Experience: Essays on Perception* (Cambridge: Cambridge University Press, 1992), pp. 79-104; 'Self, Reference and Self-Reference', *Philosophy* 68 (1993), pp. 15-33; 'The Causal Autonomy of the Mental', *Mind* 102 (1993), pp. 629-44; and 'Perception: A Causal Representative Theory', in Edmond Wright (ed.), *New Representationalisms: Essays in the Philosophy of Perception* (Aldershot: Avebury, 1993), pp. 136-52.

I am also particularly grateful to the following individuals and members of the following Departments of Philosophy for helpful comments on previous drafts of various parts of the book, many of which were presented at one time or another as seminar or conference papers: Peter Carruthers, David Cockburn, Tim Crane, Roger Fellows, Irwin Goldstein, Andy Hamilton, John Heil, Susan Lowe, Graham Macdonald, Al Mele, David Oderberg, Anthony O'Hear, David Over, David-Hillel Ruben, Peter Smith and Edmond Wright, the Philosophy Departments of the Universities of Bradford, Durham, Liverpool, Nottingham, Sheffield, Stirling and York, of Davidson College, King's College London, the London School of Economics, and St David's University College at Lampeter. Finally, I owe a special debt of thanks to an anonymous reader for Cambridge University Press, who made many helpful suggestions for improving an earlier version of the book and raised several challenging queries which I have tried to address, not perhaps always at full enough length to do them complete justice.

1

Introduction

The central topic of this book is what would traditionally be called the 'mind-body problem'. In my view, however, part of what has historically generated a problem of this name is the very choice of these terms, 'mind' and 'body', to denote entities whose relationship to one another supposedly calls for explanation. I would prefer to speak of the *self*-body problem, for I do not wish to reify the 'mind' as an entity on a par with the body. Selves or persons 'have' both minds and bodies – but 'having' is not to be understood univocally for both cases. Selves 'have' minds inasmuch as they are essentially subjects of mental states – of thoughts, experiences, intentions and the like. But they 'have' bodies in a quite different and genuinely relational sense: for persons and their bodies are each distinct kinds of entity in their own right. Bodies (in the sense of the term now relevant) are organized material objects, capable of undergoing growth and change in their material parts, subject to the retention of certain basic characteristics of form and function. However, neither they nor their parts are genuine subjects of mental states: it is *persons* or *selves* who think, feel and act intentionally, not their bodies or their brains. This, if true, is enough to establish the non-identity of selves with their bodies, though by no means implies that selves are wholly *im*material and separable from their bodies. I myself may still be, strictly and literally, the bearer of certain physical properties and the occupier of a location in physical space, even though I am not identifiable with that organized material object which serves as my physical body, and through which I exercise my capacities of perception and agency.

The picture that I am recommending, though I think it accords well with common-sense ways of talking, is not without difficulties. If I am not the same as my body, nor yet an essentially immaterial thing, how *am* I related to my body, and what makes my body peculiarly

1

mine? Could I survive a change of my body for another, perhaps radically different in form or material constitution? Again, if it is I and not my body or brain that have thoughts and feelings, how are those thoughts and feelings related to events and processes going on in my body and brain? How is it that, through a mental decision, I can make my body move in a desired way; and how is it that through the neural processing of optical information in my eye and brain I can experience my physical environment as a three-dimensional arrangement of coloured surfaces? Finally, how could mentally endowed beings like ourselves have evolved naturally, given that we are more than just the biological organisms which constitute our bodies?

I attempt to answer, or at least to begin to answer, all of these questions and many related ones in the course of this book. But a fundamental assumption of my approach throughout is that satisfactory answers to questions in the philosophy of mind presuppose a satisfactory metaphysical framework of ideas. It is to that framework that I shall now turn, and more particularly to the notion of *substance*, which is pivotal to much of what I have to say about mind, self and body.[1]

1. WHAT IS A SUBSTANCE?

What do we – or, more to the point, what *should* we – mean by a 'substance'? I am prepared to defend what I take to be a more or less Aristotelian conception of this notion. That is, I shall follow the Aristotle of the *Categories* in taking a 'primary' substance to be a concrete individual *thing*, or 'continuant'.[2] Paradigm examples are such entities as an individual horse (say, Eclipse) and an individual house (say, the one I live in). If, as some commentators believe,[3] Aristotle changed his mind about this between composing the

---

[1] A very much fuller account of my metaphysical position can be found in my book *Kinds of Being: A Study of Individuation, Identity and the Logic of Sortal Terms* (Oxford: Basil Blackwell, 1989). What follows is only an outline sketch.

[2] See further my chapter on 'Substance', in G. H. R. Parkinson (ed.), *An Encyclopaedia of Philosophy* (London: Routledge, 1988), pp. 255-78. The term 'continuant' was coined by W. E. Johnson: see his *Logic, Part III* (Cambridge: Cambridge University Press, 1924), ch. 7.

[3] See, e.g., Alan Code, 'Aristotle: Essence and Accident', in R. E. Grandy and R. Warner (eds.), *Philosophical Grounds of Rationality* (Oxford: Clarendon Press, 1986), and Michael Frede, 'Substance in Aristotle's *Metaphysics*', in his *Essays in Ancient Philosophy* (Oxford: Clarendon Press, 1987).

Categories and the *Metaphysics*, then so be it; I am really only interested in the doctrine, not in whether or when Aristotle held it.

Such substances (henceforth I shall drop the word 'primary') belong to kinds, that is, to species and genera (which Aristotle, in the *Categories* but not elsewhere, called 'secondary' substances). The kinds to which substances belong I shall call *substantial* kinds. Not *all* kinds are substantial kinds, of course, since there are kinds of non-substantial individuals: for example, kinds of events and kinds of sets. Events, though concrete individuals, are not substances by the 'Aristotelian' account because they are not entities capable of persisting through qualitative change – indeed, they just *are*, broadly speaking, the changes which substances undergo. Sets are not substances because – assuming indeed that they really exist at all – they are purely abstract entities.[4]

Substantial kinds may be *natural* (like the kind *horse*) or they may be *artefactual* (like the kind *house*). This distinction is mutually exclusive and perhaps also exhaustive – though arguably there genuinely exist substantial kinds, like perhaps the culinary kind *vegetable*, which are neither natural nor artefactual.[5] But to call a substantial kind 'natural' is not to imply that individual exemplars of it could not be artificially synthesized. Rather, the characteristic feature of natural substantial kinds (henceforth, simply 'natural kinds') is that they are *subjects of natural law*. This requires some expansion. Obviously, it is not that an artefact, such as a watch, is not subject *to* natural law: if a watch is dropped, its fall will be governed by the law of gravity, quite as much as will the fall of a tree. The point rather is that there are no natural laws that are distinctively *about* watches or other human artefacts of comparable kinds: artefactual kinds are not subjects *of* natural law. By contrast, there *are* laws about plants and animals and stars and atoms and all other such natural kinds.[6] The laws in question belong to the

---

[4] A more detailed presentation of the ontological scheme I favour, and the place of substances within it, may be found in my 'Primitive Substances', *Philosophy and Phenomenological Research* 54 (1994), pp. 531-52.

[5] See T. E. Wilkerson, 'Natural Kinds', *Philosophy* 63 (1988), pp. 29-42. It must also be acknowledged that animal artefacts, such as the bee's honeycomb and the beaver's dam, are quite as 'natural' as the creatures which make them – but they differ for that very reason from the products of intentional human design, such as houses and watches, with which I am presently contrasting exemplars of 'natural' kinds.

[6] It might be objected that one needs to be able to identify which kinds are *natural* kinds (as opposed, say, to various 'gruesome' or 'gerrymandered' kinds) in order to identify which

various special sciences: biology, astronomy, nuclear physics, and so forth. Each of these sciences is about substances of certain appropriate natural kinds. The kinds that are proper to one science are not, in general, proper to another: thus astronomy has something to say about stars but not about starfish, while the reverse is true of biology. Furthermore, I see no good reason to believe that all laws about natural kinds are even 'in principle' reducible to, or wholly explicable in terms of, laws about some privileged set of 'basic' or 'fundamental' natural kinds – such as sub-atomic particles. That is to say, I consider the various special sciences to be for the most part relatively autonomous, despite numerous theoretical interconnections between them.

One reason why I reject reductionism about laws is that I reject it about substantial individuals of the kinds which are the subjects of laws. For instance, I reject the view that a biological entity such as a tree can simply be regarded as being nothing over and above an assemblage of sub-atomic particles, even though we now believe that the ultimate constituents of trees (and of everything else material) are indeed such particles. (I am inclined to take the same non-reductionist view of artefacts, but would still insist that these differ from members of natural kinds in lacking an associated network of natural law.) It may perhaps be true that the existence of a tree in some sense 'supervenes' upon that of its constituent particles at any given time (though saying this is no clearer than the somewhat obscure notion of supervenience permits it to be). But that these particles constitute a *tree* rather than an entity of some quite different non-biological kind crucially depends upon their organization (that is, in Aristotelian terms, upon their realizing the 'form' of a tree). And this organization can only be appropriately described (I would contend) in distinctively *biological* terms. Thus, what is crucial as far as the presence or absence of a *tree* is concerned, is that the particles in question should be so organized as to subserve the characteristic life-sustaining functions of the various typical parts of a tree – respiration, photosynthesis, nutrition, and so forth. (By a tree's 'typical' parts I mean such parts as its leaves, branches and roots, all of which play distinctive biological roles in its overall structure and economy.) Saying what these typical

generalizations are to count as natural laws. But my view is that our knowledge of laws and our knowledge of the sortal structure of the world develops in tandem, by a process of continual mutual adjustment: see the last three chapters of my *Kinds of Being*.

parts and characteristic functions are, and explaining their proper interrelationships, are precisely matters for the science of biology, and will involve the recognition of various distinctively biological laws. Biological laws are laws about living organisms *qua* living organisms (rather than, for example, *qua* material bodies), and since talk of living organisms is not reducible to talk of assemblages of sub-atomic particles, neither are biological laws reducible to the laws of nuclear physics.

2. THE CONCEPT OF SELFHOOD

I take *persons* or *selves* (terms I use interchangeably) to be subjects of experience, and hence consider theories of the self to be absolutely central to the concerns of this book. It will be helpful, then, if I say at this point what I take a theory of the self to be a theory *of* – but my characterization of the self for this purpose should be neutral as between various rival views of the self's ontological status. By a *self*, then, I mean a possible object of first-person reference and subject of first-person thoughts: a being which can think that *it itself* is thus and so and can identify itself as the unique subject of certain thoughts and experiences and as the unique agent of certain actions. Such a being may well also be able to recognize itself as the unique possessor of a certain body, but it cannot plausibly be insisted that a capacity for such recognition is a logically necessary condition of selfhood, even if it can be argued – which I do not say it can – that embodiment itself is a logically necessary condition of selfhood. (A fuller exposition and defence of this account of selfhood will be found in chapter 7.)

When I characterize the self as a being which can identify itself as the unique subject of certain thoughts and experiences, I mean that it is a logically necessary condition of selfhood that a self should know, of any concurrent conscious thought or experience which is its own, that it *is* its own thought or experience and no one else's. For instance, if a certain presently occurring pain is mine, then I must now know of that pain that it *is* mine and mine alone – a thought which I might express in words by means of the sentence '*This* pain is *my* pain' (although I do not insist that a self be capable of articulating such thoughts). That is why I believe we cannot really render intelligible the curious reply of Mrs Gradgrind in *Hard Times*, when asked on her sick bed whether she was in pain: 'I think there's a pain somewhere in the room, but I couldn't positively say that I have got it.'[7] I should stress, however, that I only insist that a self must know of its *conscious* thoughts and experiences that they are its own, and only insist that it must know this *at the time at which they are occurring* (though it is arguable that it must know this of at least *some* of its past thoughts and experiences as well).

It may be suspected that even these qualified claims are threatened by the existence of such clinical disorders as schizophrenia and multiple personality. Though I shall touch on these disorders later in the book, I do not have space to discuss their implications for our conception of the self in any detail. However, I am willing to allow – since this is all I really need for my purposes – that it is strictly only psychologically *normal* selves that fully meet my condition for selfhood, and that other cases only approximate to it in varying degrees. I should add, though, that it may be possible to have *de re* knowledge of two experiences, e_1 and e_2, that each is mine, without necessarily having *de dicto* knowledge that e_1 and e_2 are both mine – and this might permit even the psychologically disordered selves to meet my condition fully.

3. SUBSTANTIVAL VERSUS NON-SUBSTANTIVAL THEORIES OF THE SELF

With these remarks on substance and on selfhood in place, let us turn to the following question: How could the *self* be a *substance*? A student of the history of philosophy might well answer that this could be so only if the self were either identifiable with a certain physical body or else identifiable with an immaterial Cartesian ego or soul. And neither view is easily defensible. The first (material substantivalism) is not because it seems to get quite wrong the conceptual connection between the self and its body. The self is necessarily conceived to be the owner or subject of its experiences and actions in a primitive sense in which the body is apparently quite ineligible for that role. That *these* experiences are *my* experiences is arguably known to me as a necessary truth; but that these experiences are associated with this body, though perhaps known by me, does not seem to constitute a necessary truth. And the obvious explanation for the contingency of

---

[7] Charles Dickens, *Hard Times* (Harmondsworth: Penguin Books, 1969), p. 224.

the association is that while these experiences are *necessarily mine*, this body is only *contingently mine*. Thus the contingency of the association of these experiences with this body is explicable – and I think only explicable – as a consequence of a contingency in the relationship between me and my body, a contingency which material substantivalism cannot countenance.[8]

A rejoinder which the material substantivalist might make here is that the reason why '*These* experiences are *my* experiences' is a necessary truth is that it is just analytic, on the grounds that 'I' just means 'the subject of these experiences' (so that 'These experiences are my experiences' just means 'These experiences are experiences of the subject of these experiences', which is as good a candidate as any for the status of analytic truth). This would then allow the material substantivalist to insist, none the less, that I – that is, the subject of these experiences – am identical with this body, even though 'These experiences are experiences of this body' is *not* an analytic truth. For, of course, analyticity is not necessarily preserved under the substitution of co-referring expressions.

But such a rejoinder is quite unsatisfactory, not least because it fails to account for the unity of consciousness that is characteristic of self-hood and the privileged access which the self has only to its own experiences. If 'I' just means 'the subject of these experiences', what is to guarantee that it in fact picks out a unique entity at all? Why should all these experiences be assignable to the *same* subject? Why should not *this* pain and *this* itch be assigned to *different* subjects? The obvious answer is that they cannot be because they are both necessarily *mine*: but this is clearly not an answer that is available to the material substantivalist who resorts to the strategy now under examination, nor does it seem to me that he has any viable alternative answer. To say that the experiences are assignable to the same subject because they are 'co-conscious' or 'co-presented' not only gets the cart before the horse, but also reduces the self's unity of consciousness to an analytic triviality. (I shall deal with these issues in much greater depth in chapters 2 and 7.)

So let us turn to the traditional alternative to material substantivalism – Cartesian or immaterial substantivalism, according to which the

---

[8] I present other arguments against identifying the self with its body in my *Kinds of Being*, ch. 6.

self is not identifiable with the body but is seen rather as an immaterial substance wholly distinct and separable from the body, albeit intimately causally related to it. The trouble with this view is that to the extent that it goes beyond a mere rejection of material substantivalism it rests on pure speculation without either *a priori* sanction or, seemingly, any hope of empirical confirmation. From the fact that I am not identical with my body it by no means follows that I am wholly distinct and separable from it, much less that I am endowed with no physical characteristics whatsoever.

Since I have nothing to say in defence of immaterial substantivalism and have rejected material substantivalism, it might seem that I should be willing to reject altogether the notion that the self is a substance. But I am not, because the alternatives are in my view untenable. What are these alternatives? In essence there are two, one more radical than the other. The less radical position is 'Humean' psychological constructivism (exemplified in modern times by the view of philosophers such as Derek Parfit), according to which the self – the object of first-person reference and subject of psychological states – is nothing *over and above* the states of which it is the subject, but is not therefore *nothing at all*, since it is a perfectly respectable entity whose identity and persistence conditions are entirely expressible in terms of relationships between those states. In short, the self is a 'bundle of perceptions'.[9] The deepest problem with this sort of view is that the entities out of which it attempts to construct the self – psychological states and processes – are themselves quite generally not individuable and identifiable independently of the selves that are their subjects, so that fatal circularity dooms the project. I shall discuss this point much more fully in chapter 2, so I shall say no more about it here.[10]

The more radical of the two alternatives to substantivalism is what I call the non-entity theory – the view that there is literally no such thing as the self, as philosophers have attempted to conceive of it, and indeed that there is *no* object of first-person reference, because 'I' is not really a referring expression at all.[11] But this view falls prey to the

[9] See David Hume, *A Treatise of Human Nature*, I, IV, sect. VI, ed. L. A. Selby-Bigge and P. H. Nidditch (Oxford: Clarendon Press, 1978), and Derek Parfit, *Reasons and Persons*, 3 (Oxford: Clarendon Press, 1984).

[10] See also my *Kinds of Being*, pp. 131-3.

[11] See, e.g., G. E. M. Anscombe, 'The First Person', in S. Guttenplan (ed.), *Mind and Language* (Oxford: Clarendon Press, 1975).

same general objection levelled at psychological constructivism, namely, that psychological states (whose existence the non-entity theory is not, wisely, attempting to deny) are necessarily owned by subjects whose individuation is quite generally presupposed by any tenable account of the identity-conditions of such states. Since, then, the existence of subjects of experience is not to be denied, it is preposterous to deny that these are the intended objects of first-person reference or indeed that there is such a phenomenon as first-person reference. And that being so, the existence of selves, as I have defined them, is not to be disputed, however much one may dispute their precise ontological status and underlying nature.

So far I have rejected what are, as far as I can see, the only two serious rivals to substantivalist theories of the self – psychological constructivism and the non-entity theory – but have also rejected the best known versions of substantivalism itself, material and immaterial or Cartesian substantivalism. Thus we are left looking for a distinctive and defensible version of substantivalism. As I see it, the two main problems that a viable substantival theory of the self has to face are these. First, how can one and the same self persist identically through time even though its persistence-conditions are not those of the body? And, secondly, how is it that the self, though not identical with the body, can support the various psychological states and processes that make up its mental life and which qualify it (rather than the body) as a subject of thought and experience and agent of deliberative actions? I hope to throw light on these problems in the remaining chapters of this book, though I do not claim entirely to solve them.

4. A LOOK AHEAD

In what remains of this introductory chapter, I shall briefly outline what I hope to accomplish in the rest of the book. (Readers who do not like the plot to be revealed in advance should skip this section.) I begin chapter 2 by discussing in much more detail than I have so far the ontological status of the self, examining the attractions and difficulties of three mutually opposing views. Two of these views have in common that they treat selves or persons as *substances* – that is, as enduring bearers of successive states and in no way reducible to mere successions of those states. Another two of the views have in common that they treat the concept of the self or person primarily as a *psychological* one. I argue in favour of the view that belongs to both of these pairs, that is, the view that the self is a *psychological substance* – though I reject the Cartesian version of this view in favour of a version which permits the self to be a bearer of physical as well as psychological states. The rival views that I dismiss have their historical roots in the philosophical thought of Aristotle and Locke respectively, but also have many modern adherents, whence I call the modern versions the neo-Aristotelian and neo-Lockean views of the self. The former treats persons as *biological substances* (that is, as a kind of *animal*), the latter treats them as *psychological modes* (that is, as appropriately unified successions of psychological states). I argue against the neo-Aristotelian view that it is excessively anthropocentric in its conception of persons, and against the neo-Lockean view that it suffers from a fatal circularity through its failure to accommodate the fact that psychological states are only individuable by reference to the selves that are their subjects.

In the later sections of chapter 2, I attempt to develop in some detail a positive account of the self consistent with my view of its ontological status as a psychological substance. I argue that the self is a *simple* substance, that is, a substance possessing no substantial parts. On this view, parts of the self's body are not literally parts of the self, though the self may still consistently be said to possess certain physical characteristics which supervene upon those of its body. Moreover, the self's substantial simplicity is in no way incompatible with its manifest psychological complexity, though that simplicity does help to explain its psychological *unity*. The simplicity of the self is seen to imply that its diachronic identity – its persistence through time – is irreducible and ungrounded, and hence criterionless. Towards the end of the chapter various physicalist objections to this picture are answered, notably the objection that it is inconsistent with a naturalistic account of the evolution of human persons. Persons or selves are argued to be quite as much a product of cultural as of biological evolution.

Chapter 3 begins with an examination of the charge, traditionally levelled by physicalists against dualists ever since the time of Descartes, that dualist interactionism conflicts with the fundamental laws of physics, particularly the conservation laws. This charge is shown to be quite unfounded. Even so, I concede that the 'Cartesian' model of psychophysical causation is unsatisfactory for a number of other reasons, but sketch an alternative interactionist scheme which escapes these difficulties. This new approach is developed in more detail later in the chapter, where I draw a distinction between 'initiating' and 'facilitating' causes and argue that the mental causes of bodily behaviour fall into the latter category. I explain how such mental causes could play an independent role supplementary to that of the neurological causes of behaviour, and indicate what sort of empirical evidence would support the claim that they do indeed play such a role. This theory presents an 'emergentist' picture of mental powers, but one which appears to be perfectly consistent with a naturalistic, evolutionary account of their origin. I should add that a good deal of this chapter is devoted to demonstrating the inadequacies of so-called nonreductive physicalism – the majority view amongst philosophers of mind at present – and thus to cutting away the supposed middle ground between a robust dualism of the sort I favour and the more extreme forms of physicalism, such as eliminativism, which at best lack plausibility and at worst threaten to prove wholly incoherent.

Chapter 4 is devoted to the development of a comprehensive theory of sense perception which emphasizes the indispensable role of conscious, qualitative states of experience both in perceptual processes themselves and in associated processes of belief-formation. I begin by arguing that perceptual processes involve a quite distinct class of mental states – perceptual experiences – which can occur even in the absence of their normal extra-mental causes. I contend that perceptual experiences are distinguished by their possession of both intentional or representational content and qualitative or phenomenal content, with the latter reflecting the sensuous or sensational element in perception. Certain uses of words such as 'look' and 'appear' are shown to be devices for capturing aspects of the qualitative content of perceptual experience, rather than just means of describing the objects of perception as such. With these distinctions in place, I next go on to give a detailed account of the way in which systematic causal dependencies between the qualitative features of perceptual experience and the properties of environmental objects enable human subjects to extract environmental information from their sensory stimulations – an account which presents a distinct alternative to both the 'ecological' and the 'computational' theories of perception currently in favour amongst philosophical psychologists. Another issue examined in this chapter is the relationship between the role of qualitative experiential states in perception and the ability of human subjects to form conceptually structured beliefs and judgements amenable to rational evaluation and revision. This issue is explored with the aid of thought-experiments envisaging extensions of the phenomenon of 'blindsight' to other sensory modalities.

In the last section of chapter 4 the focus of inquiry shifts from the qualitative or phenomenal content of perceptual experience to its intentional or representational content, though also to the question of how these two kinds of content are related. I hold that the intentional content of a perceptual experience is best characterized in terms of the belief-content that it is typically apt to induce in its subject, and that its aptness to induce a given belief-content is a product of the role which experiences with similar qualitative content have played in that particular subject's history of perceptual learning. Such an account serves to connect a subject's ability to form beliefs about environmental objects with his or her perceptually acquired knowledge of what such objects 'look like' (or otherwise 'appear' to other sensory modalities), and thus confirms the conclusions of the 'blindsight' thought-experiments discussed earlier on. More generally, though, the purpose of chapter 4 is to assemble all the ingredients of a causal theory of perception which is at once a 'representative' theory of perception and a 'direct realist' theory (surprising though such a combination may seem to those who assume that theories of these kinds are mutually incompatible).

Chapter 5 returns to the topic of voluntary agency which was one of the central concerns of chapter 3. A 'volitional' theory of such agency is defended, according to which a distinctive class of mental states – volitions – play an indispensable role in the genesis of voluntary behaviour. Volitions are shown to be distinctive not least in respect of their intentional content, which is self-referential but not propositional in character. Though beliefs and desires are amongst the causal determinants of volition, a philosophy of action which appeals only to states of the former kinds is inadequate. In other words, 'conative' or 'executive' mental states must be invoked in addition to cognitive and appetitive or motivational states in any satisfactory account of human agency. The theory of chapter 5 does not, however – unlike some other recent approaches – simply equate 'willing' with 'trying', or attempt to eliminate the former notion in favour of the latter, because the concept of trying, though apt enough for everyday purposes, cannot bear sufficient weight for theoretical deployment in an account of the aetiology of human action.

In chapter 6, I develop the thesis, initially advanced in chapter 4, that our capacity for thought is intimately related to our capacity to enjoy qualitative experiences of environmental objects in sense-perception. I argue that thought at its most basic is a non-discursive process of imaginative (re)construction akin to, and ultimately dependent upon, processes of perceptual recognition, and that higher-level linguistic thinking is only rendered possible by these more basic psychological processes. To some extent this serves to restore the credentials of Locke's unjustly vilified 'ideational' theory of linguistic signification.

In the last chapter, chapter 7, I expand on the claim made in section 2 above that certain kinds of self-knowledge are definitive conditions of selfhood – notably a knowledge of the identity of one's own present, conscious thoughts, experiences and actions. This sort of reflexive self-knowledge is shown to be compatible only with a substantival theory of the self of the kind defended in chapter 2. At the same time, I explain why it is that, even though the self is not to be identified with its body, the specially intimate relationship in which it stands to its own conscious states is in some respects extensible to certain parts of its own body, namely, those over which it can exercise direct voluntary control and those in which it can phenomenologically localize bodily sensations. These considerations help to fill out an account, already begun in chapter 2, of what it is that qualifies a particular physical body as peculiarly *mine*.

It is my hope that, collectively, the chapters of this book present a rounded picture of human subjects and their mental powers which is at once non-reductive, naturalistic, metaphysically coherent and consistent with our own subjective intuitions concerning ourselves.

2

Substance and selfhood

Are persons substances or modes? The terminology in which this question is framed may seem archaic, but the problem itself is a live and important one. Two currently dominant views may be characterized as offering the following rival answers to this problem. According to the first view, persons are just *biological substances*. According to the second, persons are *psychological modes* of substances which, as far as human beings are concerned, happen to be biological substances, but which could in principle be non-biological. There is, however, also a third possible answer, and this is that persons are *psychological substances*. Such a view is inevitably associated with the name of Descartes, and this helps to explain its current unpopularity, since substantial dualism of his sort is now widely rejected as 'unscientific'. But one may, as I hope to show, espouse the view that persons are psychological substances without endorsing Cartesianism. This is because one may reject certain features of Descartes's conception of substance. Consequently, one may also espouse a version of substantial dualism which is distinctly non-Cartesian. One may hold that a person, being a psychological substance, is an entity distinct from the biological substance that is (in the human case) his or her body, and yet still be prepared to ascribe corporeal characteristics to this psychological substance.[1] By this account, a human person is to be thought of neither as a non-corporeal mental substance (a Cartesian mind), nor as the product of a mysterious 'union' between such a substance and a physical, biological substance (a Cartesian animal body). This is not to deny that the mind-body problem is a serious and difficult one, though it *is* to imply that there is a version of substantial dualism which does not involve regarding the 'mind' as a distinct substance in its own right.

[1] Such a view has close affinities with that advanced by P. F. Strawson in his *Individuals: An Essay in Descriptive Metaphysics* (London: Methuen, 1959), ch. 3.

14

Subjects of experience

1. BIOLOGICAL SUBSTANCES AND THE NEO-ARISTOTELIAN VIEW OF PERSONS

I hope I have already sufficiently explained what I mean by 'substance' and 'substantial kind' in the previous chapter, and with this explanation in place we can turn at once to the question of the ontological status of persons. According to the first view mentioned in my opening remarks, persons are biological substances – that is, they are members of a substantial kind which is a kind of living organism. Briefly: persons are a kind of animal. This seems to have been Aristotle's view, and in modern times it is well represented in the work of David Wiggins.[2]

One striking feature of this view is that it threatens either to promote what is (to my mind) an ethically dubious anthropomorphic 'speciesism' or else to play havoc with zoological taxonomies.[3] To see this, it should be noted that it is normally the case in zoology that if a species a is subordinate to both of two genera b and c, then either b is subordinate to c or c is subordinate to b. (I use the term 'genus' here in a broad sense just to mean a higher kind than another, relative to which the latter is correspondingly a 'species'.) Formally, we may state this principle as follows (where '/' symbolizes the subordinancy relation):

$$P_1 \ (a/b \ \& \ a/c) \ \rightarrow \ (b = c \ \text{V} \ b/c \ \text{V} \ c/b).$$

For instance, goats are both ruminants and ungulates – and, as it turns out, ruminants are (i.e., are subordinate to) ungulates, in accordance with the requirements of principle P_1. Consequently, if two distinct species a and a' are both subordinate to a genus b, while a is also subordinate to a genus c and a' is subordinate to a genus c', then (by our principle P_1) it is *both* the case that either b is subordinate to c or c is subordinate to b, *and* the case that either b is subordinate to c' or c' is subordinate to b. It follows (assuming that our principle P_1 also applies to the genera and that the subordinancy relation is transitive) that in

---

[2] See David Wiggins, *Sameness and Substance* (Oxford: Basil Blackwell, 1980), p. 187.

[3] Wiggins himself (ibid., pp. 174f.) gravitates towards the first horn of this apparent dilemma. Another recent author who gravitates towards the anthropocentric position is Kathleen Wilkes: see her *Real People: Personal Identity without Thought Experiments* (Oxford: Clarendon Press, 1988), pp. 97ff., 230ff.

such a case either c is subordinate to c', or c' is subordinate to c, or else c and c' are both subordinate to b.

Now, an adherent of the view that persons are a kind of animal will doubtless want to say that *humans* (i.e., members of the species *homo sapiens*) are *persons* and are also (for example) *mammals*. But could an adherent of this view also accept the possibility of there being a hitherto unknown species of *amphibians* (say), call them *bolgs*, which were likewise *persons*? Not if our taxonomic principle P_1 is correct, for this would commit them to the proposition that either mammals are amphibians, or amphibians are mammals, or else both mammals and amphibians are persons – and none of these disjuncts is true. (The last disjunct is of course false because if amphibians are – i.e., are subordinate to – persons, then, since frogs are amphibians, frogs would have to be persons, by virtue of the transitivity of the subordinancy relation. But frogs are not persons, outside the realms of fairy tale.) So either a widely applicable taxonomic principle must be rejected or else it must be claimed that creatures such as our imagined bolgs cannot be persons – which seems to require an intolerable degree of anthropocentric prejudice.

Perhaps, however, all that this shows is that our principle P_1 should indeed be rejected in favour of a weaker one, expressible formally as follows:[4]

$$P_2 \ (a/b \ \& \ a/c) \rightarrow (b = c \ \text{V} \ b/c \ \text{V} \ c/b \ \text{V} \ (\text{E}x)(b/x \ \& \ c/x)).$$

(In words: if a is subordinate to both b and c, then either b and c are identical, or b is subordinate to c, or c is subordinate to b, or there is some species x to which both b and c are subordinate.) Appealing to this principle, an adherent of the biological substance view of persons could hold that both humans and bolgs are indeed persons, even though humans are mammals and bolgs are amphibians. For the only constraint that P_2 imposes here is that mammals, amphibians and persons should all be subordinate to some one higher genus – and an adherent of the biological substance view will of course be quite happy to allow this, seeing the genus *animal* as occupying precisely such a role. The proposed set of relationships is displayed in figure 1.

---

[4] Cf. Wiggins, *Sameness and Substance*, p. 202.

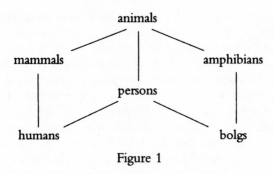

Figure 1

Such a taxonomic structure cannot, I think, be ruled out *a priori*, since I am certainly prepared to allow that structures isomorphic with it may obtain amongst artefactual kinds. However, amongst *natural* (and more specifically *biological*) kinds this seems most improbable. This is connected with the fact that natural kinds are subjects of natural law (see chapter 1, section 1). If persons are a natural, biological kind, as is now being proposed, then one would expect there to be distinctive biological laws relating to personkind – laws intimately linked to the evolution of persons as a biological kind. Such laws would have to be applicable to both humans and bolgs, these both being *ex hypothesi* species of person. However, humans and bolgs, being mammals and amphibians respectively, must be presumed to have had quite different evolutionary histories, tenuously linked only by a very remote common ancestor species: and this seems to make it little short of miraculous that they should none the less *both* have evolved to be governed by the *same* distinctive network of biological laws, even to the extent of qualifying them as species of a single biological kind, personkind. It is rather as if we were to discover that although all the frogs we have hitherto encountered are amphibians, there is in fact also a mammalian species of frogs, exhibiting many of the features we are familiar with in frogs and yet warm-blooded and given to suckling their young. As an imaginary contribution to biological science (which is what it appears to be), the theory of persons just adumbrated is no less incredible.

At this point various responses are available to my opponent. One is to remark that in fact evolution *has* thrown up species sharing many morphological features despite their having no close common antecedent, a phenomenon which is often reflected in the popular names of these species: for instance, *wolves* and *marsupial wolves*.[5] But such examples do not really help my opponent, since biological science does *not* in fact classify such species as genuinely falling under the same genus by virtue of the shared morphological features in question. Marsupial wolves are *not* regarded by zoologists as a species of dog, unlike true wolves (*canis lupus*). However, to this my opponent may respond that I have unfairly stacked the cards against him by taking zoological species as my paradigm of biological kinds.[6] 'Obviously', he may say, 'persons can't be regarded as a zoological species on a par with *canis lupus* or *homo sapiens*, and so can't be expected to fit in neatly with zoological taxonomies; but this doesn't mean that they can't constitute a biological kind – a kind of animal – which finds a place in some alternative (though not for that reason *rival*) taxonomic scheme.'

My reply to this suggestion is that it is threatened by the following dilemma. Either it will be compelled to regard persons as constituting a purely 'nominal' (as opposed to 'real') kind – and this will undermine the supposedly biological status of persons. Or else it will have difficulty in establishing compatibility between the zoological taxonomy and the proposed alternative biological taxonomy in which persons are supposed to find a place. To see this, we must recall that an adherent of the suggestion will want to claim that individual human beings are *both* members of the zoological species *homo sapiens* and *also* members of the allegedly biological kind *person*. Now, if *person* is regarded as a purely nominal kind – that is, as a 'kind' membership of which is secured merely by the possession of some set of 'defining characteristics' (so that, in my view, it deserves the name 'kind' by courtesy only) – then the claim in question is not threatened by inconsistency. However, it does now appear obscure in what sense it could still be insisted that the concept of a person is essentially a *biological* one. For if personhood is determined by the satisfaction of a set of defining characteristics, it seems clear that the favoured candidates for such characteristics would have to be broadly *psychological* ones: an ability to reason, the possession of consciousness, a capacity

[5] Cf. ibid., p. 203.
[6] Cf. ibid.

18

to perceive and engage in intentional activity, and so forth.[7] It certainly is not clear why we should have to include amongst these characteristics any mention of a biological substrate or distinctively biological functions. There seems to be no good reason, either *a priori* or *a posteriori*, to suppose that the psychological capacities mentioned earlier could not in principle be associated with an inorganic body, and indeed even with a wholly artefactual one.[8]

So let us turn to the other horn of the dilemma, by supposing that persons are to be regarded as constituting a *real* biological kind. My point now is that it is difficult to see how this can be consistent with regarding individual members of the species *homo sapiens* as also being instances of the kind *person*, given the relative independence of the two taxonomic schemes within which these kinds are supposed to find their places. The reason for this is as follows. Specifying what real or substantial kind(s) a particular belongs to is, in Aristotelian terms, tantamount to determining its *essence*. Thus, bound up with such a specification will be an account of the particular's *persistence conditions*; that is, an account of the sorts of admissible changes it can undergo while yet surviving as a particular of that kind. Changes that are admissible for particulars of one kind are very often not admissible for particulars of another kind. And in general the range of admissible changes will (in the case of natural kinds) be intimately tied to the range of natural laws of which the kind in question is the subject.[9] For example, the change from possessing gills and a tail to possessing lungs and four legs is admissible in the case of frogs but not in the case of

---

[7] For a view of personhood along these lines, see Daniel C. Dennett, 'Conditions of Personhood', in his *Brainstorms* (Hassocks: Harvester Press, 1979). I criticize this sort of approach in my *Kinds of Being: A Study of Individuation, Identity and the Logic of Sortal Terms* (Oxford: Basil Blackwell, 1989), pp. 112–18. Thus I agree with Wiggins that persons constitute a real rather than a merely nominal kind, but differ from him in denying that the kind in question is a *biological* one.

[8] David Wiggins challenges this view in his *Sameness and Substance*, pp. 174–5. It has of course also been challenged, if more obliquely, by John Searle, most recently in his *The Rediscovery of the Mind* (Cambridge, MA: MIT Press, 1992), ch. 9. But I find neither challenge convincing: see my *Kinds of Being*, p. 111.

[9] Here it may be objected that we can imagine all sorts of 'gruesome' and 'gerrymandered' persistence conditions which can be associated with correspondingly gerrymandered kinds, and that this threatens to undermine the objectivity of my approach. I would reply in the same way as I did to a similar objection raised (in a footnote) in section 1 of chapter 1, concerning my view of the relationship between natural laws and natural kinds.

trout, because the laws of morphological development differ for creatures of these two different kinds. Now, if *person* and *homo sapiens* are *both* real biological kinds, then both will apparently have associated with them a range of admissible changes determined by the developmental laws governing these kinds. However, given the relative independence of the two taxonomic schemes within which these kinds are supposed to find their places, there is no reason to suppose compatibility between these ranges of admissible changes – and indeed every reason to suppose incompatibility.[10] For instance, suppose that our imagined bolgs are accepted as *bona fide* members of the kind *person*, and yet are also similar to their amphibian cousins the frogs in undergoing metamorphosis from a larval to an adult phase. Then bolgs *qua* amphibians can survive a change from having gills and a tail to having lungs and legs, whereas humans *qua* members of the mammalian species *homo sapiens* cannot. But both bolgs and humans are supposedly *also* members of the allegedly biological real kind *person*, governed by its own developmental laws. Either these laws permit the change from having gills and a tail to having lungs and legs or they do not permit it. If they do, then it follows, absurdly, that an individual human being *can* survive the change *qua* person but *cannot* survive it *qua* member of *homo sapiens*. If they do not, then it follows, equally absurdly, that an individual bolg *cannot* survive the change *qua* person but *can* survive it *qua* bolg.[11]

---

[10] Wiggins would deny this, on the grounds that both schemes are supposedly dominated by the genus *animal*. Thus he writes: 'Cross-classifications that are resolved under a higher sort do not ultimately disturb a system of natural kinds. It is always (say) animals that are under study; and different classifications will not import different identity or persistence conditions for particular animals' (*Sameness and Substance*, p. 204). This seems to presume that all animals, of whatever kind, are governed by the same persistence conditions. But that is patently false, at least if one means by the 'persistence conditions' for a given kind of animals the range of changes which, as a matter of natural law, members of that kind can undergo. Of course, it may be *conceptually* possible for an individual member of one animal kind to survive a transmutation which renders it a member of another kind governed by persistence conditions different from those of the first. But the bare logical possibility of such fairy-tale transmogrifications obviously does nothing to lessen the tension between our two supposed taxonomic schemes, conceived as contributions to empirical biological science.

[11] If it is felt that this argument is suspect on the grounds that human beings do not have gills and a tail in the first place, or indeed on the opposing grounds that human beings do in fact undergo a metamorphosis not unlike that of amphibians but prenatally during their embryo stage, then it is easy enough to substitute for the bolgs an imagined species undergoing a metamorphosis which human beings undoubtedly *cannot* undergo despite

It may be objected, perhaps, that the foregoing argument is too strong, in that it would equally imply that the kinds *homo sapiens* and *frog* cannot both belong to the higher kind *animal*. However, there is clearly no *single* set of persistence conditions that applies to *all* animals, and to this extent we cannot talk of 'the' persistence conditions of animals *simpliciter*. So this line of objection can only be exploited by someone who, analogously, believes that *persons* are not governed by a single set of persistence conditions, and consequently that there may be quite different kinds of persons just as there may be quite different kinds of animals. Here I protest that the concept of a person is not as polymorphous and indeterminate as this account would make it, implying as it does that persons may differ *essentially* from one another. Recall, too, that what I am arguing against is the sort of taxonomic structure depicted in figure 1 above, and it is implicit in that diagram that persons as a kind occupy a level of generality no *higher*, at least, than that of the distinction between mammals and amphibians. If this is now denied, by moving persons as a kind to the same level of generality as that of animals, then a new tension is created for the position under attack, in that it now becomes increasingly implausible to insist that only *biological* species can be admitted as possible sub-kinds of the kind *person*. (Compare the difficulty which arose earlier for the 'nominal kind' version of the biological view of persons: the general lesson is that the more robustly *biological* the view is made, the more anthropocentric it threatens to be.)

This concludes my discussion of the first view mentioned in my opening remarks – the view that persons are biological substances.[12] I hope I have made the unattractiveness of that view abundantly clear, and in particular I hope I have made it clear why adherents of that view are driven towards anthropocentrism. It is true that I have offered no explicit arguments against such anthropocentrism itself – against the opinion, that is, that human beings are the only persons that there could be (whether in the weaker sense that the only *naturally possible* persons are human beings or in the stronger sense that the only *conceivable* persons are human beings). But this is because I find such anthropocentrism (in both its stronger and its weaker form)

---

possessing the morphological features of its initial phase – for instance, a change from having hair and arms to having feathers and wings.

[12] I raise other objections against it in my *Kinds of Being*, pp. 108–21.

21

not only morally repugnant and dangerously arrogant, but also symp-tomatic of a philosophically inadequate imagination. I cannot really take the suggestion seriously as one meriting detailed examination and discussion. (Clearly, the weaker version is less objectionable than the stronger, but even to hold that dolphins and chimpanzees, say, are excluded from personhood *as a matter of natural law* strikes me as being intolerably dogmatic.)

2. PSYCHOLOGICAL MODES AND THE NEO-LOCKEAN VIEW OF PERSONS

The next view I shall consider – that of persons as psychological modes – is essentially the view of Locke and Hume; though, of course, Locke and Hume also had their important differences on matters to do with substance and identity. Here I should explain that by a *mode* I understand any concrete non-substantial individual, or any entity wholly constituted by concrete non-substantial indivi-duals. Paradigm examples of concrete non-substantial individuals are events, processes and states. And the view of persons which we are now considering takes persons to be wholly constituted by *psychological* or *mental* events, processes and states.

It must be conceded that Locke's adherence to the psychological mode view of persons is less clear-cut and explicit than Hume's. Hume of course quite expressly regards the self as being 'nothing but a bundle or collection of different perceptions'.[13] On the other hand, Locke's official doctrine seems to be that 'person' denotes a nominal kind whose defining characteristics are all psychological in nature.[14] Even so, Locke's account of the identity conditions of per-sons and his concomitant treatment of the puzzle cases certainly appear to imply that, on his view, neither material nor (finite) 'spiritual' *substances* can qualify as persons.[15] Furthermore, there is a passage in

[13] See David Hume, *A Treatise of Human Nature*, ed. P. H. Nidditch (Oxford: Clarendon Press, 1978), I, IV, sect. VI, p. 252.
[14] See John Locke, *An Essay Concerning Human Understanding*, ed. P. H. Nidditch (Oxford: Clarendon Press, 1975), II, ch. XXVII, sect. 9. Of course, Locke thought that *all* sortal terms denote merely nominal kinds, so that his classification of 'person' as a nominal kind term reflects no special treatment of it.
[15] See further my review of Harold W. Noonan's *Personal Identity*, in *Mind* 99 (1990), pp. 477-9, and chapter 5 of my *Locke on Human Understanding* (London: Routledge, 1995).

the *Essay* in which Locke, having claimed that the only three kinds of substance of which we have ideas are God, finite spirits and material particles, goes on to say that 'all other things [are] but modes or relations ultimately terminated in substances'.[16] Given that persons (other than God, at least) are not substances, this would certainly appear to imply that for Locke they have the status of *modes*. Anyway, ignoring further exegetical complications, I shall henceforth just assume that Locke does indeed belong to the same broad camp as Hume.

In recent years, a view of persons very much like that of Locke and Hume has enjoyed a revival in the writings of such philosophers as Derek Parfit.[17] Modern adherents of the view are, however, usually concerned to represent it as a physicalist theory, or at least as being compatible with a thoroughgoing physicalism. This, they suppose, may be achieved by maintaining that mental events, processes and states are – or at least could well be – identical with physical events, processes and states. Such psychophysical identities may, it is further supposed, obtain either on a 'type-type' or on a 'token-token' basis (with the latter suggestion currently enjoying rather more popularity than the former).

How are persons supposed to be constituted by mental states? (Henceforth, for the sake of brevity, I shall use 'state' in a broad way to include both events and processes.) Here theorists diverge somewhat. According to what we may call the 'Lockean' school, personal identity consists in the obtaining of relationships of 'co-consciousness' between mental states. That is to say, on this approach a person is constituted by a manifold of mental states by virtue of these states being connected to one another, but not to any other mental states, by relationships of co-consciousness. Just what these relationships are is a matter for further theorizing on the part of adherents of the Lockean school, but it is generally agreed that in the case of coexisting mental states they involve some sort of 'unity of consciousness' condition while in the case of mental states separated by time they involve memory of a special sort (sometimes called 'experiential memory' or 'first person memory'). Adherents of what we may call the 'Humean' school differ from those of the Lockean

[16] Locke, *Essay*, II, ch. XXVII, sect. 2.
[17] See Derek Parfit, *Reasons and Persons* (Oxford: Clarendon Press, 1984), 3.

school chiefly in contending that the relationships between mental states which are crucial to personal identity are not so much cognitive as *causal* in character[18] (though since both schools will typically also advance causal accounts of cognitive relations such as memory, the differences between the Lockean and Humean schools are more ones of emphasis than of fundamental principle). It is probably fair to say that most modern proponents of the view of persons now under consideration espouse an amalgam of neo-Lockean and neo-Humean ideas. For brevity, and in recognition of Locke's historical priority, I propose however simply to call such modern accounts collectively the *neo-Lockean theory*.

It is to the credit of the neo-Lockean theory that, unlike the neo-Aristotelian theory, it is untainted by anthropocentrism (this indeed is the lesson of Locke's story of the rational parrot). This explains, too, why the neo-Lockean theory should appeal, as it clearly does, to enthusiasts for the prospects of artificial intelligence. The existence of a neo-Lockean person is popularly likened to the running of a computer program, which is largely independent of the detailed 'hardware' of the machine on which it is run. Human brains and nervous systems provide, on this view, highly efficient hardware (or 'wetware') for the 'running' of a person, but there is no reason in principle why the 'program' should not be run on an altogether different kind of machine, constructed on electronic rather than on biological principles. This even offers human persons – albeit only in the distant future – the prospect of immortality by means of transfer to a solid state device (though equally it offers an embarrassment of riches in the form of simultaneous transfer to more than one such machine).

However, the neo-Lockean theory is untenable. Neo-Aristotelians indeed are likely to abhor it as reviving the 'myth of the ghost in the machine', and as grotesquely abstracting from the bodily and social dimensions of personality. It is not clear to me that this line of criticism is at all fair, though, since it is perfectly open to the neo-Lockean to insist that persons must indeed be *embodied*, and moreover furnished with bodies apt for the performance of physical actions, including those necessary for social co-operation and communication. (After all – to pursue the computer analogy – you cannot run a program

[18] Cf. Hume, *Treatise*, p. 261: 'the true idea of the human mind, is to consider it a system of different perceptions . . . which are link'd together by the relation of cause and effect.'

on a chunk of rock or a tin can, much less on nothing at all; nor would anyone see fit to denigrate the notion of a program as introducing the 'myth' of a ghost in the hardware.) I suspect that all that this neo-Aristotelian line of criticism amounts to is once again the expression of anthropocentric prejudices. Yet for all that the neo-Lockean theory *is* untenable, and this for reasons of fundamental principle.

What is wrong with the neo-Lockean theory is that, in purporting to supply an account of the individuation and identity of persons it presupposes, untenably, that an account of the identity conditions of psychological modes can be provided which need not rely on reference to persons. But it emerges that the identity of any psychological mode turns on the identity of the person that possesses it. What this implies is that psychological modes are essentially modes *of persons*, and correspondingly that persons have to be conceived of as psychological *substances*. This is what I now hope to show.

By psychological modes I mean, as I have already explained, individual mental events, processes and states. (It is important to emphasize that we are talking about *individual* entities here – 'tokens' rather than 'types'.) Paradigm examples would be: a particular belief-state, a particular memory-state, a particular sensory experience, a particular sequence of thoughts constituting a particular process of reasoning, and so on. But, to repeat, such individual mental states are necessarily states *of persons*: they are necessarily 'owned' – necessarily have a *subject*. The necessity in question arises from the metaphysical-cum-logical truth that such individual mental states cannot even in principle be individuated and identified without reference to the subject of which they are states. (The point has been argued before by Strawson,[19] but it is none the less worth insisting on it again since Strawson's arguments seem to have gone quite widely unheeded.)

Consider thus the example of a particular experience of pain, which is a 'token' mental event occurring at a specific time. (Whether it occurs at a specific *place* is more contentious. We should not confuse the phenomenological location of the pain – where it is felt 'at', for instance in a certain tooth – with the place, if any, at which the token experience occurs. Physicalists would of course presume that the token experience is identifiable with a token neural event located in the brain, at least in the case of a human person; but the truth – and

---

[19] See Strawson, *Individuals*, ch. 3.

indeed the intelligibility – of physicalism is something that I have grave doubts about.[20]) Now, clearly, the qualitative character and time of occurrence of this token experience do not suffice to individuate it uniquely: two qualitatively indistinguishable token experiences could, logically, occur simultaneously (and quite probably often do, given the vastness of the world's population). What is additionally required to individuate the token experience, it appears, is precisely reference to its *subject*. For instance, if the pain is *mine*, then that it seems will serve to distinguish it from any other qualitatively exactly similar pain occurring at the same time.

But two questions arise here. First, can we be sure that there is no *other* way of individuating the token experience uniquely which does not require reference to its subject? And secondly, can we be sure that one and the same subject could *not* simultaneously have two qualitatively indistinguishable token experiences? Both of these questions have been interestingly addressed quite recently by Christopher Peacocke.[21] Peacocke suggests that although it is a necessary truth that one and the same subject cannot have two qualitatively indistinguishable token experiences at the same time, this is not because token experiences are individuated by reference to their qualitative character, time of occurrence and subject: rather, the explanation is quite the reverse of this, namely, that subjects themselves are individuated by reference to token experiences in such a way that where we have evidence for the occurrence of two simultaneous and qualitatively indistinguishable token experiences, this should *ipso facto* be taken to imply the existence of two distinct subjects of experience. In support of this suggestion, Peacocke appeals to an example involving a so-called 'split-brain' patient. We could, he contends, have good evidence for supposing that in the case of such a patient there might be, on a given occasion, 'two distinct but qualitatively identical experiences grounded in (different) states of the same brain'.[22] And, he goes on, 'It seems that if we speak of two distinct minds or centres of consciousness in these circumstances, we do so because the token experiences are themselves distinct.'[23] This presupposes, of course, a

---

[20] See further my *Kinds of Being*, pp. 113-14, 132-3, and chapter 3 below.
[21] See Christopher Peacocke, *Sense and Content: Experience, Thought and their Relations* (Oxford: Clarendon Press, 1983), pp. 176ff.
[22] Ibid., p. 177.
[23] Ibid.

favourable answer to the *first* question raised a moment ago: that is, it presupposes that we can individuate token experiences independently of their subject, and hence have independent evidence, in the case of the split-brain patient, for the simultaneous occurrence of two qualitatively indistinguishable token experiences.

Now Peacocke *does* consider that a favourable (to him) answer to our first question is available. He suggests that in order to individuate token experiences it suffices, apart from referring to their qualitative character and time of occurrence, to refer to their *causes and effects*. Thus, he says,

There is a clear motivation for saying that in the split brain there are two token experiences, a motivation which does not appeal to the identity of persons. The two experiences have different causes – for example, one results from the stimulation of one nostril, the other from the stimulation of the other nostril – and they may have different effects too.[24]

(Peacocke's example here involves, of course, olfactory experiences rather than pains, but this is beside the point.) However, I consider this line of argument to be fatally flawed. No doubt it is true that whenever two distinct token experiences occur, they will differ in respect of at least some of their causes and effects: but it is far from clear that one can effectively appeal to such causal distinctions to individuate token experiences quite independently of any reference to the subjects of those experiences. For it may be, as indeed I believe to be the case, that such causal distinctions themselves cannot be made independently of reference to subjects. But before pursuing this point it is worth remarking that to the extent that Peacocke's proposed criterion for the individuation of token experiences – sameness of causes and effects – is merely a special application of Davidson's well-known criterion for the individuation of events in general, it falls foul of the latter's fatal defect, which is a kind of circularity.[25] Briefly, the trouble with Davidson's criterion is that if (as Davidson himself proposes) the causes and effects of events are themselves events, then the question of whether events e_1 and e_2 have the *same* causes and effects (and

---

[24] Ibid.

[25] See Donald Davidson, 'The Individuation of Events', in his *Essays on Actions and Events* (Oxford: Clarendon Press, 1980). For an exposure of the defect, see my 'Impredicative Identity Criteria and Davidson's Criterion of Event Identity', *Analysis* 49 (1989), pp. 178–81.

hence turn out to be the same event according to the criterion) is itself a question concerning the identity of events, so that in the absence of an independent criterion of event identity Davidson's criterion leaves every question of event identity unsettled: hence it is either super-fluous or ineffectual. Moreover, Peacocke's special application of Davidson's criterion to mental events inherits this difficulty. For even if we suppose, for the sake of argument, that the individuation of *non*-mental events is unproblematic, it is none the less the case that no mental event has purely non-mental causes and effects: that is to say, every mental event has other mental events amongst its causes and effects. And hence the proposal to individuate mental events in terms of the sameness of their causes and effects will again presuppose answers to questions of the very sort at issue, namely, questions con-cerning the identity of mental events.

It will be of value to expand upon the point that mental events never have wholly non-mental causes and effects, not only in order to support a premise of the foregoing argument, but also because it will help to support the more ambitious claim I made a moment ago that causal distinctions between token experiences (and other mental states) cannot be made independently of reference to subjects. The point is that a mental event, such as a token sensory experience, can only occur *to* a subject, and moreover only to one in a condition which involves the simultaneous possession by that same subject of a whole battery of other mental states – at least some of which will stand in causal relations to the sensory experience in question, helping to determine such features as its intensity and duration and in turn being affected by it in various ways. For instance, if one directs one's attention away from a pain, its intensity may be diminished; again, if one believes that the pain is symptomatic of a serious illness, it may cause one to have fears which one would otherwise have lacked; and so on. That a pain should have such causal liaisons with other mental states of the same subject is partially constitutive of the very concept of pain. Thus we can make no sense at all of a subject undergoing a single sensory experience in the complete absence of all other mental activity, much less of a single sensory experience – a twinge of pain, say – occurring out of the blue to no subject at all. *Pace* Hume, 'perceptions', even if they are 'distinct', are frequently not 'separable'.[26] Mental events, even of the most rudimentary kinds, are only conceivable as elements within relatively well-integrated mental economies – that is, as parts of the mental lives of subjects.[27] At root, this is just a corollary of Davidson's own well-known thesis of the 'holism of the mental'.[28]

But let us now see how all this bears upon Peacocke's suggestion that causal distinctions can motivate a claim that two distinct token olfactory experiences occur in his imagined split-brain patient without relying on any consideration as to the number or identity of the subjects involved. What sorts of causal distinctions might be appealed to? Unfortunately, Peacocke only gestures in the direction of an answer, merely saying (as we have already seen) that 'The two experiences have different causes – for example, one results from the stimulation of one nostril, the other from the stimulation of the other nostril – and they may have different effects too.' But so far all we know about the imagined case is that it is one in which the *corpus callosum* of a living human brain is severed and subsequently the two nostrils neurally connected to the different hemispheres are simultaneously stimulated in the same way. Thus far, however, we have been given no reason for supposing that *either* stimulation results in an olfactory experience. For that, we need to know the answers to such questions as 'Was the patient awake?', 'Did he still possess a sense of smell?', 'Was he paying attention to the stimulus?', and so on. But these are all questions which precisely make reference to a putative *subject* of olfactory experience. Moreover, they presume – perhaps wrongly – that there is just a *single* subject present. But how is this presumption, if mistaken, to be recognized as being in error? That is, how are we to discover that we are dealing with two subjects rather than just one? Peacocke's suggestion seems to be that we *first* determine that each stimulation results in a distinct but qualitatively exactly similar token experience, and *then* on that basis assign each to a different subject, hence concluding that we have two subjects rather than one. But we have just seen that the question of whether a stimulation results in any

<hr/>

[26] Cf. Hume, *Treatise*, pp. 233, 634.

[27] This has been disputed recently by Andrew Brennan, in his 'Fragmented Selves and the Problem of Ownership', *Proceedings of the Aristotelian Society* 90 (1989/90), pp. 143-58. He cites in his support clinical cases of patients suffering from Korsakov's syndrome, which involves severe amnesia. However, my thesis is not an empirical one, vulnerable to the alleged findings of such psychiatric case studies, but rather a logico-metaphysical one which imposes an *a priori* constraint on what could *count* as an experience or as evidence for the occurrence of one.

[28] See Davidson, *Essays on Actions and Events*, p. 217.

olfactory experience at all is only answerable in the light of information concerning the prospective subject of that experience (whether he is awake, and so on). So Peacocke's suggested procedure presupposes an answer to the very question that it proposes to settle: for it presupposes, with respect to each stimulation, that we already have in view a subject to which any resulting experience may be assigned. The key point is that whether the stimulation of a particular nostril results in an olfactory experience depends precisely on whether that nostril is functioning as an olfactory sense organ of a subject who is identifiable as the possessor of a suitable range of further mental states at the time of stimulation. Hence it emerges that we cannot effectively motivate a claim that each stimulation results in a distinct token experience without relying on presumptions concerning the existence and identity of the prospective subject(s) of those experiences. And the more general lesson is that one cannot reasonably form judgements about the causation of mental events – including sensory experiences – independently of forming judgements about the subjects of those states, and so cannot expect judgements of the former sort to underpin the individuation of such states in a way which makes no reference to those subjects.[29]

But what then *are* we to say about the split-brain patient? *Do* we have two subjects here or only one? Let me say at once that I think it is a mistake to regard the psychological subject as a 'centre of consciousness'. (Peacocke himself shifts uneasily between the terms 'centre of consciousness', 'mind' and 'person' – all of which, in my view, demand quite different treatments.) The notion of the subject as a 'centre of consciousness' seems to involve precisely that Lockean conception of the self which I am now engaged in challenging: for it suggests that 'unity of consciousness' is somehow criterial for the identity of the self, and this I wish to deny. The case of the split-brain patient is indeed a difficult and puzzling one: but I am strongly inclined to urge that even in such a case we have only a single subject, albeit a subject quite possibly suffering from a partial bifurcation of consciousness, or 'divided mind'. Perhaps, however, this is really no more than an extreme case of a condition to which all psychological

[29] This elaborates and strengthens an argument to be found in my *Kinds of Being*, pp. 131-3.

subjects are prone.[30] At various times we all find ourselves 'dividing our attention' (as we say) – for example, engaging in conversation while negotiating busy traffic.

There remains one line of defence of the neo-Lockean theory which I have not yet tackled. The burden of my criticism of that theory has been that it fails to accommodate the fact that mental states have to be individuated as states *of persons*, for this introduces a vicious circularity into its attempt to specify the identity conditions of persons in terms of relations between mental states. But, it may be urged, the truth is only that mental states – being modes – have to be individuated as states *of something*, that is, as states of substances of *some* sort. And why, it may be asked, should not the neo-Lockean simply say that mental states are states *of the body* – allowing indeed that the body might in principle vary enormously in nature from one person to another? In fact, of course, the neo-Lockean who is also a physicalist does hold precisely this to be true. But the problem is that reference to the body is simply incapable of playing the individuative role here demanded of it. This is because by the neo-Lockean's own lights there can be no guarantee of a one-to-one correspondence between bodies (of whatever sort) and persons. Hence, in a case (however hypothetical) of co-embodiment by two distinct persons (as in the Jekyll and Hyde story), referring a mental state to a particular body will not determine to which person it belongs nor, hence, which token state it is. For persons cannot share token mental states, and so while it is left undetermined to which person a token state belongs, the identity of that token state must equally be left undetermined. For example, if the token state – say, a token belief-state – is referred to the Jekyll-Hyde body, this leaves it open whether it is Jekyll's belief-state or Hyde's belief-state: it cannot be *both* Jekyll's *and* Hyde's, but whose it is matters if we are to identify which particular belief-state it is.

Perhaps this argument will be objected to as question-begging, however. Perhaps it will be urged that reference to the Jekyll-Hyde body *will* serve to *identify* the belief-state, but merely leave undetermined whether this state belongs to Jekyll or to Hyde. But what if, as seems perfectly conceivable, Jekyll and Hyde *both* have token belief-states of exactly the same type? Still these token belief-states cannot be identical because, as has been remarked, token mental states are not

[30] Cf. Wilkes, *Real People*, ch. 5.

shareable between persons. In that case there will be two exactly similar token belief-states referrable to the same body, so that reference to that body will not, after all, serve to distinguish them. The plain fact is (and we should hardly be surprised by it) that in rejecting the biological substance view of persons in favour of the psychological mode view, the neo-Lockean theory has cut itself off from any possibility of treating the *body* as the 'owner' of mental states and thus as playing an essential role in their individuation. The 'owner' of mental states for the neo-Lockean theory must be the person *as opposed to* the body, even though the person itself is, according to that theory, a construct of mental states – the very mental states indeed of which it is the 'owner'. And it is of course precisely this circularity in the theory to which I object.

3. THE SELF AS A PSYCHOLOGICAL SUBSTANCE

The conclusion I draw from the preceding arguments is that a person or subject of mental states must be regarded as a *substance* of which those states are modes, and yet not as a *biological* substance (as the neo-Aristotelian theory would have it). What sort of substance, then? Clearly, a *psychological* substance. That is to say, a person is a substantial individual belonging to a natural kind which is the subject of distinctively psychological laws, and governed by persistence conditions which are likewise distinctively psychological in character. But thus far this is consistent with regarding a person as something like a Cartesian ego or soul, and this is a position from which I wish to distance myself. The distinctive feature of the Cartesian conception of a psychological substance is that such a substance is regarded as possessing *only* mental characteristics, not physical ones. And this is largely why it is vulnerable to certain sceptical arguments to be found in the writings of, *inter alia*, Locke and Kant. The burden of those arguments is that if psychological substances (by which the proponents of the arguments mean *immaterial* 'souls' or 'spirits') are the real subjects of mental states, then for all I know the substance having 'my' thoughts today is not the same as the substance that had 'my' thoughts yesterday: so that, on pain of having to countenance the possibility that my existence is very much more ephemeral than I care to believe, I had better not identify myself with the psychological substance (if any) currently having 'my' thoughts (currently 'doing the thinking in me').

But if *I* am not a psychological substance, it seems gratuitous even to suppose that such substances exist (certainly, their existence cannot be established by the Cartesian *cogito*).

By why should we suppose, with Descartes, that psychological substances must be essentially immaterial? Descartes believed this because he held a conception of substance according to which each distinct kind of substance has only one principal 'attribute', which is peculiar to substances of that kind, and such that all of the states of any individual substance of this kind are modes of this unique and exclusive attribute.[31] In the case of psychological or mental substances, the attribute is Thought; whereas in the case of physical or material substance(s), the attribute is Extension. On this view, no psychological substance can possess a mode of Extension, nor any physical substance a mode of Thought. However, I am aware of no good argument, by Descartes or anyone else, in support of his doctrine of unique and exclusive attributes. Accordingly, I am perfectly ready to allow that psychological substances should possess material characteristics (that is, include physical states amongst their modes). It may be that there is no material characteristic which an individual psychological substance possesses *essentially* (in the sense that its persistence conditions preclude its surviving the loss of this characteristic). But this does not of course imply that an individual psychological substance essentially possesses *no* material characteristics (to suppose that it did imply this would be to commit a 'quantifier shift fallacy' of such a blatant kind that I am loath to accuse Descartes himself of it).

How, though, does this repudiation of the Cartesian conception of psychological substance help against the sceptical arguments discussed a moment ago? Well, the main reason why those arguments seem to get any purchase is, I think, that in presupposing that psychological substances would have to be wholly non-physical, they are able to take it for granted that such substances are not possible objects of ordinary sense perception. They are represented as invisible and intangible, and as such at best only perceptible by some mysterious faculty of introspection, and hence only by each such substance in respect of itself. But once it is allowed that psychological substances have physical characteristics and can thus be seen and touched at least as 'directly' as any ordinary physical thing, the suggestion that we

[31] See René Descartes, *Principles of Philosophy*, I, sect. 53.

33

might be unable to detect a rapid turnover of these substances becomes as fanciful as the sceptical suggestion that the table on which I am writing might 'in reality' be a succession of different but short-lived tables replacing one another undetectably. Whether one can conclusively refute such scepticism may be an open question; but I see no reason to take it seriously or to allow it to influence our choice of ontological categories.

I believe, then, that a perfectly tenable conception of psychological substance may be developed which permits us to regard such substances as the subjects of mental states: which is just to say that nothing stands in the way of our regarding *persons* precisely as being psychological substances. The detailed development of such a conception is the topic of the remaining sections of this chapter, and for now it must suffice to say that I conceive of psychological substances as the proper subject-matter of the science of psychology, which in turn I conceive to be an autonomous science whose laws are not reducible to those of biology or chemistry or physics. However, it will be appropriate to close the present section with a few remarks on the relationship between psychological and biological substances, that is, between persons and their bodies. (I restrict myself here to the case of persons who – like human persons – have animal bodies.)

With regard to this issue I am, as I indicated at the outset, a *substantial dualist*. Persons are substances, as are their bodies. But they are not identical substances: for they have different persistence conditions, just as do their bodies and the masses of matter constituting those bodies at different times. (I should perhaps emphasize here that where a person's body is a biological substance, as in the case of human persons, the body is to be conceived of as a *living organism*, not as a mere mass of matter or assemblage of physical particles.) Clearly, though, my version of substantial dualism is quite different from Descartes's. Descartes, it seems, conceived a human person to be the product of a 'substantial union' of two distinct substances: a mental but immaterial substance and a material but non-mental substance. How such a union was possible perplexed him and every subsequent philosopher who endeavoured to understand it. The chief stumbling block was, once again, Descartes's doctrine of unique and exclusive attributes. How could something essentially immaterial be 'united' with something essentially material? But psychological substances as I conceive of them are *not* essentially immaterial. Moreover, in my

view, human persons are themselves just such psychological substances, not a queer hybrid of two radically alien substances. (I should
stress that my criticism of Descartes here pertains solely to his doctrine
of 'substantial union' and not to his conception of psychophysical
causation, which – as I shall explain in chapter 3 – I consider to be
far more defensible.)

So, as for the relationship between a person and his or her body, I
do not see that this need be more mysterious in principle than any of
the other intersubstantial relationships with which the natural sciences
are faced: for instance, the relationship between a biological entity
such as a tree and the assemblage of physical particles that constitutes
it at any given time. Most decidedly, I do not wish to minimize the
scientific and metaphysical difficulties involved here. (I do not, for
example, think that it would be correct to say that a person is
'constituted' by his or her body in anything like the sense in which
a tree is 'constituted' by an assemblage of physical particles.[32]) None
the less, it is my hope that by adopting a broadly Aristotelian conception of substance and by emphasizing not only the autonomy but also
the continuity of the special sciences, including psychology and biology, we may see a coherent picture begin to emerge of persons as a
wholly distinctive kind of being fully integrated into the natural
world: a picture which simultaneously preserves the 'Lockean' insight
that the concept of a person is fundamentally a psychological (as
opposed to a biological) one, the 'Cartesian' insight that persons are
a distinctive kind of substantial particulars in their own right, and the
'Aristotelian' insight that persons are not essentially immaterial beings.

4. THE SELF AS A BEARER OF PHYSICAL CHARACTERISTICS

Let us recall that we are not required to *deny* that a person or self has
physical characteristics, and though we have to regard it as distinct
from its body, we are not required to think of the two as separable
(except perhaps purely conceptually, or purely in imagination). But
what physical characteristics can we allow the embodied self to possess?
All those ascribable to its body? Only some of these? Some or all of

---

[32] For criticism of this suggestion, see my *Kinds of Being*, pp. 119-20.

these plus others not ascribable to it? We need above all a principled way of distinguishing between those statements of the form 'I am *F*' (where '*F*' is a physical predicate) which are more properly analysed as 'I have a body which is *F*', and those which can be accepted at face value. Here it may help us to consider whether or not the self is a *simple* substance – that is, whether or not it has *parts*. For if not, no statement of the form 'I am *F*' can be taken at face value if being *F* implies having parts. My own view is that the self is indeed a simple substance, and I shall argue for this later.

But does not *every* physical predicate imply divisibility into parts (as Descartes held – this being the basis of one of his main arguments for the immateriality of the self)? No, it does not. For instance, 'has a mass of seventy kilograms' does *not* imply having parts. A self could, thus, strictly and literally have a mass of seventy kilograms without it following logically that it possessed various parts with masses of less than that amount. (After all, an electron has a finite rest mass, but it does not, according to current physical theory, have parts possessing fractions of that rest mass.) Again, 'is six feet tall' does *not*, I consider, imply having parts, *in the relevant sense of 'part'*. The relevant sense of part is this: something is to be counted a 'part' of a substance in this sense only if that thing is itself a substance. We may call such a part a 'substantial part'. Simple substances have no substantial parts. We must, then, distinguish between a substantial part of a thing and a merely *spatial* part of it. A spatial part of an extended object is simply some geometrically defined 'section' of it (not *literally* a section, in the sense of something *cut out* from it, but merely a region of it defined by certain purely geometrical boundaries). Thus, for example, the left-hand third of my desk as it faces me is a *spatial* part of it. It is doubtless the case that there is *also* a substantial part of my desk which at present coincides exactly with that spatial part – namely, the mass of wood contained within that region. But it would be a category mistake to *identify* that mass of wood with the left-hand third of my desk.[33] Now, 'is six feet tall' certainly implies having *spatial* parts, but does not imply having *substantial* parts. Extended things – the claims of Descartes and Leibniz notwithstanding – *can* be simple substances.

[33] For further discussion of these issues, see my 'Substance, Identity and Time', *Proceedings of the Aristotelian Society*, supp. vol. 62 (1988), pp. 61-78, and my 'Primitive Substances', *Philosophy and Phenomenological Research* 54 (1994), pp. 531-52.

So far, then, I can allow that physical statements such as 'I weigh seventy kilograms' and 'I am six feet tall' may be taken at their face value. But a statement such as 'I am composed of organic molecules' *cannot* be so taken, but must be analysed rather as 'I have a body which is composed of organic molecules'. Even so, it is surely evident that if 'I weigh seventy kilograms' is literally true of me, it will be so only in virtue of the fact that I have a body which weighs seventy kilograms. And, indeed, it seems clear that all of the purely physical characteristics which are literally ascribable to the self will be thus ascribable in virtue of their being ascribable to the self's body – we can say that the self's purely physical characteristics 'supervene' upon those of its body.

But what, now, *is* it for the self to 'have' a certain body as 'its' body? Partly, it *is* just a matter of that self having certain physical character-istics which supervene upon those of *that* body rather than any other – though it is clear that this fact must be derivative from some more fundamental relationship. More than that, then, it must clearly also be a matter of the self's perceiving and acting 'through' that body, and this indeed must be the crucial factor which determines *which* body's physical characteristics belong also to a given self. But what *is* it to perceive and act 'through' a certain body rather than any other? As far as agency is concerned, this is a matter of certain parts of that body being directly subject to the agent's (that is, the self's) will: I can, of necessity, move certain parts of *my* body 'at will', and cannot move 'at will' any part of any body that is not part of mine.[34] (Here it may be conceded that someone completely paralysed may still possess a certain body, though only because he *could* once move parts of it 'at will', and still perceives through it; but someone completely paralysed *from birth* – if such a condition is possible – could only be said to 'have' a body in a more attenuated sense.) As far as perception is concerned, apart from the obvious point that one perceives the world from the position at which one's body is located (except under abnormal circumstances, as when one looks through a periscope), it may be remarked that one's own body is perceived in a different manner from others in that one's sensations of it are phenomenologically localized in the parts per-

---

[34] In another terminology, we may say that movements of certain parts of its own body can necessarily be executed as 'basic' actions by the self. The *locus classicus* for the notion of a 'basic' action is Arthur C. Danto's 'Basic Actions', *American Philosophical Quarterly* 2 (1965), pp. 141-8. In chapter 5 below I discuss the nature of 'basic' action more fully, offering an account of it which differs from Danto's in important respects.

ceived: when one feels one's foot, one locates that feeling *in the foot*, whereas when one feels a wall, one does not locate that feeling *in the wall*. (I discuss these and related issues more fully in chapter 7 below.)

Now it is true that in a less interesting sense all action and perception is 'through' a certain body, namely, in the sense that as an empirically ascertainable matter of fact I need my limbs to move and my eyes to see. But *these* facts do not as such serve to qualify my limbs and eyes as especially *mine*, as parts of *my* body. For, of course, I can be fitted with prosthetic devices for locomotion and vision, yet these do not *thereby* become parts of my body (though they *may* do so if they enter into the more intimate relationships discussed a moment ago). What makes my body peculiarly *mine*, then, is not determined merely by the empirically ascertainable dependencies that obtain between its proper functioning and my ability to engage in perception and agency. Thus, for example, even if it should turn out that I need a brain in order to think, it does not follow that this relationship suffices to make that brain peculiarly *mine*. In fact I should say that a certain brain qualifies as mine only derivatively, by virtue of being the brain belonging to *my* body, where the latter qualifies as mine by virtue of having parts related to me in the more intimate ways mentioned earlier. As far as these more intimate relationships are concerned, my brain is as alien to me as a stone or a chair.

My thoughts, feelings, intentions, desires and so forth all belong properly to me, not to my body, and are only to be associated with my body in virtue of those intimate relationships which make it peculiarly mine. It is impossible to associate such mental states with a body non-derivatively, that is, without relying upon their ascription to the self or person whose body it is – or so I would claim. No mere examination of brain-function or physical movement can warrant such an association, without a detour through a recognition of the existence of a self or person to whom the body belongs. This recognition, in interpersonal cases, will of course have to issue from empirical evidence – but it will be evidence of embodied selfhood in the first instance, not directly and independently of particular mental goings-on.[35]

---

[35] See further this chapter, section 2.

5. THE SELF AS A SIMPLE SUBSTANCE

But what now of my crucial claim that the self is simple, or lacks substantial parts? Well, what substantial parts *could* it have, given that the self is not to be identified with the body? Parts of the body cannot be parts of the self. If the self and the body had exactly the same parts, they would apparently have to be identical substances after all (certainly, standard mereological theory would imply this).[36] Similarly, if it were urged that all and only parts of the brain, say, were parts of the self, this would imply that self and brain were identical. So I conclude that the self can have *none* of the body's parts as parts of itself, unless perhaps the self could have other substantial entities *in addition* to bodily parts as parts of itself. However, no other substantial entity *does* appear to be a tenable candidate for being a substantial part of the self, whether or not in addition to bodily parts. For instance, the self patently does not consist of a plurality of lesser 'selves' acting cooperatively, despite the picturesque 'homuncular' descriptions of mental functioning advanced by some philosophers.[37] Such descriptions are not intelligible if taken literally. (Similarly, we should not take literally overblown talk of 'corporate persons', that is, the idea that institutions like clubs and firms are genuinely persons in their own right.[38] At neither level – subpersonal nor suprapersonal – does the concept of a person find anything other than metaphorical application.) Nor should we regard the mind's various 'faculties' – will, intellect, appetite, or modern variants thereof, such as linguistic or visual processing 'modules' – as being 'parts' of the self. For in the first place it is a mistake to reify faculties, and in any case they certainly

---

[36] See, e.g., Nelson Goodman, *The Structure of Appearance*, 3rd edn (Dordrecht: D. Reidel, 1977), pp. 33ff. Standard mereological theory is possibly wrong on this score, if it is correct (as I believe) to differentiate between a tree, say, and the mass of wood which temporarily composes it – for these may seem to have the same parts, at least during the period in which the one composes the other. However, while the tree and the wood arguably have the same *spatial* parts, it is much more debatable whether they have the same *substantial* parts. For instance, a certain root will be a substantial part of the *tree*, but hardly of the wood composing the tree. (By contrast, a substantial part of the wood composing the tree arguably *is* also a substantial part of the tree.) The issue is a complex one, which I cannot go into in further depth here. But, in any case, I think it independently reasonable to deny that substantial parts of the body are literally parts of the self (and I do not think of the body as in any sense *composing* the self).

[37] See, e.g., Daniel C. Dennett, *Brainstorms*, pp. 122-4.

[38] See, e.g., Roger Scruton, 'Corporate Persons', *Proceedings of the Aristotelian Society*, supp. vol. 63 (1989), pp. 239-66.

could not qualify as *substantial* parts, which are what are now at issue. Faculties have no possibility of independent existence and should properly be seen as no more than abstractions from the mental lives of persons. For instance, the notion of a will without an intellect, or of a language faculty in the absence of belief and desire, is just nonsense. Finally, it will not do to speak of the self's psychological states and processes themselves – its beliefs, intentions, experiences and so forth – as being 'parts' (much less as being substantial parts) of it: for this would only be at all appropriate on a Humean constructivist view of the self (the 'bundle' theory), which we have rejected. I conclude, therefore, that if the self is a substance, it must indeed be a *simple* substance, entirely lacking substantial parts.

The simplicity of the self goes some way towards explaining its *unity*, including the unity of consciousness that characterizes its normal condition. Where this unity threatens to break down – as in various clinical conditions such as those of so-called multiple personality, schizophrenia, brain-bisection, and so on – we are indeed inclined to speak of a plurality of selves, or of divided selves. In fact I think such talk should again not be taken literally, and that the psychological unity that most fundamentally characterizes the self is not merely to be located at the level of consciousness.[39] A divided consciousness is, I think, in principle consistent with self-identity: what is not is a radical disunity of beliefs and values, manifested in a radical inconsistency of thought and action. (Of course, we all display mild inconsistencies, but no *one* person could intelligibly be interpreted as possessing the incompatibilities of belief and value that typically characterize different persons.) Now, a complex entity can act in disunified ways because the various incompatible or conflicting activities can be referred to different parts of the entity. Thus a corporate entity such as a firm or a club can act inconsistently because its members may act in conflicting ways. But the actions of the self – those that are truly predicable of it (because they are genuinely intentional) and not of the body (such as so-called reflex actions) – cannot in this way be ascribed to different elements or parts within the self. So we see that the simplicity and the unity of the self are indeed intimately related, even though there must clearly be much more to the matter than these brief remarks disclose.

[39] See again section 2 of this chapter.

Another consequence of the simplicity of the self is this. If the self is a simple substance, then it appears that there can be no diachronic criterion of identity which grounds its persistence through time.[40] This is not to say that there may not be some *cause* of its persistence. It may well be, thus, that the continued normal functioning of the brain is a causally necessary condition of the persistence of the self, at least in the case of embodied, human persons. But it would not follow from this that the identity of the self over time is grounded in continuity of brain-function, or indeed anything else. Nor should we think it contrary to the self's status as a substance that its existence may be thus causally dependent upon the functioning of another, distinct substance – the brain or, more generally, the body. No tenable account of substance can insist that a true substance be causally independent of all other substances. For instance, a tree is as substantial an entity as anyone could wish for, yet of course its continued existence depends upon the maintenance of a delicate balance of forces in nature, both within it and between it and its environment. But a tree is a *complex* substance, and accordingly its persistence can be understood as grounded in the preservation of certain relationships between its substantial parts, despite the gradual replacement of those parts through natural processes of metabolism and growth. Not so with a self, any more than with, say, an electron or other 'fundamental' particle. Thus the reason why the self – or any simple substance – cannot be provided with a criterion of diachronic identity is that such a criterion (in the case of a substance or continuant) always makes reference to a substance's constituent parts, of which simple substances have none.[41]

That the diachronic identity of simple substances, including the self, is primitive or ungrounded should not be seen as making their persistence over time somehow mysterious or inscrutable. In the first place, as I have already pointed out, it does not preclude us from recognizing the involvement of various causal factors in their persistence. Secondly, we can still concede, or better insist, that there are certain

---

[40] For more general discussion of persistence and criteria of identity, see my 'Substance, Identity and Time' and also my 'What is a Criterion of Identity?', *Philosophical Quarterly* 39 (1989), pp. 1-21.

[41] See further my 'Lewis on Perdurance versus Endurance', *Analysis* 47 (1987), pp. 152-4, my 'The Problems of Intrinsic Change: Rejoinder to Lewis', *Analysis* 48 (1988), pp. 72-7 and, especially, my 'Primitive Substances'.

necessary constraints on the possible history of any simple substance of a given kind, that is to say, limits on the sorts of changes it can intelligibly be said to undergo, or limits arising from empirically discoverable natural laws governing substances of this kind. Thus in the case of the self, a possible history must have a certain internal coherence to be intelligible, not least because perception and action are only possible within a temporal framework that includes both forward and backward-looking mental states (intention and memory). Finally, the persistence of at least some simple substances is, I consider, presumed at the very heart of our understanding of time and change in general, so that we should not expect to be able to give a reductive or exhaustive account of all such persistence.[42] Indeed, since the only simple substances directly known to us without benefit of scientific speculation and experimentation are precisely *ourselves*, I would urge that the pretheoretical intelligibility of time and change that is presupposed by all scientific theorizing actually rests upon our acquaintance with ourselves as simple persisting substances. So, although in the *ontological* order of nature it may well be the primitive persistence of fundamental physical particles that underpins objective time-order – makes the world *one* world in time – still, in the *conceptual* order of thought it is the persistence of the self that underpins our very grasp of the notion of objective time-order. If this is indeed so, it would clearly be futile to expect the concept of the self to reveal upon analysis an account of the self's identity over time which did not implicitly presume the very thing in question.

A consequence of the ungroundedness of the self's identity over time is that there is, and can be, no definitive condition that necessarily determines the ceasing-to-be (or, indeed, the coming-to-be) of a self. In the case of complex substances which are governed by criteria of identity the conditions for substantial change (that is, their coming or ceasing-to-be) can be specified fairly exactly, even though these conditions may in some cases be infected by some degree of vagueness. But not so with simple substances – and this is not, with them, a matter of *vagueness* at all (not, at least, in the sense in which 'vagueness' implies the existence of 'fuzzy' boundaries, whose 'fuzziness' may be measured in degrees). This observation certainly seems to apply in the realm of fundamental particle physics, as far as

[42] See further my 'Substance, Identity and Time'.

I can judge. Thus if, in a particle interaction, an electron collides with an atomic nucleus and various fission products arise, including a number of electrons, it would seem that there may be no determinate 'fact of the matter' as to whether the original electron is, or is not, identical with a given one of the electrons emerging from the impact event. There is here, it would seem, a genuine indeterminateness (I do not say *vagueness*) of identity.[43] But this should not lead us to view with suspicion the idea that electrons *do* genuinely persist identically through time. Note, too, that known constraints on the possible history of an electron *may* enable us to rule out *some* reidentifications as impossible in a case such as that described – so the indeterminacy is not totally unconstrained, which would be bizarre indeed; but the point is that even when all such constraints are taken into account, there may still be a residual indeterminacy in a given case.

Returning to the self, we see, thus, that while we may well believe that we have good scientific grounds for believing that the functioning of the brain is *causally* necessary for the continued existence of the self, none the less, in the nature of the case, such evidence as we possess for this is bound to be inconclusive (and not just for the reason that all empirical evidence is defeasible), since we lack any proper grasp of what would *constitute* the ceasing-to-be of a self. Lacking that grasp, we cannot really say what empirical evidence would or would not support a claim that a self had ceased to be. This is why the prospects for life after bodily death must inevitably remain imponderable and unamenable to empirical determination.

Against this it may be urged that, since I have allowed that perception and agency are essential to selfhood, I must allow that the cessation of these *would* constitute a terminus for the self's existence. However, it is the *capacity* for perception and agency that is essential, not its perpetual *exercise*. Very well, so can we not say that the demise of this capacity – and certainly its *permanent* demise – would constitute the demise of the self? But this is not really informative. For what would *constitute* the permanent demise of this capacity? Only, as far as I can see, the demise of the self – that is to say, no non-circular answer

---

[43] A sizeable literature related to this issue has grown out of Gareth Evans's paper 'Can There be Vague Objects?', *Analysis* 38 (1978), p. 208, though this is no place for me to attempt to engage with it. I discuss the electron case more fully and challenge Evans's argument against indeterminate identity in my 'Vague Identity and Quantum Indeterminacy', *Analysis* 54 (1994), pp. 110–14.

can be given. It will not do to say that the permanent cessation of brain-function would *constitute* the demise of the capacity for perception and agency. For the most we can really say is that there seems to be an empirical correlation between mental activity and brain-function, at least in the case of human persons. But the capacity for perception and agency does not of its nature *reside* in any sort of cerebral condition. Indeed, there is nothing whatever unintelligible about supposing the existence of a capacity for perception and agency in a being lacking a brain.

6. PHYSICALISM, NATURALISM AND THE SELF

Is physiological psychology, or neuropsychology, a contradiction in terms, then? Not at all, so long as it is seen as telling us empirical facts about the condition of embodied human persons or selves – telling us what sorts of processes as a matter of fact go on in their brains and nervous systems when they think or feel or act. This is not, though, and cannot be, an account of what *constitutes* thought or feeling or agency in a human person. Thought can no more *be* (or be constituted by) a brain-process than a chair can *be* (or be constituted by) a set of prime numbers.[44] Nor should we be tempted into saying such things as that a brain-process may 'realize' an episode of thinking (as more cautious modern physicalists sometimes put it) – for what on earth is this really supposed to *mean*?

In answer to this last question, it will perhaps be said that what it means to say that brain-processes 'realize' thought-episodes is that thought-episodes 'supervene' upon brain-processes, at least in the case of human persons. But this sheds no real illumination either, for the notion of supervenience (however useful it may be in some contexts) is out of its depth here. Suppose we ask what it means to say that thought-episodes supervene upon brain-processes. We shall perhaps be told that what this means is that if *A* and *B* are two human persons who share (type-)identical brain-states at a given time (that is, whose brain structures are atom-for-atom, neuron-for-neuron indistinguishable at that time, with all of these neurons in identical states of

---

[44] Cf. P. T. Geach, *Truth, Love and Immortality: An Introduction to McTaggart's Philosophy* (London: Hutchinson, 1979), p. 134.

excitation), then of necessity *A* and *B* will be enjoying (type-)identical thought-episodes at that time. (Perhaps not thought-episodes identical in *content*, if we are to accept the conclusions of Putnam and Burge regarding so-called 'Twin-Earth' cases,[45] but none the less ones that are subjectively indistinguishable – whatever that means!) But the empirical status of this sort of claim (and presumably it cannot be paraded as anything more than an empirical claim, since it can have no *a priori* justification) is highly problematic.

Let us first be clear that the thesis must be that thought-episodes supervene *globally* or *holistically* (rather than just piecemeal) upon brain-processes, since it is clear that to the extent that thought is dependent on the brain it can be so only in a holistic way which will not permit us to make any empirically confirmable claims about individual dependencies between particular ('token') thought-episodes and particular ('token') brain-events or processes.[46] So the thesis must be that a person with a brain exactly replicating mine at a level of neuronal organization and excitation will enjoy a mental life (feelings, beliefs, memories and so on) indistinguishable from mine, but not that any partial replication would engender any corresponding partial similarity in mental life. Nothing short of whole-brain replication will do. But what we now need to ask is this: what causal constraints would there be upon the process of bringing two distinct brains into such a state of exact neural replication? It is irrelevant that one might in some sense be able to *imagine* this being done, perhaps instantaneously, by a device that we tendentiously dub a 'brain replicator': you walk in through one door, the operator throws the switch, and then you and your Doppelgänger walk out hand in hand. One might as well say that the trick could be performed by magic. So might pigs fly. But in fact it seems clear that there is simply *no* non-miraculous way in which this feat could be achieved. It would not even suffice, for instance, to take identical twins from the moment of conception and attempt to submit them to exactly similar environ-

---

[45] See, especially, Tyler Burge, 'Individualism and the Mental', *Midwest Studies in Philosophy* 4 (1979), pp. 73-121.

[46] This appears to be an inescapable implication of Donald Davidson's well-known thesis of the 'holism of the mental', for which see his *Essays on Actions and Events*, p. 217. I do not, for reasons which I have already made plain earlier in this chapter, accept Davidson's own view of the relations between mental and physical events, which is a 'token-token' identity theory. See further my *Kinds of Being*, pp. 113-14, 132-3.

mental and social stimuli. For, first of all, the growth of nerve cells involves a good deal of randomness,[47] and secondly, it seems likely that brains, at the relevant level of organization, constitute a class of so-called 'chaotic systems'.[48] Thus it could be that because the twins are subjected to minutely different influences for brief periods during their early development (as is effectively unavoidable), neural connections end up getting laid down in quite different ways in the two brains. The more one reflects on the matter, the more evident it should become that the whole idea of bringing two brains into identical neural states is so completely fanciful that it merits no place in serious philosophical inquiry.[49]

It will not do for the physicalist to protest here that all he is interested in or committed to is the bare conceptual possibility of such whole-brain replication: for even if you can really get your mind around this notion, what are you supposed to *do* with it? Precisely because the notion of such replication is the stuff of pure fantasy utterly beyond the realm of scientific possibility, it cannot be conjoined with any genuine scientific findings from neuropsychology in order to yield a verdict on the truth or falsehood of the supervenience thesis. Nor can we justify such a verdict by consulting our 'intuitions' regarding the upshot of the imagined replication experiment – for we are simply not *entitled* to any 'intuitions' about the matter, and any we do have we probably owe simply to our own prejudices. So my conclusion is that even if the supervenience thesis is coherently statable (and even this may be in question), we can have no possible basis, either empirical or *a priori*, for judging it to be true.

But now it may be objected that this rejection of physicalism even in the comparatively weak form of the supervenience thesis is unacceptably at odds with a 'naturalistic' view of human beings and the mind. The emergence of mind must, it may be said, be recognized as

---

[47] See further Gerald M. Edelman, *Neural Darwinism: The Theory of Neuronal Group Selection* (Oxford: Oxford University Press, 1989), pp. 33-7.

[48] See, e.g., James P. Crutchfield *et al.*, 'Chaos', *Scientific American* 255 (December 1986), pp. 38-49, and Ary L. Goldberger *et al.*, 'Chaos and Fractals in Human Physiology', *Scientific American* 262 (February 1990), pp. 34-41.

[49] It has also been pointed out that if quantum states of the brain have to be taken into account (as they will be if mental states are at all dependent on them), then exact duplication at the relevant level of organization will be ruled out by quantum mechanical principles: see Roger Penrose, *The Emperor's New Mind: Concerning Computers, Minds, and the Laws of Physics* (Oxford: Oxford University Press, 1989), p. 270.

being a result of evolutionary processes working upon the genetic make-up of animal life-forms, through wholly biochemical means. Hence a biological account of mentality is inescapable if one has any pretence to being 'scientific'. There cannot be anything more to thought than can be exhaustively explained in biochemical terms, for otherwise the emergence of mind seems to be an inexplicable freak or accident. But again this is an objection which just reflects a dogmatic prejudice. Indeed, it is thoroughly question-begging and circular. It is just assumed from the outset that any wholly adequate explanation of the *emergence* of mind must be purely biological in character, because it is already presupposed that mind or mentality is a wholly biological characteristic of biological entities – animal life-forms. But the whole burden of my position is precisely that the mind is *not* a biological phenomenon and that mentality is *not* a property of the biological entities which constitute human bodies. That such entities should be apt to embody selves or persons can, indeed, be no accident – but why presume that the evolution of such bodies or organisms is to be explained in exclusively biochemical terms? It is the environment of organisms that determines the evolutionary pressures on them to adapt and change: but the 'environment', in the present instance, cannot necessarily be specified in wholly physical and biochemical terms. All that can be said is that the *proximate* cause of genetic mutation is biochemical, as are the *proximate* causal factors favouring selection. But these causal factors are themselves effects, and the chain of causation can easily take us beyond the biochemical sphere. After all, we *know* that minds can affect the evolution of organisms, for the intelligent activities of human beings have done so within historical time. So there is nothing miraculous or non-naturalistic in the idea that the evolution of mind and that of body are *mutually interactive*, just as (on my view) individual minds and bodies are themselves mutually interactive. Thus, my answer to the 'evolutionary' objection is that, unless it is presumed, question-beggingly, that only if the mental were biologically based could it affect the environmental selective pressures on organisms, it cannot be held that a non-biological view of the mental such as mine is at odds with evolutionary theory.

But we need not take a purely defensive stance on this issue. It is worth remarking that archaeological evidence points to the occurrence of a fundamental intellectual transition in the human race some 35,000 years ago, not apparently connected with any radical biological or neurological development in the human organism.[50] This was a transition from a primitive condition in which human creativity was limited to the production of the most rudimentary and severely practical tools to a condition recognizably akin to our own, with the flourishing of visual and plastic arts reflective of a sophisticated aesthetic sensibility. The development of this condition, we may reasonably suppose, went hand-in-hand with that of true language, systems of religious thought, and the beginnings of political structures. At the root of these developments, it seems, was the emergence of genuine systems of *representation*, without which the sophisticated level of thought, communication and social structure essential for personal being would be impossible. Now, as I say, it seems likely that these developments were *not* the upshot of any radical change in human brain structure or neural processing capacity, but arose rather through concomitant changes in patterns of social interaction and organization.[51] And indeed we can observe essentially the same phenomenon in microcosm today in the education and socialization of human infants – who, unless they are subjected to appropriate social, cultural and linguistic stimuli at an early age, are doomed never to develop a truly human personality and character. The implication of all this, I suggest, is that selves or persons are not created through biological processes but rather through socio-cultural forces, that is, through the cooperative efforts of other selves or persons. Persons create persons, quite literally.

The picture I am sketching of self-creation and the evolution of human personality is not all fanciful or 'unscientific'. On the contrary, what seems utterly fanciful and facile is the biological reductivism which we see promoted so forcefully by many philosophers

---

[50] See Randall White, 'Visual Thinking in the Ice Age', *Scientific American* 261 (July 1989), pp. 74–81, and 'Rethinking the Middle/Upper Paleolithic Transition', *Current Anthropology* 23 (1982), pp. 169–92. See also the papers by White and others in Paul Mellars and Chris Stringer (eds.), *The Human Revolution: Behavioural and Biological Perspectives on the Origins of Modern Humans* (Edinburgh: Edinburgh University Press, 1989), especially section 2.

[51] This would be consistent with much of the recent work of psychologists, anthropologists and ethologists presented in Richard Byrne and Andrew Whiten (eds.), *Machiavellian Intelligence: Social Expertise and the Evolution of Intellect in Monkeys, Apes, and Humans* (Oxford: Clarendon Press, 1988).

today.[52] When we reflect on how much we depend for our human condition upon the artificial and social environment that we ourselves have created, it seems quite incredible to suppose that one could hope to explain the human condition as having a basis solely in the organization of the human brain. Indeed, where human brain development and structure *do* differ significantly from those of the higher primates like chimpanzees – for instance, in connection with our respective linguistic capacities – it seems proper to regard the difference as being at least as much a *product* as a *cause* of the different life-styles of human beings and primates. For, of course, the neural structures in these distinctive parts of the human brain develop in human infants only in response to the right sorts of educative and social influences. It is true that a chimpanzee cannot, by being treated from birth like a human child, be made to develop in the way that the latter does, and this seems to betoken some innate biological difference. But we cannot assume that what we possess and the chimpanzees lack is some innate propensity specifically to develop human personality, language-use, aesthetic appreciation, mathematical abilities, and so forth. For it may be that what debars the chimpanzees from taking advantage of our human processes of socialization and personality-creation is not an innate inability to acquire the capacities which these processes confer upon us, but rather just an inability to engage appropriately with these particular processes, geared as they are to specifically human needs and characteristics. After all, a human being could probably never learn to swim if it had to take lessons from dolphins: but this does not show that it is impossible for human beings to acquire a capacity to swim, only that the acquisition process must be one that is geared to human limitations. In like manner, it is not inconceivable that chimpanzees could be inducted into processes of personality-creation, if only processes appropriately tailored to their particular limitations could be discovered.[53] (Whatever

---

[52] My opposition extends even to the most sophisticated modern proponents of the biological approach, such as Ruth G. Millikan: see her *Language, Thought, and Other Biological Categories* (Cambridge, MA: MIT Press, 1984). However, a detailed critique must await another occasion.

[53] I should remark, incidentally, that I by no means wish to deny *mentality* to chimpanzees and other higher primates, though I very much doubt whether any such animal may be said to possess or embody a 'self', as I have defined that term. Thus, inasmuch as mental states necessarily attach to psychological subjects which are not to be identified with biological bodies (see further section 2 of this chapter), I am committed to the view that persons or selves are not the only species of psychological substance, and that – in

one makes of the attempts to teach chimpanzees such as Washoe the genuine use of language, it is clear that they only even began to look successful when they took into account chimpanzees' severely restricted capacities for vocalization, and substituted sign-language for speech.[54])

Perhaps the following analogy will help to convey the general sense of my proposal. A potter takes a lump of clay – which has, as such, no specific *propensity* to be formed into any sort of artefact, such as a statue or a vase, though it is *suitable* material for such a purpose, in a way that a bunch of feathers, say, would not be – and he forms it into, let us say, a vase. In creating the vase he has created a new substantial particular, distinct from, though of course embodied in, the lump of clay. In like manner, I suggest, human persons acting cooperatively take the biological 'clay' of their offspring and 'shape' it into new persons. And this 'clay', though of course it has to be *suited* to the 'shaping' processes applied to it, need not be thought of as having a specific *propensity* to receive such a 'shape'. Finally, to complete the analogy, a human person, emerging from this 'shaping' process, is a new substantial particular, distinct from though embodied in the biological entity that is the 'clay'. It is no accident, surely, that it is precisely this metaphor for the creation of persons that we find so often in religious and mythic literature. Note, furthermore, one aspect of the analogy which is particularly apt: what constitutes 'suitable' material for formation into an artefact of any given sort is not purely a function of the inherent properties of that material together with the nature of the sort of artefact in question, but *also* a function of the sorts of creative processes that the artificer is equipped to apply to the material. Clay is a suitable material to make into vases as far as *human* artificers are concerned, but only because human beings have hands with which they can shape the clay. It should also be said, though, that many processes of artefact-creation are facilitated, or sometimes only made possible, through the use of previously created artefacts (for example, the potter's wheel). In like manner, now, what makes *human* biological material 'suitable' for the creation of persons is not just a function of the inherent biological characteristics of that material

an older terminology – there are 'animal souls' which find a place 'below' ourselves in a hierarchy of psychological substances. I hope to discuss this issue more fully elsewhere.

[54] See, e.g., Eugene Linden, *Apes, Men and Language* (Harmondsworth: Penguin Books, 1976).

together with the nature of the psychological capacities which need to be conferred, but also a function of the creative processes available to us given our own particular limitations, although indeed some of these limitations may be progressively transcended through the exploitation of previous products of our own creativity, that is, through exploitation of our growing socio-cultural, linguistic and technological heritage.

I should just stress, in conclusion, that what I have just been developing *is* only an analogy: I do not want to suggest that persons literally *are* artefacts, other than in the liberal sense that they are products of personal creativity. Above all, unlike material artefacts, persons or selves are *simple* substances: parts of their bodies are not parts of *them*, as bits of clay are parts of a vase. Moreover, whereas it is plausible to hold that all of a vase's intrinsic properties supervene upon certain properties of its constituent clay, it is not, as we have seen, reasonable to regard the self's psychological properties as supervening upon any properties of its body, such as neurophysiological properties of its brain. The self is what it is, and not another thing.

3

Mental causation

It is widely supposed that dualist theories of the mind–body relation face an intractable difficulty concerning psychophysical causation – even if it is not always agreed what, precisely, the nature of the difficulty is. Perhaps two main, if vague, areas of concern can be identified, one more serious than the other. The first is that dualism, in allegedly representing the mind as utterly distinct from and unlike anything physical, has a problem in rendering intelligible any kind of causal nexus between the two domains. But the proper response to this, first given by Hume, is to deny that we should expect *any* causal nexus to be 'intelligible' in the sense in which dualism allegedly fails to represent psychophysical causation as being. One does not have to adopt a 'Humean' theory of causation – the 'regularity' or 'constant conjunction' theory – to avail oneself of this response (and, incidentally, it doesn't presently concern me whether Hume himself *was* a 'Humean' in this sense). All one has to draw from Hume is the idea that causal relations are not, in general, knowable *a priori*, like logico-mathematical relations. Anyway, I have no intention of discussing further this (to my mind) spurious aspect of the supposed problem that psychophysical causation poses for the dualist. The more serious area of concern is created by the suspicion that dualist views of the mind–body relation – and certainly those that are interactionist – are somehow at odds with the findings of modern physical science: not only physiology and neurology, but also, more fundamentally, physics itself. Although, for reasons given in chapter 1, I prefer to represent my form of dualism as a dualism of *self* and body rather than as a dualism of *mind* and body, I cannot afford to ignore this challenge and shall devote the whole of the present chapter to meeting it.

1. DUALISM VERSUS PHYSICALISM: THE TERMS OF THE DEBATE

Before addressing the challenge that has just been raised, some more general remarks are in order concerning the term *dualism* – which, as I have already indicated, is open to different interpretations. It is customary nowadays to distinguish between 'substance dualism' and 'property dualism', and to treat the former – with Descartes as its archetypal proponent – as the principal target of criticism. (I should stress that I am only concerned to discuss *interactionist* dualisms, not epiphenomenalist or parallelist theories, which avoid the problem of psychophysical causation only by denying – utterly implausibly – that such causation occurs and is a two-way affair.) *Substance dualism* is traditionally conceived as the view that mind and body are distinct and separable substances, the former unextended and conscious, the latter extended and non-conscious. *Property dualism* (attributed to Spinoza by some commentators) is then the view that mental and physical properties are quite distinct, but may none the less be properties of the same substantial particular – which by some accounts might be the brain (a physical substance).

But this familiar dichotomy is clearly not an entirely satisfactory basis for classifying dualisms, partly for reasons that I have already given. For one thing, there are non-Cartesian dualisms which are classifiable as substance dualisms according to some accounts of the term 'substance' – not least, Strawson's dualism of persons and bodies (a version of which I have just defended in the previous chapter), which treats persons as distinctive in being subjects of *both* psychological *and* physical predicates.[1] Secondly, 'property dualism' as hitherto defined subsumes a variety of different positions, some but not all of which are fairly straightforwardly *physicalist* theories of mind – for a great deal turns on the bearing that one takes property dualism to have on the status of mental events and processes. An espousal of property dualism might only indicate a rejection of so-called 'type-type' identity theories of mental events (and need not even entail that, depending on one's theory of events and event-types). Certainly one could espouse a 'token-token' identity theory of mental events –

---

[1] See P. F. Strawson, *Individuals: An Essay in Descriptive Metaphysics* (London: Methuen, 1959), ch. 3.

identifying individual mental events with individual physical events in the brain – while upholding property dualism.

Further needless discussion can however be avoided at this stage by observing that since (as I shall for the moment be assuming, at least) causation is a relation between individual events, if any form of dualism has a problem as regards psychophysical causation, it has one *only if* it represents individual mental events as being distinct from – non-identical with – individual physical events. I should stress that I say 'only if', not 'if'. For it is possible to reject token identity between mental and physical events and yet still be a species of physicalist concerning the mind, and hence avoid the (dualist) problem of psychophysical causation – for one may espouse some form of *supervenience* theory, whereby mental events supervene upon, but are not necessarily identical with, physical events. According to such a view – which holds, roughly, that there is never a mental difference without an underlying physical difference – mental events have no independent causal powers: for any causal difference they make to the train of physical (and other mental) events they do so in virtue of the difference made by the physical events upon which they supervene. In short, a dualist theory is faced by a problem over psychophysical causation if and only if it maintains that mental events have *independent causal powers* – that they make a difference to how the world goes over and above any difference made by physical events.

Now, why should we concern ourselves with the problems of any such form of dualism? Well, I have a personal concern because I believe that some such form of dualism is probably *true* – because I reject both token-token identity theories and supervenience theories of mental events and processes. I shall not repeat now my various reasons for this in any detail, beyond saying that I consider token-token theories to be of dubious intelligibility because I think that mental events and physical events have different and incompatible criteria of individuation and identity, while I regard supervenience theories as being inherently unamenable to empirical (much less *a priori*) support or confirmation.[2] One thing worth saying in this connection, however, concerns some of the philosophical arguments that are commonly adduced in favour of identity and supervenience

---

[2] On token-token identity theories, see further my *Kinds of Being: A Study of Individuation, Identity and the Logic of Sortal Terms* (Oxford: Basil Blackwell, 1989), pp. 113–14, 132–3. On supervenience theories, see further chapter 2, section 6, above.

theories: very often these arguments effectively proceed from an assumption that *only* the physical can (ultimately) have causal powers – so that if mental events have causal powers they can do so only by virtue of being identical with, or supervening upon, physical events. But, fairly transparently, this is a form of argument that illicitly assumes precisely what it attempts to establish. Non-question-begging arguments for identity or supervenience theories are hard – indeed, I think impossible – to find.[3]

Let me give a simple example. It is sometimes urged that if a mental event M is to be regarded as the (or even *a*) cause of a physical event P, then since (as it is assumed) P will have a *wholly physical* causal explanation in terms of the occurrence of a set of prior physical events P_1 - P_n, the mental event M must either be identical with one of P_1 - P_n (or with the 'fusion' of two or more of these), or at least somehow 'supervene' upon or be 'realized' by one or more of P_1 - P_n – for to deny this is to imply, quite implausibly, that P and indeed all other mentally caused physical events are systematically causally overdetermined. But the assumption that P has a 'wholly physical' causal explanation precisely begs the question against the dualist who maintains that M is a non-physical event with independent causal powers.[4]

To be fair, however, charges of question-begging have to be handled delicately, and in the present case matters are perhaps more complicated than I have so far represented them as being. The claim that only the physical can have causal powers – or, at least, that only the physical can causally affect the physical – may be seen by many not just as some question-begging antidualist prejudice, but as a cornerstone of modern physical science. It is the principle that the physical world is a *causally closed system* – a principle which might be viewed as the metaphysical implication of the various conservation laws of physics: the laws of the conservation of energy and of linear and angular momentum. And these laws, surely, are not mere prejudices but, on the contrary, very high-level but none the less empirical generalizations discovered over the centuries by hard thought and backed by countless observations and experiments.

But now that we are going to take these complications seriously, we must see that we haven't yet reached the end of them. For one thing,

---

[3] Cf. T. Crane, 'Why Indeed? Papineau on Supervenience', *Analysis* 51 (1991), pp. 32-7.
[4] See further my 'Against an Argument for Token Identity', *Mind* 90 (1981), pp. 120-1.

we shall see shortly that the principle that the physical world is causally closed by no means follows from the conservation laws of physics alone, and that what has to be added to them to get that principle is by no means uncontroversial. For another thing, we can no longer afford to go on taking for granted what we mean by the words 'physical' and 'physics'.[5] If either expression is partially defined in terms of the causal closure principle itself (as is sometimes effectively assumed), then the victory of the 'physicalist' over the 'dualist' will be an empty one. That is, if we insist that partly what we *mean* by describing an event as 'physical' is that it can enter into causal relations with other 'physical' events (where these include such paradigm physical events as, say, limb-movements), then mental events will inevitably qualify as 'physical' if we accept the existence of psychophysical causation at all. But if, on the other hand, we *don't* write the causal closure principle into the very meaning of the word 'physical', how *do* we demarcate the realm of the physical? (It won't do to say that the physical is the subject-matter of the current science of physics, for that is far too parochial; nor can we usefully appeal to some ideal 'completed' physics of the distant future, about which we have no right to speculate.) However, if we have no principled and non-question-begging way of demarcating the realm of the physical, 'physicalism' as a metaphysical position appears to be drained of all substance (as perhaps is 'dualism' too, at least if it is defined partly in terms of opposition to physicalism).[6]

2. DUALISM VERSUS PHYSICALISM: THE HISTORY OF THE DEBATE

So are we in fact still left with a genuine *problem* for dualism concerning psychophysical causation? Well, perhaps, yes. If physics poses a serious threat to dualism, I think it does so in virtue of the possible clash of dualism with the conservation laws. (By 'physics', here, I mean

[5] See further Crane, 'Why Indeed?: Papineau on Supervenience', and also T. Crane and D. H. Mellor, 'There is No Question of Physicalism', *Mind* 99 (1990), pp. 185-206.

[6] I myself do not offer a definition of the physical in this chapter, but since no positive thesis of mine hinges on the provision of one, this is excusable. I am content to characterize dualism as the view that mental events and processes are neither identical with nor supervenient upon brain events and processes, and to assume that the latter must qualify as 'physical' by any criterion.

physics as it is currently formulated according to leading informed opinion.) Indeed, if we look to the history of dualist interactionism's supposed problems, we find in Leibniz's criticism of Descartes's theory of psychophysical causation precisely this focus on the apparent incompatibility of Descartes's account with the law of the conservation of momentum.[7]

Descartes – so the familiar story goes – thought that the mind exercised causal influence on the body by altering the direction of motion of animal spirits (a form of rarefied matter) in the pineal gland of the brain, these motions then being communicated purely mechanically to the extremities of the body through the flow of the animal spirits in the nerve filaments, giving rise to movements of the various limbs in accordance with the mind's desires. But Descartes was unaware that this process conflicts with the law of the conservation of momentum, partly because he lacked the modern concept of momentum as a vector (the product of mass and *velocity*) and was under the misapprehension that what had to be conserved was what he called *quantity of motion* (effectively, the product of mass and *speed*, a scalar quantity). That is, he failed to realize that even altering the *direction* of flow of the animal spirits, while leaving their *rate* of flow unaltered, would result in a change of momentum, a conserved quantity which could not be supplied from the non-physical mind but only from matter in motion (or at least by the operation of physical forces of some sort, even if one does not insist – as Descartes did – that these are all contact forces of a mechanical nature).

Now this analysis of Descartes's difficulty is essentially that provided by Leibniz – but we need not assume that Descartes would have agreed with this diagnosis had he lived to hear of it. For one thing, although it is true that Descartes himself believed in a principle of conservation of quantity of motion, it is not clear that he thought that this principle applied to cases of *psychophysical* interaction (as opposed to purely material interactions), and so not clear that he thought he needed to demonstrate the compatibility of his account of mental causation with this conservation law. By the same token, then, had Descartes lived to learn that his scalar law was mistaken and required

---

[7] The next few paragraphs owe much to R. S. Woolhouse, 'Leibniz's Reaction to Cartesian Interactionism', *Proceedings of the Aristotelian Society* 86 (1985/86), pp. 69-82 and D. Garber, 'Mind, Body, and the Laws of Nature in Descartes and Leibniz', *Midwest Studies in Philosophy* 8 (1983), pp. 105-33.

to be replaced by the modern law of the conservation of linear momentum, it is conceivable that he would have taken the view that that law only reigns in the realm of inanimate matter – in short, that momentum simply is *not* conserved in mind-brain interactions, however perfectly it may be conserved in purely material interactions.

Nor would this have been as *ad hoc* a proposal as might initially be supposed – at least from a Cartesian point of view. For one thing, to the extent that the law of conservation of momentum is conceived of as an empirical generalization supported by observation (rather than as a regulative principle of experimental method, with a quasi *a priori* status), it must be remarked that the evidence in support of it to date has come exclusively from the observation of purely material interactions (a point which the physicalist, to be sure, is in no position to dispute!). Secondly, Descartes as a theist supposed that God, at least – an infinite mind – could create matter in motion (and hence momentum) *ex nihilo*, and yet clearly did not think of this as violating any natural law of Cartesian physics. So why should not finite minds likewise be conceived of as being capable of affecting the quantity of motion or momentum in existence without thereby contravening the physical conservation laws, appropriately construed as only applying unreservedly to purely material interactions?

However, if Descartes had taken this line of defence he would still have been open to a line of criticism the force of which was clear to Leibniz. This is that if, as is now being supposed, a law like that of the conservation of linear momentum is regarded as applying exceptionlessly only to purely material interactions, because the non-physical mind can create momentum *ex nihilo*, or conversely annihilate it, then it will prove impossible to state any simple, universal law governing the kinematic and dynamic behaviour of all material bodies – because of the ever-present possibility of the interference of mind. There will be no guarantee that there *are* any 'purely material' interactions, much less that we shall be able to ascertain which they are. (Indeed, since *observation* is a mental activity, we won't be able to be sure that in observing a material interaction we don't render it 'impure' – a suggestion which may remind one of some contemporary views of the role of the observer in quantum mechanics, but now made more general.)

Leibniz thought that the wisdom and goodness of God implied the existence of a world combining the greatest possible variety of particular matters of fact with the least possible number and complexity of general laws governing those matters of fact: and the Cartesian world just described would fail miserably on the latter score. Nor need we share Leibniz's theological perspective to feel the unsatisfactoriness of such a position. On criteria of simplicity and parsimony, such as are regularly appealed to in both scientific and metaphysical theory-construction, the Cartesian picture just sketched is an unattractively messy one. (But I should stress that this does not conclusively remove it from the field of competition: after all, in our own times continuous creation *ex nihilo*, in contravention of supposed conservation laws, has been proposed by Hoyle and others as a perfectly respectable scientific hypothesis, albeit one now out of favour for purely empirical reasons.[8])

Suppose, now, that we accept this Leibnizian line of criticism of the dualist who is prepared to reject the universal applicability of the physical conservation laws in order to 'make room' for an independent causal contribution from the mind in physical affairs. Does that leave no other strategy for the dualist interactionist – is he compelled to follow Leibniz's lead by opting for some form of parallelism in order to cling on to dualism? By no means. For an important fact which has so far gone unnoticed is that classical particle mechanics – Newton's laws of motion, which form the basis of the conservation laws – *is not a deterministic theory*. This has been pointed out in an important paper by Richard Montague, and before him by Ernest Nagel, but it is really quite obvious on a little reflection.[9]

A simple example will illustrate the point. Suppose two worlds, w_a and w_b, in each of which a particle of mass m_1 is falling from rest at time t_1 and height h_1 towards the centre of the earth, which has mass m_2. In each world, suppose that energy and momentum are conserved. It is still perfectly possible for the two particles to differ in their positions and velocities at a subsequent time t_2. This is because those positions and velocities will depend on the value of g, the strength of the earth's gravitational field, and hence ultimately

---

[8] See H. Bondi, *Cosmology*, 2nd edn (Cambridge: Cambridge University Press, 1961), ch. 12.

[9] See R. Montague, 'Deterministic Theories', in his *Formal Philosophy* (New Haven: Yale University Press, 1974), and E. Nagel, *The Structure of Science* (London: Routledge & Kegan Paul, 1961), ch. 7.

(given that we are assuming the earth's mass to be fixed at m_2) upon the value of the universal gravitational constant G. Each particle will gain in kinetic energy ($1/2m_1v^2$, where v is its velocity at time t_2) exactly what it loses in potential energy ($m_1g(h_1 - h_2)$, where h_2 is its height at t_2). Also, the net momentum of the earth-particle system will remain unaltered (assuming the operation of no external forces), since the particle's gain of momentum in the downward direction (m_1v) will be exactly compensated for by the earth's gain of momentum in the upward direction (m_2u, say). But the crucial point is that by setting g (and G) at different values for worlds w_a and w_b, the value v of the particle's velocity at time t_2 can be made to vary as we please between those two worlds. Furthermore, we have been presupposing so far that only gravitational forces are in play – but of course there might be others, such as electromagnetic forces, the strengths of which in the two worlds will depend ultimately on the value of the charge on the electron, which again may be supposed to differ between the two worlds (not to speak of the possibility that one of the worlds might contain forces not present at all in the other). In the terminology of Nagel and Montague, what has to be added to classical particle mechanics to transform it into a deterministic theory is a specification of the *force-function*, which will tell us what laws of force are in play and specify the values of the various constants which feature in those laws.

But how does all this bear upon the issue of dualist interactionism? Well, there are two ways in which a proponent of that view might exploit the points that have just been made. One strategy would be to propose the existence of distinctive *psychic forces* – forces supplementary to the familiar physical forces of gravitation and electromagnetism and so forth. (Contemporary wisdom has it that there are just four fundamental physical forces – the two just mentioned plus the so-called 'strong' and 'weak' nuclear forces: though the electromagnetic and 'weak' nuclear force are now thought to be aspects of the same phenomenon, and attempts continue to 'unify' all four forces.) Postulating laws of psychic force would just be one way of contributing to a specification of the force-function. Just as adding electromagnetic forces to a situation hitherto supposed only to involve gravitational forces makes a difference to the predicted kinematic behaviour of (charged) material particles in that situation – without in any way threatening a conflict with the conservation laws – so adding psychic forces would have this effect.

But there is an obvious objection to this sort of proposal. It is that these so-called 'psychic' forces would have to be construed as being just a new variety of *physical* force, and so would provide no comfort for the genuine dualist. Why so? Well – or so I anticipate the answer to be – anything which *can* exert a force on physical objects, that is, which can do work on a physical system, is *ipso facto* something 'physical' and the force it exerts is consequently a 'physical' one. The very definition of the 'physical', one is tempted to say, is that it is something capable of *exerting force*, or equivalently of *doing work* or *contributing energy* to a system. But this answer should remind us at once of an idea we encountered earlier, that a 'physical' event is by definition one which can enter into causal relations with other 'physical' events: the problem with both suggestions is that they threaten to render the self-styled physicalist's victory over dualism a purely empty one. Suppose that the existence of the postulated 'psychic' forces was confirmed empirically, and suppose that the laws governing them differed markedly from those governing the more familiar physical forces (suppose, say, that there was absolutely no prospect of 'unifying' the psychic forces with any of the latter) – *would* it really be so obvious and natural to classify them as just a new species of 'physical' force? It simply isn't clear what a decision of this sort ought to turn on, but I certainly don't think that it can properly be made a mere matter of stipulative definition. (I don't want to suggest that physicalists typically think that it *can*, only to warn against the temptation to do so.) We have again struck one of the chief obstacles to fruitful discussion of the dispute between physicalism and dualism – the absence of any agreed and principled definition of the 'physical', which doesn't just beg the question one way or the other.

Even so, the dualist proposal now under consideration – the postulation of 'psychic' forces – has another serious drawback, to which I shall draw attention shortly, after I have explained a second strategy which might be exploited by a dualist who doesn't want to come into direct conflict with the conservation laws while yet remaining an interactionist. According to this second line of thought, the mind exerts causal influence on the body not through the exercise of psychic (non-physical) *forces* of any sort, but through influencing the values of the so-called 'constants' which feature in various *physical* force laws – for instance, by influencing (presumably only locally and to a vanishingly small degree) the value of the universal constant of gravitation G or the value of the charge on the electron. Thus it would turn out that these so-called 'constants' are strictly speaking *variables*.

This is not in principle such a shocking or heretical idea. There are indeed cosmological theories – such as E. A. Milne's kinematic relativity – according to which the so-called 'constant' of gravitation undergoes a secular increase, with the consequence that the sum of the universe's mass/energy increases with time.[10] It is true, then, that postulating variability in such constants is *in a sense* at odds with the classical principle of the conservation of energy, but not in the way that the earlier proposal made on Descartes's behalf was. For it is not now being suggested that the mind has a power of creating energy *ex nihilo* or conversely annihilating it. The latter proposal has a disagreeable air of hocus pocus about it, nor is it apparent how such a process could be conceived of as operating in a lawlike way. But the idea that what have hitherto been assumed to be constants of nature are in reality variables open to influence by mental operations is not obviously vulnerable to either of these objections. And it has the advantage over the alternative idea of 'psychic' forces that it does not require us to think of the mind as being capable of contributing energy to, or absorbing it from, a physical system.[11]

However, notwithstanding these advantages, this latest proposal still has a fundamental difficulty which also besets the idea of psychic forces, and indeed the 'Cartesian' proposal mooted earlier. This is that all three theories seem to be inherently incapable of explaining why the mind's causal influence upon the material world has to be channelled through the brain: none of them can readily explain why telekinesis is not a ubiquitous phenomenon. Of course, it might be urged on behalf of all three that the mind – or the human mind, at least – can exert only a very weak influence on matter, an influence which has to be amplified by many orders of magnitude if it is to give

[10] See Bondi, *Cosmology*, ch. 11 and E. A. Milne, *Modern Cosmology and the Christian Idea of God* (Oxford: Clarendon Press, 1952), ch. 6.

[11] This is not to say that I find the idea of such 'absorption' unintelligible: all it implies is that energy will have to be thought of as a conserved quantity which can be transferred between radically different kinds of system – an idea which is easier to grasp now that we identify such apparently different forms of energy as thermal, kinetic, electromagnetic, gravitational and mass energy. For an interesting discussion of some of the issues involved here, see W. D. Hart, *The Engines of the Soul* (Cambridge: Cambridge University Press, 1988), ch. 9 (aptly entitled 'Psychic Energy').

rise to macroscopic effects such as limb-movements: and that the human body is precisely such an amplifier, partly having evolved to serve that very function. But then there still remains a puzzle as to why one mind should not be able to exploit the amplifying capacities of *another* mind's body, but only those of its own, and indeed why telepathy is not a ubiquitous phenomenon. All three theories, then – even the last one to be presented – have a quasi-magical aura by virtue of their apparent commitment to the possibility of mysteriously elusive psychic phenomena, such as telekinesis and telepathy. Of course, those who are convinced that such phenomena *do* occur will not regard what I have just said as a valid objection to any of those theories. But they still have to explain why the phenomena are so elusive, and that may not be at all easy.

Perhaps the fundamental problem with all three of the dualist inter-actionist proposals that we have been examining is one which they inherit from Descartes's own conception of the nature of mind-body interaction, according to which the mind exerts causal influence on the body by *setting matter in motion* (or at least by affecting the motion of matter). On one level, of course, this *must* be what the mind does, inasmuch as mental events and processes are ultimately causally responsible for the gross movements of our limbs that we make in performing (intentional) bodily actions, such as walking or raising an arm. But Descartes, because his conception of physics was wholly mechanical, assumed that these gross movements of our limbs must be mediated by movements of *other* quantities of matter – the flow of animal spirits in the nerve filaments – so that at some stage in the process the mind would have to act *directly* upon matter to produce or alter motion in it: a stage which he famously located in the pineal gland, the 'seat of the soul'. But in fact one can espouse dualist inter-actionism without accepting this aspect of Descartes's position at all – especially as it is no longer appropriate to think of physics, in Cartesian style, as being just the science of mechanics. In supposing that the mind can causally influence the course of physical events, we need never suppose that it does so by (directly) affecting the state of motion of physical particles. Hence we need not ascribe to the mind some mysterious power of telekinesis, creating for ourselves the problem of explaining why this power can only be exercised on the brain (and not just any brain, but only one's own).

3. GROUNDWORK FOR A NEW SYSTEM OF
INTERACTIONISM

In this section I want to sketch an altogether new picture of dualist interactionism, which will escape the difficulty that I have just identified.[12] Rather than ask how a mental event (conceived dualistically as non-physical) can directly cause a physical event in the brain (such as an alteration in the flow of animal spirits, or some modern variant thereof) thus initiating a causal chain leading thereafter through purely physical links to a movement of the limbs, it may be more profitable to begin from the other end – the limb-movement – and consider what happens when causal chains are traced backwards from this. It seems likely that as these causal chains are traced backwards through neural pathways leading to and into the brain, the chains will begin to display a tree-structure – quite possibly one exhibiting a 'fractal' pattern (so that branches of the tree are smaller trees, the branches of which are still smaller trees, and so on indefinitely).[13] Moreover, trees emanating from different peripheral events (limb-movements and the like) will soon become inextricably intertwined. (I should stress that I am not talking about the neural pathways as such – though they will certainly also display branching: I am talking about causal chains of events occurring in those pathways.[14] Also, I am not assuming fully deterministic physical causation at all the nodes in the branching causal chains: we can suppose if we like – and as seems plausible on empirical grounds – that at least some of the physical causation is probabilistic, with antecedent events only fixing the chances of their effects at values between 0 and 1.)

---

[12] I must stress that what follows *is* only a sketch of an alternative approach for dualists to explore: a fully-fledged theory along the lines to be proposed would require a great deal more work, not least of an empirical nature. More detailed suggestions are made in section 6 below.

[13] There is indeed empirical evidence that the pattern of brain activity which characteristically precedes voluntary movement is (until very shortly before the movement) non-specific, widely distributed over the cortex, and gradual in build-up: for details, see K. R. Popper and J. C. Eccles, *The Self and its Brain: An Argument for Interactionism* (Berlin: Springer, 1977), pp. 282ff, 293f. I might remark that I am not wholly sympathetic to Eccles' own interactionist theory, though some features of his approach accord with mine.

[14] That neural structures themselves exhibit a fractal geometry is well attested: see further A. L. Goldberger *et al.*, 'Chaos and Fractals in Human Physiology', *Scientific American* 262 (1990), pp. 34–41.

Now, if that is a correct description of the topology of the causal chains involved in deliberative action, then the implication appears to be that it would just be quite wrong to imagine that the mind's role in action could be to *initiate* causal chains leading to peripheral events. For these causal chains – or rather trees, as we now see them to be – don't have 'tips' which could provide the locus of the mind's interaction, nor are the trees which are traced back from different peripheral events distinguishable or separable once their branches have become inextricably intertwined.[15] In all this maze of neural events there are simply *none* of which we can say that *they* are the ones directly caused by some specific mental event which is ultimately responsible for a given peripheral event.

The picture, then, is as follows: I desire or will to raise my arm, and *as a result* my arm goes up – the movement being the terminus of a causal tree branching in a fractal pattern backwards into the maze of antecedent neural events. But though that causal tree *mediates* the causal relation between my desire or volition and the movement of my arm, it does not do so by virtue of my volition or desire initiating the 'growth' of the tree from the 'tips' down: for the tree has *no* tips, and certainly none that it can call exclusively its own.[16]

But now it may be objected that if this is the picture we want to adopt of the causal antecedents of peripheral events, why do we need

---

[15] I am not suggesting that the trees lack 'tips' because the fractal branching proceeds literally *ad infinitum*, with each pathway constituting an infinite series of causally related events the totality of which occurs within a finite period of time – an idea reminiscent of one invoked by Lukasiewicz in attempted refutation of determinism: see J. Lukasiewicz, *Aristotle's Syllogistic from the Standpoint of Modern Formal Logic*, 2nd edn (Oxford: Clarendon Press, 1957) pp. 207-8. For although such a scheme is mathematically possible, it seems unlikely from a physical point of view. Rather, the trees lack 'tips' because the fractal branching proceeding from any one peripheral event eventually merges seamlessly into the prior causal history of the whole brain, fusing with the branching of other trees. Incidentally, empirical confirmation of my claim that the mind does not *initiate* causal chains of neural events leading to peripheral events is provided by Libet's finding that conscious awareness of the will to act occurs some 350 msec *after* the onset of the pattern of brain activity ('readiness-potential') which characteristically precedes voluntary movement, though still some 200 msec before the movement itself occurs: see B. Libet, 'Unconscious Cerebral Initiative and the Role of Conscious Will in Voluntary Action', *Behavioral and Brain Sciences* 8 (1985), pp. 529-66, reprinted in his *Neurophysiology of Consciousness* (Boston, MA: Birkhäuser, 1993). This point is discussed further in section 6 below.

[16] I speak here of 'volition or desire' so as to maintain neutrality about the mental antecedents of intentional action: but in chapter 5 I shall abandon that neutrality in favour of a volitionist account.

to invoke the mind at all, conceived dualistically? *Every* physical event in a causal tree has purely physical antecedent causes, precisely because there are no 'tips'. So haven't we conceded, in effect, that the body-cum-brain is a *causally closed physical system* (ignoring inputs from the physical environment, at least, which are not relevant to present considerations)? And in that case the mind (conceived dualistically) surely has no causal role to play: it is causally quite superfluous. But since it is just *false* that the mind is in fact causally superfluous (mental events *do* have physical effects), we have no option but to abandon dualism by identifying mental events with certain neural events (or at least saying that they supervene upon them).

No: the objection is mistaken. First of all, we can capitalize on the accepted fact that peripheral events (like limb-movements) have clearly identifiable mental causes – desires or volitions or intentions or whatever you like to call them. This particular limb-movement – my arm's going up just now – had a quite specific mental cause: my particular desire or volition just now to raise that very arm at that moment. But, as we have seen, on the physical side there is plausibly *no* clearly individuable neural event or set of neural events which can similarly be identified as the cause of the limb-movement – and hence nothing on the physical side which constitutes a suitable candidate for identity with the desire or volition (or even a suitable candidate for 'realizing' that desire or volition, as a supervenience theorist might have it). The *physical* causes of different peripheral events become inextricably interwoven beyond a certain point – unlike the *mental* causes, which accordingly cannot be identified with the physical causes since the latter can't be individuated in a way which will allow us to put them into one-to-one relation with the mental causes (and the same applies, *mutatis-mutandis*, for a 'realization' account). Incidentally, let us not be sidetracked here by worries about the propriety of ever speaking of 'the' cause of a given event – worries motivated by the familiar suggestion that one person's 'cause' is another person's 'background condition'.[17] It suffices to point out that individual desires or volitions have an indisputable salience in the causal explanation of deliberative action which is not mirrored

---

[17] See further J. L. Mackie, *The Cement of the Universe: A Study of Causation* (Oxford: Clarendon Press, 1974) pp. 34ff.

by any of the neural events individuable on the physical side. (I shall develop this line of argument in more depth in section 6 below.)

Very well, the physicalist may reply, then this just shows that we were mistaken after all to accept the common-sense view that distinctly individuable mental causes – particular desires or volitions – really exist: we should espouse some version of eliminative materialism, whereby the categories of 'folk psychology' have no place in a scientific account of the aetiology of human behaviour.[18] But if that is the extreme to which physicalism is driven, then so much the worse for physicalism, say I – the boot now begins to look as though it is on the dualist's foot. For I don't need to rehearse here all the difficulties which beset eliminative materialism.

However, it still remains for the dualist to explain how mental causes can fail to be superfluous, given the picture sketched earlier of the causal antecedents of peripheral events. My proposed solution to this problem is as follows. As we have seen, when a peripheral event E (such as a limb-movement) has a distinct mental cause M (such as a particular volition or desire), it is not the case that M is the direct (that is, unmediated) cause of *any* physical event in the causal tree of neural events terminating in E: every event in that tree has, as its immediate causes, other wholly physical events – which is why we can in a sense allow that a principle of physical causal closure is satisfied and discern no threat to the physical conservation laws. Even so, it seems to me, we can still insist that M is genuinely causally efficacious in the production of E because M is responsible for (is, in the circumstances, necessary and sufficient for) the very fact that there exists a causal tree of neural events culminating in E. I am *not*, to repeat, saying that M is the direct cause of each or any member of the particular maze of neural events which happens to converge upon E, but rather that it is causally responsible for the fact that *there exists a maze at all with that particular convergence characteristic.*[19] For this fact, it seems to me, is *not*

---

[18] See, e.g., P. M. Churchland, *A Neurocomputational Perspective: The Nature of Mind and the Structure of Science* (Cambridge, MA: MIT Press, 1989), ch. 1. For forceful criticism, see L. R. Baker, *Saving Belief: A Critique of Physicalism* (Princeton: Princeton University Press, 1987), ch. 7.

[19] This commits me to holding that events can stand in causal relations to *facts*, and not just to other events, contrary to the assumption that I have been working with until now: but I am happy to accept the commitment. On the distinction between event causation and

causally explicable purely by reference to physical events antecedent to
E.

From a purely physical perspective, the convergence upon *E* looks
like (indeed, I should say *is*) a quite remarkable and inexplicable
coincidence – rather like rings on the surface of a pond miraculously
converging upon a central point, instead of spreading out from a
disturbance there towards the pond's edges. (Or – to continue the
tree metaphor – it is like supposing that a tree might grow from the
tips of its branches down to its trunk, instead of *vice versa*.) And, of
course, what makes the case of deliberative action importantly different from that of *actual* pond disturbances is that rings in ponds *never do*
display convergence patterns but only ones of divergence, whereas in
deliberative action convergence is the norm. From the purely physical
point of view, thus, such convergence in the action case makes it look
like a time-reversed process involving backward causation. But that
can't be what is really going on, of course: and that is why it is not
only legitimate but highly plausible to assign a distinctive causal role to
an antecedent mental event *M* – an event which, like a desire or
volition, has the later peripheral event *E* as its object. And here I
mean 'object' in a dual sense: *E* is the *intentional* object of *M* – in
that *M* is a volition or desire for *that particular event E* to occur – and *E*
is also the objec*tive* or *goal* of the agent's endeavour. Thus the intentionality – in both senses of the word – of volition or desire is quite
crucial to its capacity to play the causal role here required of it.

I should emphasize that the foregoing proposal is not compatible
with a supervenience theory of mental states, for its implication is that
mental states such as volitions or desires have genuinely independent
causal powers – that they make a difference to how the world goes
over and above any difference made by physical events. I might add
that if this view of mental causation is correct, it may help to explain –
as previously mentioned dualist accounts apparently could not – why a
particular mind is incapable of exercising its influence on physical
objects other than its own brain and body: for causal networks of
physical events susceptible to the sort of convergence now being
discussed are quite probably only to be found within unified nervous

fact causation, see further J. Bennett, *Events and their Names* (Oxford: Clarendon Press,
1988), pp. 21ff. Incidentally, don't ask me *how* the mind can do what I am now proposing that it does, if what you want is an answer which will render its mode of operation
'intelligible' in the sense discussed in the opening paragraph of this chapter.

systems, with patterns of convergence in different nervous systems being idiosyncratic and highly dependent upon the individual historical development of those systems.

If one still feels uneasy, even so, about the causal role which is now being assigned to mental events like desires or volitions, then perhaps a theological parallel will be of some help (though I don't mean to suggest that the parallel is an exact one). It is a familiar enough point that even in a deterministic physical universe with an infinite past a distinctive causal role can still be assigned to God: not, indeed, as a 'prime mover' or temporally first cause, for *ex hypothesi* in such a system every physical event has wholly physical antecedent causes which are necessary and sufficient for its occurrence. But − as Leibniz made us aware − God can still be invoked to explain why *this* universe was actualized rather than any of the infinitely many other possible universes equally well exhibiting determinism with an infinite past: for, of course, there can be any amount of difference between all these universes in respect of both particular matters of fact and general laws (even if there are certain very high-level conservation principles which they all obey). The point of these remarks is to impress upon us that there can be more to explaining a pattern of events than is explained by specifying the immediate causes of each event in the pattern. And that 'more', I suggest, is precisely what minds can characteristically contribute to the causal explanation of physical phenomena. Minds − whether infinite or merely finite − can explain some of the otherwise inexplicable patterns in nature. For it is of the essence of intelligence to seek patterns and to attempt to impose them upon otherwise chaotic phenomena.

An objection that I anticipate here is that the history of science already reveals to us ways in which order can emerge out of chaos without any need to appeal to the intervention of mind, however attractive such an appeal might pretheoretically have been. The classic example is provided by the evolution of animal life-forms, which are no longer explained by appeal to divine providence but rather in terms of the 'blind' mechanisms of random variation and natural selection. But to carry this strategy over to the case of deliberative action itself − in which of all cases appeal to the intervention of mind is surely *not* out of place − is effectively to commit oneself to some form of eliminative materialism, denying any genuine causal role (and hence even genuine existence) to mental states like volitions or desires. Thus suppose it is suggested, say, that modern 'chaos theory' could in principle explain why a particular maze of neural events should converge upon a specific peripheral event E, in a case of what we would pre-theoretically describe as intentional action.[20] Then that is in effect to deny that the agent's *volition* or *desire* for E to occur could after all have a genuine causal role to play in the genesis of E. For a 'chaos theory' explanation of the convergence upon E would precisely *deny* that E had a highly salient and virtually sure-fire singular cause, such as a volition or desire is conceived to be with respect to the peripheral event that is its object.

To be sure, evolutionary theory and chaos theory *can* explain how a wide variety of forms and patterns – from wing-feathers to weather-fronts – may emerge out of apparently random sets of events.[21] But such explanations are *rivals* to explanations in terms of mental or intentional causation if directed at the same explananda, and hence are not representable as ways of showing how the latter kind of causation might be implemented in physical systems. I should add, however, that I see not the slightest reason to suppose that chaos theory, or some evolution-inspired theory of neural functioning, *could* in fact provide an alternative – much less a superior – explanation of (what we would have to cease calling) deliberative action to that which is provided by appeal to intentional mental states such as volition or desire.[22] So, in sum, the alternative to my dualist approach that is now being canvassed is neither particularly promising on its own terms nor acceptable in principle to any but a committed eliminativist. And, finally, I should in any case stress that my main aim in this section has not been to argue conclusively that dualism must be *true*, but only to show that it *can* handle the problem of psychophysical causation, and consequently that it remains a viable competitor in the field of rival theories of the mind-body relationship.

---

[20] For a general and not unduly technical account of chaos theory, see J. P. Crutchfield *et al.*, 'Chaos', *Scientific American* 255 (1986), pp. 38-49.

[21] It appears that chaos theory has an important role to play in explaining certain patterns of behaviour in the autonomic nervous system, such as the normal heartbeat: see Goldberger *et al.*, 'Chaos and Fractals in Human Physiology'. But such bodily activity is, of course, precisely *not* deliberative.

[22] For one recent evolution-inspired theory of brain function, see G. M. Edelman, *Neural Darwinism: The Theory of Neuronal Group Selection* (Oxford: Oxford University Press, 1989).

At this point let us take stock. That mental phenomena are part of the natural, causal order of events is surely not to be denied. But mental causation, while apparently real enough, seems to be utterly distinct from physical causation.[23] On pain of denying either its reality or its distinctness, therefore, the natural order must be conceived to embrace more than just the physical: mental events must be endowed with independent causal powers. At the same time, the mental must surely be in some way a product of physical processes, and more particularly a product of the genetic evolution of biological organisms (albeit only in conjunction with social and cultural processes, as I urged in section 6 of chapter 2). This suggests an 'emergent' status for mental phenomena, in a strong sense of 'emergence' which is consistent with the causal autonomy of the mental. The coherence and empirical tenability of such a view of the mind are what the remainder of this chapter principally seeks to demonstrate. But first I want to move from defence to attack in my opposition to physicalism.

4. INTERLUDE: THE PHYSICALIST PROBLEM OF MENTAL CAUSATION

A peculiar feature of the notion of mental causation is that it can seem equally problematical whether one espouses dualism or physicalism. That dualism faces problems over psychophysical causation is almost universally taken for granted these days, without much argument – a situation I much deplore, for reasons which I hope have already become plain. But physicalists too have recently begun to realize that their position renders the notion of mental causation problematic – ironically enough, since the initial attraction of physicalism lay chiefly in its promise to cast light where dualism allegedly only offered obscurity. The problem for the physicalist is to steer a middle path between reductionism and eliminativism. Psychophysical reductionism, of the sort purveyed by old-fashioned type-type identity theories

---

[23] I don't necessarily want to suggest that mental and physical causation are different kinds of *causation*, as opposed to causation by different kinds of item – though it will emerge later that I do think that an important distinction can be drawn between ways in which an item can contribute causally to the production of an effect, and that this distinction has a bearing on our understanding of mental causation (see section 6 below).

constructed on the 'lightning = electrical discharge' model, renders mental causation 'unproblematical' only by denying, effectively, that it is anything other than straightforward physical causation (albeit conveniently wrapped up in a different vocabulary). Eliminativism does away with the problem of mental causation even more radically by denying that such causation occurs at all (any more than alchemical or astral causation do). Either way, the only causation there really is, on these views, is ordinary physical causation: the mental, *qua* mental, does not cause anything at all – contrary to everything that common sense and intuition suggest.

For some time it seemed as though a middle path *could* be found in a kind of non-reductive physicalism, forged in the context of token-token identity theories or supervenience accounts of the mental.[24] Apparently, such theories do not threaten to 'reduce' the mental to the physical along the supposedly 'scientific' lines of the *lightning = electrical discharge* or *temperature = mean kinetic energy* model, because they emphasize the possibility of the *multiple realization* of mental phenomena. Now, in fact it must be conceded that type-type identity theories *also* permit possibilities of multiple realization because, for instance, the temperature of a gas can be realized by many different assignments of velocity to its constituent molecules.[25] Thus it is invalid to argue, as is sometimes carelessly done in introductory texts, that because pain is – allegedly – multiply realizable, it is therefore not type-identical with any physical feature: for then, by parity of reasoning, we should equally have to conclude that since *temperature* is multiply realizable, it is not type-identical with any physical feature – when in fact it is plausibly type-identical with mean kinetic energy, which *is* a physical feature. What is significant, however, is that temperature is multiply realizable precisely *because* it is type-identical with mean kinetic energy and the *latter* admits of multiple realization[26] – whereas on token-identity theories of the mental there is, supposedly,

[24] The *locus classicus* is Donald Davidson's 'Mental Events', reprinted in his *Essays on Actions and Events* (Oxford: Clarendon Press, 1980).

[25] Cf. John Heil, *The Nature of True Minds* (Cambridge: Cambridge University Press, 1992), pp. 133-4. Heil exploits the point to deflect one common line of criticism of type-type identity theories of the mental, though not with a view to positively supporting such theories.

[26] Strictly speaking, it is in fact false to say that temperature is type-identical with mean kinetic energy because, for instance, even empty space can apparently be assigned a temperature: see Tim Crane, 'Mental Causation and Mental Reality', *Proceedings of the*

no corresponding physical type which admits of multiple realization. So when it is said that token-identity theories of the mental avoid reductionism by emphasizing the multiple realizability of mental phenomena, it must be understood that they achieve this only to the extent that such multiple realization seems to defy a type-type treatment.

Be that as it may, after a while it began to be objected that these theories, though 'non-reductive', nonetheless effectively conferred a merely *epiphenomenal* status upon the mental.[27] Even though individual ('token') mental events could be said to be causally efficacious, by virtue of being identical with or 'realized by' individual physical events (neural events in the brain, or fusions of such events), it seemed that it was only the *physical* properties of these events that conferred causal efficacy upon them, and that their mental properties were causally superfluous or idle.[28] A key point here is that given that their possession of the physical properties is *sufficient* for the causal efficacy of these events, such efficacy cannot also be attributed to their possession of the mental properties, on pain of admitting a kind of systematic causal overdetermination.

One line of response to this difficulty is that advocated recently by Cynthia Macdonald, namely, that 'an instancing of a mental property by an event just *is* an instancing by it of a physical one'.[29] John Heil, who has independently made a very similar suggestion, explains that the response works by focusing on property *instances* or 'tropes' rather than on the mental or physical properties which those instances

Aristotelian Society 92 (1991/92), pp. 185-202 (see p. 195). But I ignore this complication for ease of exposition.

27 See, e.g., Ted Honderich, *Mind and Brain: A Theory of Determinism, Volume I* (Oxford: Clarendon Press, 1990), pp. 89ff.

28 In point of fact it is questionable whether Davidson's version of the token-identity theory (his 'anomalous monism') is vulnerable to the epiphenomenalist objection, because on his view of causation it is illegitimate to ask in virtue of *which properties* of an event it causes its effect – though it is strongly arguable that for this very reason his view of causation (as a purely extensional relation between particulars) is unsatisfactory. See further Tim Crane, 'Mental Causation and Mental Reality', p. 189. Davidson clarifies his position and defends it against the epiphenomenalist objection in his 'Thinking Causes', in J. Heil & A. R. Mele (eds.), *Mental Causation* (Oxford: Clarendon Press, 1993); this defence is, however, subjected to severe scrutiny by Kim, McLaughlin and Sosa, in Heil & Mele (eds.), *Mental Causation*.

29 Cynthia Macdonald, *Mind-Body Identity Theories* (London: Routledge, 1989), p. 162. This position was first developed by Cynthia and Graham Macdonald in a earlier paper, 'Mental Causes and Explanation of Action', *Philosophical Quarterly* 36 (1986),

exemplify.[30] However, Heil's explanation notwithstanding, it is still not entirely clear to me what notion of instantiation is supposed to be at work here; and, certainly, there are strict constraints, not obviously met in the cases envisaged, upon the possibility of identifying instances of different properties.[31] Moreover, as Heil himself seems to concede, the proposal threatens to obliterate differences between the capacities of different properties possessed by an event to confer causal efficacy upon it: for, surely, even if one accepts the terms of the proposal, one will have to concede that an event's instancings of *some* properties are causally irrelevant notwithstanding their (allegedly) just *being* instancings by that event of other, causally relevant properties. Heil himself cites the example (due originally to Fred Dretske) of a woman's singing of a phrase causing a glass to shatter, but only in virtue of its *pitch*, not its *meaning* – and this despite the fact that, on the proposal now under consideration, her singing of a phrase with that pitch 'just *is*' her singing of a phrase with that meaning.[32] Thus the proposal, as it stands, doesn't avert the threat posed by the 'epiphenomenalist' objection, since it is compatible with the mental properties of an event being as causally inert as the semantic properties of the singing event are in the case just described.

As against this 'epiphenomenalist' objection, however, it could be argued that causal *explanation* in mentalistic terms can still be regarded as autonomous with respect to physical explanation, on the grounds that mentalistic explanations invoke generalizations (and associated subjunctive conditionals) which are simply not at all salient at the purely physical level. To this end, one could exploit a strategy adopted by Heil, who appeals to the existence of 'a system or network of projectable counterfactual and subjunctive conditional truths' to

pp. 145-58, and is further defended by Graham Macdonald in his 'The Nature of Naturalism', *Aristotelian Society Supplementary Volume* 66 (1992), pp. 225-44, where he writes: 'On this view it is only one instance which is causally efficacious, thus ruling out overdetermination. The instance is an instance of both a physical and . . . a mental property, . . . thus ruling out epiphenomenalism. The only remaining puzzle is why such a neat solution is not more widely accepted' (p. 231).

[30] See John Heil, *The Nature of True Minds*, pp. 138-9. On 'tropes' more generally, see Keith Campbell, *Abstract Particulars* (Oxford: Basil Blackwell, 1990).

[31] See further my *Kinds of Being*, p. 113.

[32] Heil, *The Nature of True Minds*, p. 139. Cf. Steven Yablo, 'Mental Causation', *Philosophical Review* 101 (1992), pp. 245-80, for a similar criticism of the Macdonalds' position (see p. 259, n. 32).

differentiate the causally relevant cases from the rest.[33] As he points out, 'there is no *systematic, projectable* connection between singings that mean "Break not my heart!" and glass-shatterings'[34] – whereas there plausibly *is* between neural events that are, say, intendings to *F* and *F*-ings.

The upshot of this line of thought would seem to be that although any particular *instance* of mental causation obtains purely in virtue of physical causation between the token events concerned, nonetheless the instances of such causation that are classified together by a mentalistic explanatory generalization may have nothing of theoretical interest in common from a purely physical perspective.[35] (This situation is made possible, of course, by the 'multiple realization' thesis.) Put another way, although all these mental events may possess some unitary and explanatorily salient mental property, the only physical property they all possess may be highly disjunctive in character (and thus dubiously even qualify as a genuine 'property' at all). Hence mentalistic causal *explanation* is still autonomous and irreducible on this view, even if particular *instances* of mental causation are not.[36]

Here I protest that taking the foregoing line is tantamount to conceding that there is, really, no such thing as distinctively mental causation – all causation is really physical causation – and all that we have are patterns of explanation which cannot usefully be picked out in physicalistic vocabulary. This is, effectively, to take a *non-realist* view of the causal and ontological status of the mental[37] – similar to the

---

[33] Heil, *The Nature of True Minds*, p. 140.

[34] Heil, *The Nature of True Minds*, p. 141.

[35] Cf. David Owens, *Causes and Coincidences* (Cambridge: Cambridge University Press, 1992), pp. 132ff.

[36] I should remark that Heil himself would not be happy to describe the upshot of his strategy in these terms, nor does he claim originality for it, giving credit for this to Al Mele (personal communication). See further Alfred R. Mele, *Springs of Action: Understanding Intentional Behavior* (New York: Oxford University Press, 1992), pp. 34ff; another recent exponent of the strategy is Yablo – see his 'Mental Causation', pp. 278-9. The verdict that this strategy denies autonomy to particular instances of mental causation is mine – not Heil's or Mele's – and turns on the fact that the strategy makes the causal relevance of an instancing of a mental property reside in the subsumability of that instance under a wider, projectable pattern of causally related events (both actual and counterfactual), rather than in the efficacy of its own intrinsic (mental) character. As far as I can see, the strategy presumes that it is *physical* causation that is exhibited by all the particular events subsumable under the pattern (say, neural events that are intendings to *F*), albeit causation in virtue of different physical properties in different cases.

view one might plausibly take of social and economic facts and explanations. And to that extent this is still a strongly counter-intuitive position. For one surely wants to say that mental facts and events *are* real and genuinely causally efficacious in their own right, in a much more robust way than socio-economic facts and events are. A particular belief, desire or intention can, one wants to say, make a causal difference to the course of physical events (and other mental events) in virtue of being the particular mental event it is, bearing the intrinsic mental features it does. To deny this is, I suggest, incompatible with ascribing to ourselves the sort of capacity for intentional action which alone enables us to make sense of our projects and plans as free and intelligent agents. When, exercising my will, I decide to move my arm in a certain way, I *cannot*, consistently with regarding this as an intentional action of mine, suppose that my decision is causally efficacious only insofar as it is putatively identical with or 'realized by' some neural event which causes my arm to move purely in virtue of its physical characteristics – or so I would urge.

It is no consolation to be told that the *explanation* of the arm movement in terms of my desire to move it is still autonomous with respect to physical explanation because it appeals to a distinctive and irreducible pattern of generalization amongst psychophysical events, a pattern not discernible at the purely physical level. For what concerns me as an agent (as opposed to a passive observer, predictor and interpreter of the actions of others) is not how my action may be retrospectively *explained* but rather what, prospectively, will *cause* it – a particular conscious decision of mine, *qua* decision to move the arm just so, or some neural event in my brain quite inaccessible (at least under that description) to my consciousness.

---

[37] I realize that this contention would be strenuously denied by authors like Heil, Mele and Yablo, as indeed would be my description of the scenario as one in which 'all causation is really physical causation'. To their number might be added Daniel Dennett: see his 'Real Patterns', *Journal of Philosophy* 88 (1991), pp. 27-51 (especially p. 43, n. 22). Although this is not the place to fight this particular battle to a conclusion, I would emphasize in my favour the point implied below, namely, that the Heil-Mele-Yablo-Dennett line, by relaxing the criterion for what is to count as 'real' causation, finds itself in no position to discriminate between mental causation and, say, 'economic' causation on the point of their 'reality', and this strikes me as being deeply implausible and counter-intuitive. Here it is perhaps worth mentioning that Dennett himself declines to answer the question of whether the view he defends is 'a sort of instrumentalism or a sort of realism' ('Real Patterns', p. 51).

5. EMERGENTISM

At this point it may be protested that, after all, what I want is nothing
less than full-blooded dualism – mental events with *independent causal
powers*, that is, causal powers not grounded in and determined by the
causal powers of physical events. Well, and why not? Here the stock
objections to dualism may once again be trotted out: that it 'violates'
the conservation laws of physics; that it requires a totally implausible
systematic causal overdetermination of many physical events; that it
conflicts with the principle of the causal closure of the physical world
which lies at the heart of modern physical theory; that it necessitates
miraculous 'gaps' in chains of physical causation; that it makes the
impossible demand that spatially unlocated items be able to act at
specific points of space; and so on. Most if not all of these objections
are fairly feeble, and many of them are just plain question-begging. A
particularly blatant example of such anti-dualist prejudice is to be
found in a recent book of Daniel Dennett's, where he question-beggingly asserts, as though it were definitional, that 'anything that can
move a physical thing is itself a physical thing'[38] – not apparently
realizing that this short way with dualism empties his 'physicalism'
of any substantive content.[39]

Now, behind the more extreme of these objections is the thought
that psychophysical causation on the dualist model must be supernatural (or at least *non*-natural) and thus 'magical' – the connotations
of this pejorative term being that such a view is 'unscientific' and
'obscurantist'. (Thus, Dennett again: '[D]ualism wallows in mystery'.[40]) And even the more moderate objections (such as the allega-
tion of conflict with the conservation laws) attempt to impugn the
scientific credibility of dualism. But can the charge that dualism is at
odds with science really be made to stick? What, positively, do we
demand of a 'naturalistic' account of the mental and of psychophysical
causation? Regrettably, many modern physicalists liberally use the
adjectives 'physical' and 'natural(istic)' to characterize their position
and declare their supposedly 'scientific' credentials, without making

---

[38] Daniel C. Dennett, *Consciousness Explained* (Harmondsworth: Penguin Books, 1991),
p. 35. In the light of its overall message, the book might have been more aptly titled
'Consciousness Explained *Away*', or even 'Consciousness Denied'!

[39] For criticism of such unthinking physicalism, see Tim Crane and D. H. Mellor, 'There is
No Question of Physicalism', and also section 1, above.

[40] Dennett, *Consciousness Explained*, p. 37.

much if any effort to specify clearly and non-circularly what properties these honorific epithets are supposed to convey. One thing that *may*, however, reasonably be demanded of a theory of mind is that it should permit consciousness and mental causation to be seen as phenomena which could have arisen through the evolution of animal life-forms – on the grounds that these phenomena are only known to exist in association with organisms possessing highly developed nervous systems. Very well, but this does not by any means exclude dualism. For it is possible to see consciousness as an *emergent* feature of biological evolution[41] – that is, as a novel feature brought into being by biological processes but not itself a biological phenomenon. After all, biological processes can and have brought into existence complex structures which are not themselves biological – the spider's web and the bee's honeycomb are obvious examples, which may encourage us to see the art and architecture of human beings in much the same light (though in the latter case consciousness itself also clearly plays an intermediary role).[42]

Here it is interesting to advert to a chapter in a recent book of John Searle's.[43] Searle himself believes that consciousness *is* a biological phenomenon, albeit in a sense an 'emergent' one. He distinguishes, however, between two different notions of emergence, a weaker and a stronger one.[44] He points out first that some features of complex systems are ascribable to them purely in virtue of the properties and organization of their constituents or elements – thus the weight, shape and velocity of a macroscopic object are due purely to the properties and organization of its microscopic parts (allowing also for their

---

[41] This idea is by no means new, of course. For some interesting recent studies of the history of emergentism, see A. Beckermann *et al.* (eds.), *Emergence or Reduction?: Essays on the Prospects of Nonreductive Physicalism* (Berlin: de Gruyter, 1992). As we shall shortly see for ourselves, some emergentist conceptions of the mental are consistent with (or tantamount to) varieties of non-reductive physicalism – whereas the emergentism that I shall be recommending is properly dualist in my terms.

[42] For an interesting discussion of the relationship between animal artefacts and genetic evolution, see Richard Dawkins, *The Extended Phenotype* (Oxford: Oxford University Press, 1982), ch. 11. One need not accept Dawkin's notion of the 'selfish gene' in order to embrace his insight that a gene 'should be thought of as having *extended* phenotypic effects, consisting of all its effects on the world at large, not just its effects on the individual body in which it happens to be sitting' (p. 4).

[43] John R. Searle, *The Rediscovery of the Mind* (Cambridge, MA: MIT Press, 1992): see ch. 5, 'Reductionism and the Irreducibility of Consciousness'.

[44] The epithets 'weak' and 'strong' are mine, not Searle's, I should point out. He talks instead of 'emergent₁' and 'emergent₂' features.

relations to the environment). But other features of complex systems are only explicable when account is taken of the *causal interactions* of the component parts or elements – Searle's examples being the liquidity and transparency of a body of water and the solidity of a lump of stone. Searle calls such features 'causally emergent', but in a weak sense – weak in that the causally emergent features do not themselves possess any causal powers which are not explicable in terms of the causal powers of the elements from which the features emerge. But he acknowledges also the notion of a stronger kind of causally emergent feature, one which *would* have independent causal powers, though he doubts whether any such exist, on the grounds that their existence 'would seem to violate even the weakest principle of the transitivity of causation'.[45]

For Searle, consciousness is an emergent, global property or feature of the whole brain, rather as liquidity is of the collection of molecules forming a body of water. He rejects, then, the notion that consciousness might be emergent in the stronger sense. As he puts it, 'The naive idea here is that consciousness gets squirted out by the behavior of the neurons in the brain, but once it has been squirted out, it then has a life of its own.'[46] For Searle, thus, consciousness has *no* independent causal powers, a point he somewhat confusingly makes by saying that 'consciousness is *causally reducible to* . . . brain processes'.[47] But he still regards it as (in another sense, plainly!) 'irreducible' – though not for any ontologically deep reason, since according to him 'the irreducibility of consciousness is a trivial consequence of the pragmatics of our definitional practices'.[48] He doesn't, however, consider that this makes consciousness epiphenomenal,[49] because on his account conscious states *do* have causal powers, albeit not independent ones. So, it seems, Searle is endorsing a species of non-reductive physicalism of the

[45] Searle, *The Rediscovery of the Mind*, p. 112.
[46] Ibid.
[47] Searle, *The Rediscovery of the Mind*, p. 116, my emphasis.
[48] Searle, *The Rediscovery of the Mind*, p. 122. His point is that standardly *reduction* invokes a distinction between 'appearance' and 'reality' which is unavailable in the case of consciousness because 'consciousness consists in the appearances themselves' (p. 122) – though quite how this allows Searle to claim that the irreducibility of consciousness 'has no deep metaphysical consequences for the unity of our overall scientific world view' (p. 122) is obscure to me.
[49] Searle, *The Rediscovery of the Mind*, p. 126.

79

sort discussed earlier.[50] But he doesn't (in my view) face up to the difficulties and inherent instability of such a position.[51] And there seems to be, besides, a certain amount of confusion in his position in any case (as the foregoing quoted remarks on 'reducibility' rather serve to show).

Now, why does Searle dismiss so perfunctorily the possibility that consciousness might be 'emergent' in his *stronger* sense? Is it really so difficult to think of a feature of a complex system which is produced by the causal interaction of elements of the system and yet which has independent causal powers, without any violation of the principle of the transitivity of causation? I don't think so. In fact, I've mentioned some already. Consider the spider and its web. This is a complex system one feature of which – the web – is wholly produced by elements within the system (the relevant organs of the spider), and yet which, once produced, has independent causal powers. The web does things for the spider which it could not possibly do for itself unaided, and yet it is wholly created by the spider. Just because the spider created the web, we don't have to say that the things which the spider does with it are in no way to be credited to the web itself, independently of the spider. (Here it may be objected that the web is not so much a 'feature' of the system, in Searle's sense, as a *part* of it. I shall return to this issue later, but for now I should just say that a merely hollow victory would be secured for Searle by allowing him to use the term 'feature' in a way which excluded *by definition* the possibility of there being strongly emergent features.)

Another putative example of a strongly emergent phenomenon is provided by the emergence of *language* amongst human populations – for it is wholly created (though not necessarily purposively) by human beings and yet once created confers upon them abilities that are completely novel and unattainable in the pre-linguistic state.[52] Why not

---

[50] This is not absolutely clear, in view of the 'trivial' status Searle accords to the irreducibility of consciousness, which most non-reductive physicalists would deny. See also Heil, *The Nature of True Minds*, pp. 125ff, where a type-identity theory is attributed to Searle, though only on the basis of Searle's earlier writings. By contrast, Tim Crane, in a trenchant and illuminating critical notice of *The Rediscovery of the Mind*, emphatically denies that Searle holds a type-identity theory: see the *International Journal of Philosophical Studies* 1 (1993), pp. 313-24.

[51] These difficulties are well articulated, incidentally, by Brian Loar in his 'Elimination versus Non-Reductive Physicalism', in David Charles and Kathleen Lennon (eds.), *Reduction, Explanation and Realism* (Oxford: Clarendon Press, 1992).

take the same view of *consciousness* as a product of biological processes in the brain – or, more plausibly (in view of the dubious possibility of solipsistic consciousness), as a product of such processes *together with* processes of social interaction between human beings? (As with language, one could espouse such an emergentist picture both at a phylogenetic and at an ontogenetic level.)

But what about the principle of the transitivity of causation, which I certainly have no wish to challenge here?[53] Well, that principle only implies that if x causes y and y causes z, then x causes z. It certainly doesn't imply that if x causes y and y possesses certain causal powers, then x likewise (and independently of y) possesses those causal powers, or that y's causal powers are wholly grounded in x's. To see this more clearly, just look more closely at the example of the spider and its web, and consider what effects the web has and how it produces them. Note, then, that the web both constrains the movements of the spider and enables it to make movements which it could not make without the web. Suppose the spider, using the web, moves from A to B, in a way it couldn't move without using the web. Are we to say, just because the spider *created* the web and thus *caused* it to possess the properties which constrain and facilitate the spider's movements, that the causes of the spider's movement from A to B lie wholly within the spider – that the web makes no independent causal contribution to that movement's occurrence? Evidently not. (It is true enough that it would be inappropriate to say that the web *caused the spider to move from A to B*: rather, the spider caused itself to do this, by moving its limbs in certain ways. But this just reflects the use of a restricted sense of 'cause' – of which more anon – and by no means implies the causal inertness of the web.)

Of course, the causal powers of the web are indeed *explicable* in terms of the causal powers of the material from which the spider weaves it together with the structure which the spider imposes upon it – but not in the same sense that, say, the causal powers of liquid water are explicable in terms of the causal powers and relations

---

[52] It may be felt that there exists a tension between this suggestion and my earlier non-realist remarks about social facts and events – but only if one takes language to be a purely social phenomenon, which I do not. For more on my views about language, and its relationship with thought, see chapter 6 below.

[53] Not that I think that this principle is perfectly unassailable: see my 'For Want of a Nail', *Analysis* 40 (1980), pp. 50-2.

of its constitutent molecules. The point is that, once produced, the web has, in Searle's phrase, 'a life of its own': its causal powers *originate from*, but are not wholly *grounded in* (or 'causally reducible to') the causal powers of those elements of the system which produced it.

6. A MODEL OF AUTONOMOUS MENTAL CAUSATION

It must be emphasized that the foregoing example of the spider and its web is only an analogy for our purposes, with all the limitations that analogies possess. What we must ask now is *how* conscious states might be at once a product of brain-processes and yet also possess independent causal powers having an impact upon brain-processes. I should say at once that my own feeling is that we only find the thought of 'dualistic' psychophysical causation mysterious and 'magical' because we are tempted to operate with unhelpful and misleading models of mental causation.[54] Descartes is perhaps partly to blame for this (though in view of the opprobrium which is liberally and unjustly heaped upon him by today's physicalists, I am loth to add to the attack). We imagine that the dualist must think of mental events as 'initiating' chains of physical events in the brain, which leaves us puzzled because we see no reason why physical chains of events in the brain should exhibit any 'gaps', much less 'gaps' in the right places for the dualist's purposes. We are persuaded that if we could look at the neural functioning of the whole brain in microscopic detail, all we would see would be a seamless net or maze of causally interconnected neural events.

But consider again the spider and its movements. If we just observed the movements and took no notice of the web, we would observe no 'gaps' in the movements – each movement would ensue from and be ensued by other movements continuously. So we might wonder how the web contributed anything at all to the movements: it didn't 'initiate' any of them, all the 'initiation' coming from the spider's limbs. The answer, of course, is that the web is what we might call an 'enabling' or 'facilitating' cause, rather than an 'initiating' cause, of the spider's movements – it enables and constrains these movements

[54] C. D. Broad felt much the same: see his *The Mind and its Place in Nature* (London: Routledge and Kegan Paul, 1925), pp. 111ff.

to take place in certain directions rather than others. Now, so too might states of consciousness both facilitate and impose constraints upon patterns of neural events.[55] I have already tentatively explored this possibility in section 3 above, but it will be in order to say a little more here.

The suggestion is that in episodes of deliberative action certain mental acts (decisions or volitions) may be thought of as inducing certain patterns of convergence amongst neural events – patterns which, in the absence of such mental causes, would appear to involve miraculous coincidences, in view of the widely distributed and chaotic character of the neural activity prior to convergence. Of course, whether this speculation is ultimately tenable is open to empirical disconfirmation, though as far as I am aware current knowledge of brain-function does not exclude the possibility of its correctness. Indeed, the suggestion draws sustenance from the fact that prior to a deliberative bodily movement there is typically a diffuse and gradual build-up of electrical activity distributed over a fairly wide area of the cortex and displaying no very specific correlation with the movement which ultimately ensues until very shortly beforehand, when there is a sudden discharge of activity along a specific efferent pathway.[56] Furthermore, according to the findings of Benjamin Libet (which, to be fair, have not gone wholly unchallenged), the agent's decision to move one of his limbs in a specific way itself occurs only just before this sudden discharge of electrical activity, and thus only after the generalized build-up of electrical activity has been for some time underway.[57] Thus the proposal is that the occurrence of

---

[55] Partly *because* I distinguish between 'enabling' and 'initiating' causes, I don't believe that this proposal can be seen as advocating the kind of 'downward causation' by the mental on the physical that some philosophers have recently considered to be problematical: see, e.g., Jaegwon Kim, '"Downward Causation" in Emergentism and Non-Reductive Physicalism', in A. Beckermann *et al.* (eds.), *Emergence or Reduction?* Incidentally, although my distinction between 'initiating' and 'enabling' causes clearly bears some resemblance to Fred Dretske's distinction between 'triggering' and 'structuring' causes, there are considerable differences between our applications of our respective distinctions to the problem of mental causation: see further F. Dretske, 'Mental Events as Structuring Causes of Behaviour', in Heil & Mele (eds.), *Mental Causation*.

[56] See L. Deecke, P. Scheid & H. H. Kornhuber, 'Distribution of Readiness Potential, Pre-Motion Positivity and Motor Potential of the Human Cerebral Cortex Preceding Voluntary Finger Movements', *Experimental Brain Research* 7 (1969), pp. 158–68.

[57] For details, see Benjamin Libet, 'Unconscious Cerebral Initiative and the Role of Conscious Will in Voluntary Action'. For one recent challenge to Libet, see Dennett, *Consciousness Explained*, pp. 162ff.

the conscious mental event of a decision to move a limb in a specific fashion, while it does not *initiate* any sequence of neural events culminating in such a movement, does serve to coordinate a host of mutually independent neural events so as to induce them to converge upon one specific pattern of efferent activity rather than another, or none at all. A rough analogy might be with the way in which a large number of balls simultaneously rolling down a bagatelle board, with an initially random distribution of positions and velocities, all end up in a limited number of stable positions on the board: the location of the pins on the board, though not responsible for initiating the movement of the balls, is responsible for their ultimate convergence upon just these positions.

Of course, as I have implicitly warned already, we shouldn't take the analogy of the spider's web (nor that of the bagatelle board) too far: after all, the web is a relatively fixed structure, whereas conscious processes are in a continuous state of flux. But at least in the case of the web we know what sort of empirical evidence supports our ascription to it of independent causal powers: so what sort of evidence would give similar support to an ascription of such powers to consciousness? (After all, what I have proposed so far might be thought to be consistent with regarding mental decisions as – perhaps widely distributed – neural events in the cortex.) Well, one crucial finding which would help to confirm the dualist status of the picture of mental causation just adumbrated would be for us to discover that it is impossible to map token neural events, or fusions thereof, onto token conscious events in a way which preserves isomorphism between their respective causal liasons. This would signify that no token neural event, or fusion of such events, has exactly the same causal liasons with other token events as any token conscious event putatively has, the implication being that the causal powers of any such conscious event must either be at least partially independent of those of neural events or else purely illusory. Such a state of affairs can certainly be envisaged, for we could discover that whereas the putative mental causes of token bodily movements are distinct and separable, the neural causes are inextricably entangled – as I suggested in section 3 above.

What I have in mind here can best be grasped by means of a (highly simplified) diagram (see figure 1), in which the neural antecedents of a number of distinct and simultaneous voluntary bodily movements are

represented together with their putative causal relationships both with
each other and with those movements.

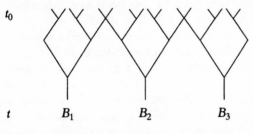

Figure 1

Here B_1, B_2 and B_3 are three distinct voluntary bodily movements of
the same agent occurring at the same time, t. The direction of time
runs from the top to the bottom of the diagram. Each line connecting
any two nodes on the diagram depicts a relationship of causation and
each node represents a neural event in the causal histories of the three
bodily movements. (We are to suppose that these branching lines
continue up the page indefinitely far backwards in time: the causal
histories have no definite 'beginning', though of course the brain in
which they occur is finitely old.)

The situation depicted in figure 1 is one in which the neural causes
of B_1, B_2 and B_3 are not wholly distinct and separable earlier than a
certain time, t_0: that is to say, at any time t_x prior to t_0 one cannot
affirm, of any set of neural events occurring at t_x, that just *these* were
causally responsible for just *one* of the three movements in question.
For, prior to t_0, some of the neural causes of B_1, say, are also causes of
B_2, and vice versa. Now, it is characteristic of a mental decision to
move a limb that it is conceived of as being a cause quite specifically of
just *that* bodily movement, and not of any other voluntary movement
which the agent happens to perform simultaneously. Moreover, the
decision is conceived of as giving rise to this bodily movement without any assistance from independent decisions to move other parts of
the body. Mental causation is, in this sense, quite *discrete*, if indeed it
genuinely occurs at all. (So central to our common sense conception
of mental causation is this feature of discreteness that if we were forced
to deny the reality of the latter we should be compelled to give up the

85

former.[58]) But suppose, now, that it were discovered that the mental decisions to perform bodily movements B_1, B_2 and B_3 could all be timed as occurring *prior* to time t_0 – certainly, it is not inconceivable that this should turn out to be the case. It would then follow that none of those mental decisions could be identified with (or in any weaker sense be put into one-to-one correlation with) any set of co-occurring neural causes of the corresponding bodily movement. For any such set of neural events would *either* be a partial cause of one of the other movements as well *or else* be such that it only gave rise to the movement in question in conjunction with neural events belonging to another set putatively identical with a decision to perform one of the other movements – and neither possibility comports with the discreteness of mental causation as we ordinarily conceive of it. For, as I have just remarked, we think of each decision as giving rise to just its 'own' movement and without any contribution from decisions to perform other, independent movements; and to abandon this thought is effectively to abandon mental causation as common sense conceives of that phenomenon.

Here it may be asked why the mental decision to perform movement B_2, say, couldn't be identified with the set of just those neural events occurring at t_x which occupy nodes dominating B_2 but not B_1 or B_3 (there are certainly some such nodes in figure 1 at t_0). This would be, admittedly, to identify the decision with only a proper subset of the neural causes of B_2 occurring at t_x, but it is in any case independently plausible to suppose that a mental decision only gives rise to its intended bodily movement in conjunction with other co-occurring neural causes. And provided corresponding constraints on the identity of the other mental decisions were also obeyed, 'discreteness' would be preserved. However, this query just reveals a minor oversimplification in figure 1 and the accompanying argument. For it is clear that if the pattern in figure 1 were extended further backward in time (that is, up the page), we could soon reach a point at which at least one of the bodily movements B_1, B_2 and B_3 was not dominated by *any* node dominating that movement alone – and strictly it is only at such a point that the argument from

---

[58] I should emphasize, though, that such discreteness is perfectly consistent with a voluntary movement's having a *plurality* of mental causes – beliefs and desires, for instance, in addition to a specific mental decision to perform that movement.

'entanglement' takes conclusive effect. That is to say, if the mental decisions can be timed as occurring at or before such a point, the discreteness of mental causation rules out a one-to-one mapping of mental decisions onto sets of neural causes. It must be conceded that obtaining clear-cut empirical evidence for the existence of such a state of affairs might be difficult in practice, but the issue is still in principle an empirical one.

Now, if a situation like the foregoing *is* the case, then, I suggest, the only admissible physicalist alternative to dualism will be eliminativism. And that, I consider, would be a *reductio ad absurdum* of physicalism.[59] In short, if, contrary to what I have surmised, there *is* always a one-to-one mapping of the sort discussed above (one which preserves the causal liasons of mental events as conceived by common sense, or 'folk psychology'), then reductionism (ontological, even if not explanatory) will be the road to take.[60] But if there *isn't*, as seems more likely, then we must either embrace dualism or else dismiss the mental as altogether 'illusory', and the latter is something which, I consider, we cannot coherently do.[61]

Let me sum up the argument of the preceding few paragraphs as follows. A mental decision to perform a certain bodily movement is conceived of as being a singular cause quite specifically of *that* movement, but not a cause (not even a partial cause) of the agent's other concurrent deliberative behaviour. By contrast, widely distributed neural events in the cortex (the only plausible physicalist candidates for identity with mental decisions) will typically be causes – but only partial causes – of many different concurrent aspects of an agent's deliberative behaviour, so that the specificity of a mental cause to its

---

[59] A somewhat similar scenario is envisaged by Ramsey, Stich and Garron with respect to the relationship between propositional attitude psychology and some connectionist models of brain-function, though they interpret the scenario as favourable to eliminativism: see W. Ramsey *et al.*, 'Connectionism, Eliminativism and the Future of Folk Psychology', in J. E. Tomberlin (ed.), *Philosophical Perspectives, 4* (Atascadero, CA: Ridgeview, 1990). Since I can't take eliminativism as a serious possibility, I would interpret such a scenario as once more supporting dualism. The key point, though, is that the middle ground between eliminativism and dualism is again seen to be under threat.

[60] Explanatory reductionism may still be deniable for reasons discussed earlier, but mental events will nonetheless just *be* physical events and mental causation just a species of physical causation.

[61] Of course, no eliminativist will concede this: but see Lynne R. Baker, *Saving Belief: A Critique of Physicalism*, for a robust reply.

intended effect would be lost if it were to be identified with such a distributed neural event. To this we may add that there will almost certainly be, in any realistic case, indefinitely many *different* distributed neural events (different combinations of separate neural events) each of which is no better a candidate than the others for identity with the mental decision to perform a particular movement: but the decision could only be *one* of these, and yet it would be arbitrary to select one rather than another for identity with it. Plausibly, no one of these distributed events will have a causal salience in the production of the bodily movement which makes it stand out from the others in the way it would have to in order to match the indisputable causal salience of the mental decision to perform just that movement. And it is precisely because, on this picture, nothing at the neural level seems apt to assume the distinctive causal role which mental decisions appear to possess that I see eliminativism as the only likely physicalist alternative to dualism, at least as far as intention and volition are concerned.

It may be objected to the picture that I have been presenting of consciousness as a strongly emergent phenomenon that it presupposes that consciousness is a substance – a kind of *stuff* – rather than a *property* (or 'feature') of the brain, as Searle regards it. After all, this is precisely what the spider's web is. Now maybe this just again demonstrates the danger of taking analogies too far. But note that Searle himself rather invites precisely this sort of analogy when he characterizes consciousness on the strongly emergent view as being 'squirted out' by the brain (after all, *stuffs* are what get 'squirted') – so that he, at least, is hardly well positioned to object if just such an analogy is taken seriously by the strong emergentist. It is indeed true that Searle himself is very much *opposed* to regarding consciousness as a kind of stuff, and takes Colin McGinn to task for suggesting that it is.[62] But in this he is perhaps a bit hard on McGinn, who was primarily pointing out that 'consciousness' is logically a stuff term[63] – as indeed on one reading it does appear to be (*not* on the reading on which it is an abstract noun in the same semantic category as 'fastidiousness', but rather on the reading on which one speaks of a *particular person's* 'consciousness', which can wax and wane and so alter in amount like a quantity). It is true that McGinn does also say that he sees nothing wrong 'metaphysically'

[62] Searle, *The Rediscovery of the Mind*, pp. 104ff.
[63] See Colin McGinn, *The Problem of Consciousness* (Oxford: Basil Blackwell, 1991), p. 60.

with regarding consciousness as being a kind of stuff – though, of course, the danger of this way of talking is that it suggests that consciousness is something like the 'ectoplasm' of nineteenth-century spiritualist séances.[64]

Be all this as it may, it is not in any case clear just what hinges on Searle's denial that consciousness is a kind of stuff and his insistence that it is a 'property' or 'feature' of the brain – for these terms, too, are obscure. Indeed, there seems nothing wrong in calling the spider's web a 'feature' of a certain ecological microsystem, despite its being (or being made of) a kind of stuff. Moreover, one can readily envisage other systems in which the relevant emergent 'feature' would *not* have this stufflike characteristic – features like force-fields, perhaps. (In fact, the web itself may be redescribed as a kind of force-field anyway; and at the level of quantum field theory perhaps that is just what it really *is*.) Certainly, another putative example cited earlier of a strongly emergent phenomenon – that of *language* – clearly does *not* have stufflike connotations.

Altogether, then, I suspect that any objection along the lines mooted earlier would just be misconceived, resting as it apparently does on a somewhat naïve and confused metaphysics. There is, indeed, a danger in Searle's line of approach that he almost rules out the possibility of consciousness being strongly emergent *by definition*. For a strongly emergent feature is one which has independent causal powers – and the possession of such powers might well be taken (by some, and so perhaps by Searle) to be one hallmark of the *substantial* status of an item. So if he is ruling out the possibility of consciousness being substantial or stufflike, he may be implicitly ruling out the possibility of its possessing independent causal powers and hence the possibility of its being strongly emergent. In short, there is a strong suggestion of circularity in Searle's classification of consciousness as a weakly emergent feature. I myself am no enemy of metaphysics, but it is important not to let uncritical metaphysical preconceptions obscure possible answers to the mind-body problem by inducing us to rule out certain forms of answer without due consideration.

Once we recognize that new kinds of phenomena, with novel and independent causal powers, can emerge naturally from the complex

---

[64] Incidentally, McGinn himself, like Searle, does not believe in the causal autonomy of consciousness: see McGinn, *The Problem of Consciousness*, p. 77.

causal interactions of other kinds of phenomena, opening up hitherto unavailable possibilities of action for the very entities involved in their production, we can hope to find a genuine role for consciousness as a 'non-physical' (and certainly non-biological) influence on biological systems whose origins nonetheless reside in the workings of those systems. Only an antiquated metaphysics and a blinkered view of causality stand in the way of taking such a possibility seriously, and thereby saving the indispensable notion mental causation from the clutches of eliminativism on the one hand and reductionism on the other.

4

Perception

The most central capacities of the self are its capacities for perception, action, thought and self-knowledge, and the remaining chapters of this book deal with each of these in turn. In each case, I present an account of the capacity in question in terms which assign a funda-mental role to the *conscious* states of the subject and their *causal* rela-tions both with one another and with physical states of the self's body and environment. In this chapter, I make a start with perception – in some ways the most primitive of the self's capacities (being shared with many of the lower animals), but in others the most remarkable and puzzling. It is my belief that, provided certain logical and con-ceptual distinctions are properly observed and due cognizance is taken of relevant empirical evidence, it is possible to defend a theory of perception which is at once a *causal* theory, a *representative* theory and a *direct realist* theory (direct realist inasmuch as it does not postulate mental entities as the immediate objects of perception). The theory that I shall be defending in this chapter possesses all three of these features.[1] The three features are not irreconcilable, as may commonly be supposed, and indeed I believe that only by combining them can an account of perception be given which is at once naturalistic and philosophically tenable.

---

[1] In many ways, my theory has affinities both to Locke's view of perception and to the kind of structural realism which Bertrand Russell expounded in, for instance, his *The Problems of Philosophy* (London: Oxford University Press, 1912), ch. 3, and in more detail in his *The Analysis of Matter* (London: George Allen & Unwin, 1927). I discuss these connec-tions more fully in my *Locke on Human Understanding* (London: Routledge, 1995), ch. 3 and ch. 8.

Subjects of experience

1. PERCEPTION AND PERCEPTUAL EXPERIENCE

I consider it vital, in the philosophy of perception, to recognize the conceptual distinction between *perceiving* and *having perceptual experiences*. One may – for instance, when undergoing a hallucination – have a perceptual experience and yet not be perceiving; or so I would claim.[2] Others, however, may urge that in such circumstances one does indeed *perceive*, but doesn't necessarily perceive any *thing* – or, more exactly, that there isn't necessarily anything that one then perceives. I say 'more exactly' because some philosophers will want to say that in at least *one* sense of 'perceive', 'I perceive an *X*' does not entail 'There is an *X* that I perceive', any more than 'I want an *X*' entails 'There is an *X* that I want' – and to conclude from this that 'I perceive something' does not entail 'There is something that I perceive'.[3] Such philosophers typically discriminate between perceiving having a 'real' or 'material' object and its having an 'intentional' object, but then go

---

[2] I should perhaps explain that I am using the term 'hallucination' here in a narrow sense which excludes non-objectified experiences of the sort involved in hypnagogic imagery and sometimes stimulated by so-called hallucinogenic drugs (swirling patterns of colour and the like): such experiences are not 'perceptual' in my terminology precisely because they are not experiences 'of' *objects* of any kind. For further discussion of such non-objectified experiences and their wholly non-epistemic character, see Edmond Wright, 'Inspecting Images', *Philosophy* 58 (1983), pp. 57-72 and 'New Representationalism', *Journal of the Theory of Social Behaviour* 20 (1990), pp. 65-92. There are some modern philosophers of perception, however, who deny that one can identify any distinctive kind of mental state – such as I take a perceptual experience to be – which could, even in principle, be common both to (veridical) perception and to hallucination: see, e.g., J. M. Hinton, *Experiences* (Oxford: Clarendon Press, 1973), P. Snowdon, 'Perception, Vision, and Causation', *Proceedings of the Aristotelian Society* 81 (1980- 1), pp. 175-92, and J. McDowell, 'Criteria, Defeasibility, and Knowledge', in J. Dancy (ed.), *Perceptual Knowledge* (Oxford: Oxford University Press, 1988). I shall not attempt to refute these philosophers directly here, but I hope that the general theory of perception which emerges from this chapter will be seen to have none of the ill consequences which philosophers of this persuasion are wont to discern in causal theories like mine (notably, an alleged tendency to promote scepticism).

[3] Actually I don't think this conclusion does follow. For it is perhaps open to one to hold (though I do not) that 'I perceive an *X*', while not entailing 'There is an *X* that I perceive', does (at least on one interpretation) entail 'There is something that I perceive *as* an *X*', where this something need not, of course, be an *X*; and from this it would seem to follow that 'I perceive an *X*' *does* entail 'There is something that I perceive'. More generally: although perception clearly does involve intentionality, I think it is misleading to attempt to draw parallels between verbs of perception such as 'see' and intentional verbs such as 'want' and 'seek' – cf. Frank Jackson, *Perception: A Representative Theory* (Cambridge: Cambridge University Press, 1977), p. 112.

on to distinguish two different *senses* of 'perceive', one for each type of object.[4]

What is one to say in explanation of this distinction between 'real' and 'intentional' objects of perception? (I should point out that I accept the distinction, but not some of the doctrines often associated with it: in particular, not the doctrine that one may be perceiving even in the absence of there being any real object of perception, nor the doctrine that there are two different senses of 'perceive'.) Well, first one might say that a 'real' object of perception is something which is perceived but which exists independently of its being perceived. (Against this it may be objected that Berkeley, on one interpretation of his views at least, held that 'ideas' were real objects of perception – that in perceiving an idea a mind stood in some genuine relation to an object distinct from itself – and yet notoriously also held that, for an idea, *esse est percipi*, and hence that ideas do not exist independently of their being perceived. However, I suspect that the right response to this objection is to say that if this *was* Berkeley's view, then his position was internally inconsistent.) An 'intentional' object of perception, one might on the other hand say, doesn't – or at least needn't – really exist at all. Inasmuch as an X is the intentional object of one's perception, there need *be* no X that one perceives, nor need there even exist any Xs at all.[5] Even a unicorn may be the intentional object of one's perception. However, I *don't* want to say that simply inasmuch as an X is the intentional object of one's perception, one is thereby entitled to say (in *any* sense of 'perceive') that one 'perceives an X'.[6] What I do want to say will emerge in a moment.

[4] See, e.g., G. E. M. Anscombe, 'The Intentionality of Sensation: A Grammatical Feature', reprinted in her *Metaphysics and the Philosophy of Mind* (Oxford: Basil Blackwell, 1981), p. 17: 'While there must be an intentional object of seeing, there need not always be a material object. That is to say "X saw A" where "saw" is used materially, implies some proposition "X saw —" where "saw" is used intentionally; but the converse does not hold.' (Note, incidentally, that a 'material' object in this sense need not be material in the physical sense, that is, composed of matter. In view of possible confusion on this score, 'real' is the preferable epithet.)

[5] I should emphasize that I use the word 'perception' as synonymous with 'perceiving', and never to denote (what I call) a perceptual experience.

[6] Perhaps against this it will be suggested that when looking at (and recognizing) a picture of a unicorn, it is proper to say, in some sense, that one 'sees a unicorn'. However, it is surely not *literally* true that one then sees a unicorn, in any sense of 'see'. 'See' is, I think, being used here in one of its many metaphorical ways or extended senses (compare 'seeing' an argument); whereas I am only concerned with the strict and literal use of perception verbs.

Consider again the case of hallucination – say, the case of Macbeth's infamous dagger (a fictitious case itself, but not an impossible one). The philosophers I have alluded to will perhaps want to say that Macbeth does indeed *see a dagger*, on the grounds that he sees and that a dagger is the intentional object of his seeing. But at the same time they will want to deny that there is *anything* – least of all a dagger – that Macbeth sees (insofar as he is hallucinating), on the grounds that his seeing has no real or material object (not even a private mental image or sense datum – for such philosophers will characteristically want to deny that there *are* any such things to be seen at all). However, what I would prefer to say is that Macbeth does not *see* at all (not, at least, inasmuch as he hallucinates a dagger). Rather, he (only) *seems to see*, or *has a visual experience as of seeing*, a dagger. We can agree that a dagger is the 'intentional object' of his visual experience (meaning thereby *simply that* he has a visual experience as of seeing a dagger). But we should not, I suggest, say that he *sees* (let alone that he sees a dagger), because to see it is not enough merely to have a visual experience: it is necessary also that one's visual experience be appropriately related to some *real object*, which one thereby sees. And the 'appropriate relation' in question is a (certain sort of) *causal* one, of which I shall have more to say in due course.

More generally, when one *perceives*, one has a perceptual experience which is appropriately causally related to some (real) object, which one thereby perceives. It needn't, however, be the case that the intentional object of one's perceptual experience 'matches' the object that one perceives. Such mismatches occur in cases of perceptual *illusion* (which are to be distinguished from cases of *hallucination*, inasmuch as the latter do not involve *perception* but only the having of perceptual experiences). Typically, in a case of illusion, one perceives a certain object (a real object, that is) of a certain sort, but has a perceptual experience as of perceiving an object of a rather different sort. For instance, in the Müller-Lyer illusion, one sees two lines of equal length, but seems to see two lines of differing lengths. (Actually, not *all* perceptual 'illusions' can be analysed in quite this way. Thus, in the case of the 'bent stick' illusion, it certainly *need not* be the case that one 'seems to see a bent stick', provided one has learnt how straight sticks look when half-immersed in water. When we say, correctly, that such sticks 'look bent', we are not, then, implying that when we see one we necessarily *seem to see a bent stick*; what we *are* implying in using 'look' in this way is something I shall examine later.)

Rather than say, then, that perceiving, while it may have both an intentional and a real or material object (and must have the former), may also – for instance, in the case of hallucination – have *only* an intentional object, I would prefer to say the following. *Perceiving* must always have a *real* object – that is, when one perceives, there is always something that one perceives (something that exists independently of its being perceived). On the other hand, a *perceptual experience* must always have an *intentional* object – that is, when one has a perceptual experience, it must always be an experience *as of perceiving something*. In other words, when one has a perceptual experience, one must always *seem to perceive something* – and not just a *mere* 'something', but something falling under some possible description, however vague (something *of some sort*). I would further say, of course, that perceiving must always involve having a perceptual experience of some suitable kind, *and consequently* that it must always have not only a real object but also an intentional object (inasmuch as the perceptual experience involved must have the latter).[7] Notice, incidentally, that when I speak of 'seeming to perceive' – an expression I use interchangeably with 'having an experience as of perceiving' – I do not, of course, mean to imply that someone who seems to perceive does *not* in fact perceive; for by my account someone who perceives must seem to perceive, though not *vice versa*.

Of course, it may well be – indeed, I strongly suspect that it *is* – the case that the difference between my position and that which I am opposing is to some extent a verbal or terminological one. Where I distinguish between perceiving and having perceptual experiences (having experiences as of perceiving, or seeming to perceive), the opposing view correspondingly distinguishes between two different senses of 'perceive', one in which perceiving requires a real or material object and another in which it requires only an intentional object. Even so, there are at least two distinct advantages in my position. First, the perennial danger of confusion in philosophy is always best avoided

---

[7] Against this last point one might raise the case of so-called 'blindsight', which precisely lacks characteristically visual experience; but blindsight is anomalous to a degree which, I think, allows us only in a peripheral sense to say that its victims genuinely 'see' things. For details, see L. Weiskrantz, *Blindsight: A Case Study and Implications* (Oxford: Clarendon Press, 1986). I discuss the issue at some length in section 4 below.

by marking real distinctions by verbal ones, rather than persisting in the use of confessedly ambiguous terminology. Secondly, the position which holds there to be two distinct senses of 'perceive' is in danger of remaining complacently unconcerned with their semantic relationship – whereas I cannot so easily avoid having to give some account of the semantic relationship between 'perceiving' and 'having an experience *as of* perceiving' (or, equivalently, '*seeming* to perceive'). Indeed, we shall see later (in section 6) that providing such an account presents quite a difficult challenge – and at the same time we shall discover, interestingly enough, a reason why one might indeed be tempted to suppose that there are two distinct senses of 'perceive'.

2. PERCEPTION AND SENSATION

Perceptual experiences are *intentional* (or, in the currently fashionable jargon, 'representational') states of mind: that is, they always take 'intentional' objects, even when they occur (as in hallucinations) in the absence of any real object being perceived. Thus Macbeth's hallucinatory visual experience was an experience as of seeing *a dagger*. An experience which lacked this characteristic 'object-directedness' simply would not be a *perceptual* experience. There certainly *are* 'objectless' experiences – notably, 'pure' sensations like pain – but they are not perceptual. However, it is important to recognize that perceptual experiences (indeed, *all* experiences – though some only derivatively, as I shall explain) do also involve a sensational or sensuous element.[8] We would perhaps not so easily lose sight of this fact if we took the trouble to speak of '*sense*-perception' rather than just of 'perception' *simpliciter*. Today philosophers generally use the word 'perception' to mean exclusively what in earlier times was called 'sense-perception', that is, perception *by means of the senses* – sight, hearing, touch, smell, taste and so on. But one consequence – or perhaps it is a cause – of this shift in philosophical usage seems to have been that the sensational element in sense-perception is now underemphasized, or even entirely neglected.

Whether there are states of mind that are *purely* intentional – that is, which are 'object-directed' but lack any characteristic sensational

[8] Cf. C. A. B. Peacocke, *Sense and Content: Experience, Thought, and their Relations* (Oxford: Clarendon Press, 1983), ch. 1.

element – is debatable; but if there are they are not, I believe, *experiential* states. One possible candidate for the status of a purely intentional state would be knowledge 'of' somebody or something. But such a state is obviously not experiential. Someone who *knows* Paris need not on that account be undergoing any particular sort of experience, in the way that someone who *sees* Paris must be. However, connected with this is the fact that the verb 'to know', unlike the verb 'to see', does not admit the present continuous tense – one can be *seeing* Paris, but not *knowing* it. Experiences are *occurrent*, as opposed to dispositional, states of mind; and the experiencing mind is being affected in some way of which it is concurrently aware, even if only confusedly. But what about occurrent intentional mental states like *thinking* of, or *remembering* somebody or something? These are experiential but surely do not involve *sensation*; so are they not 'purely' intentional experiential states? No, because although they do not involve sensation directly, I believe that they do involve it derivatively inasmuch as they involve *imagination*.[9] (And thus remembrance, like perception, has its different sensory modes – visual, auditory and so forth; which it would apparently not be appropriate to say if it were a 'purely' intentional state of mind.)

Each mode of (sense-)perception has its characteristic range of sensations: we have visual sensations, auditory sensations, tactile sensations, olfactory sensations, kinaesthetic sensations and so forth. I realize, however, that the very existence of such sensations has been queried or disputed by some philosophers.[10] One objection which might be raised against their existence is this: if such sensations exist, why is it that we (apparently) never trouble to describe them, and indeed lack any characteristic expressions in ordinary language wherewith to describe them? This is not the case with *bona fide* sensations like pains and tickles (so it may be said).

My response is that in fact we *do* have *and use* expressions enabling us to describe our perceptual sensations, though the descriptions in question take an oblique form for reasons which are perfectly understandable. The expressions I have in mind fall into two

[9] This claim is a controversial and important one in its own right, and one which I discuss in more detail in chapter 6; however, it is somewhat peripheral to my immediate concerns, so I need not and shall not press it here.

[10] See, e.g., Gilbert Ryle, *The Concept of Mind* (London: Hutchinson, 1949), p. 191, pp. 228ff. It seems to me that Ryle's doubts are partly the upshot of excessive deference to (what he takes to be) 'ordinary usage'.

categories: certain cross-modal words such as 'appear' and 'seem', and certain monomodal words such as 'look' (for vision), 'sound' (for hearing), 'feel' (for touch), 'smell' (for olfaction) and so forth. Consider vision. Often we speak about how objects *look* or (visually) *appear* in certain circumstances. Thus one may say that a round coin 'looks elliptical' when seen at a certain angle to the line of sight, or that a red book 'looks grey' at twilight. Now *this* sense of 'look' or 'appear' – what we may call the *phenomenal* sense – is to be distinguished from another sense, which might be called the *doxastic*. Sometimes I may say that an object 'looks *F*', thereby giving my auditor to understand that I am inclined to believe (but am not sure) that it *is* in fact *F*. However, when, using 'look' in the phenomenal sense, I say that a certain coin 'looks elliptical', knowing full well that it is round, I am obviously *not* giving anyone to understand that I am inclined to believe that the coin *is* elliptical; nor does it seem reasonable to suppose that I am doing anything so sophisticated as to give a (possible) auditor to understand that I *would* be inclined to believe that the coin is elliptical if I didn't already know or believe that it is round. What I *am* doing, I suggest, is reporting, in an oblique fashion, a certain similarity between the visual experience I enjoy in seeing the round coin in these circumstances (when it is at an angle to the line of sight) and the sort of visual experience I typically enjoy in seeing a flat elliptical object in certain other circumstances – in particular, the sort of circumstances which are optimal for forming a visual judgement as to the shape of a flat object (namely, when it is held at right-angles to the line of sight). This itself may seem a pretty sophisticated thing to report; but I am not suggesting that someone making such a report need himself grasp this analysis of 'look', only that he be alive to the experiential similarity in question and have been trained to make such a report in the right circumstances. No such 'de-sophisticating' move is available to those who would suggest that 'look' is still being used doxastically, but counterfactually, in such cases: for it is not similarly open to them – without giving the game away – to appeal to the subject's primitive awareness of an experiential similarity as the cue for his utterance.

Now, in what *respect* are these two visual experiences similar? What *sort* of experiential similarity am I alluding to in using 'look' in this way? I am plainly not alluding to any similarity between the *intentional objects* of the experiences in question, for these are on the contrary being *contrasted*: the one experience is an experience as of seeing *a flat round object at an angle*, the other an experience as of seeing *a flat elliptical object face-on*. What I suggest is that I am alluding to a similarity between the *visual sensations* I enjoy in each experience: the two visual experiences resemble each other *sensuously* in a certain way. This is confirmed by the fact that the relevant *sense-organ* – here the eye – is in fact similarly affected in each such case of seeing (in both cases a roughly similarly shaped area of the retina will be stimulated by light from the objects in question).

What I am saying, then, is that we *do* describe our perceptual sensations, albeit in an oblique fashion, when we use the language of (phenomenal) *appearances*. The obliquity consists in the fact that in saying how objects 'look' or 'appear', we are ostensibly describing the *objects*, not our experiences of them; yet what we say in fact conveys information about the sensuous aspects of our perceptual experiences. Nor is it surprising that we lack any more direct mode of description in ordinary language.[11] For we obviously, and necessarily, learn to describe the *objects* of perceptual experience (tables, chairs, coins, books) before we learn to describe perceptual experiences themselves. But having learned to describe the objects of perceptual experience we *already have* an ample vocabulary which can be adapted (through the use of locutions like 'look' and 'appear') to convey information about the sensuous aspects of our perceptual experiences indirectly, by reference to the objects which characteristically give rise to those experiences – thus rendering an alternative vocabulary (a 'language of perceptual sensations') otiose.[12] In the case of 'objectless' experi-

---

[11] I should point out that more exact, technical modes of describing perceptual sensations are certainly available to empirical psychologists – see section 3 below – and such descriptions (as befits their scientific role) lack the obliquity of the kind of ordinary language descriptions that I have been discussing. My reason for concentrating on the latter here is to rebut the contentions of those philosophers who deny that ordinary language contains *any* resources for describing perceptual sensations and who try to use this claim to cast doubt on the very existence of such sensations.

[12] In saying that we can use the language of 'looks' to convey information about the sensuous aspects of our perceptual experiences by reference to the objects which *characteristically* give rise to those experiences, I do not mean to imply that, for instance, round objects *more often* 'look round' than 'look elliptical'. 'Characteristic', in this context, is a normative (rather than a statistical) epithet, tied to a notion of *optimal* circumstances for forming a perceptual judgement as to whether or not an object possesses a given property (here, roundness). Thus, 'looks round' is to be cashed out in terms of the way a round object looks when a plane in which it has a round cross-section is orthogonal to the line of sight.

ences such as pains the development of descriptive terminology is less straightforward; though of course we still describe pains quite largely in terms of their typical causes, or by analogy with pains caused in specific ways – 'stabbing' pains, 'burning' pains and so on. (I say 'by analogy' because, for instance, someone who has never been stabbed may describe his pain as a 'stabbing' pain and – obscure though this may be – it seems that he means that his pain feels rather how one might expect a pain caused by stabbing to feel.)

Incidentally, we are now in a position to distinguish between two different kinds of perceptual illusion – 'cognitive' ones like the Müller-Lyer illusion, in which one *seems to perceive* an object somewhat different from the one that one actually perceives; and 'sensory' ones such as the 'bent stick' illusion, in which the object that one perceives *appears* (phenomenally) rather similar to an object which differs in some way from the object perceived. The very fact that there plainly *are* two different classes of perceptual illusion, whose extensions match those expected on the present theory of perception, goes some way towards confirming this theory – particularly insofar as it insists on distinguishing between the intentional and sensuous aspects of perceptual experience. Thus, when a straight stick is half-immersed in water, its 'looking bent' can at most be described as a case of *sensory* illusion, for it carries no implication whatever that in seeing the stick in such circumstances one *seems to see something bent*; whereas, by contrast, in the case of the Müller-Lyer illusion, one really does *seem to see two lines of different lengths*. As I shall explain more fully in section 6, I hold that 'seeming to see something bent' is a matter of being in an experiential state of the sort one typically enjoys when, because of the experiential state one is in, one is inclined to believe that one *is* seeing something bent. But the sort of experiential state typically enjoyed in seeing a straight stick which 'looks bent' is *not* the sort of state one typically enjoys when, because of the experiential state one is in, one is inclined to believe that one is seeing something *bent*. After all, when one is in an experiential state of the former sort, one is, on the contrary, normally inclined to believe that one is seeing something *straight*, but half-immersed in a transparent medium. But in the case of the Müller-Lyer illusion, by contrast, one is indeed in an experiential state of the sort one typically enjoys when, because of the experiential state one is in, one is inclined to believe that one is seeing two lines of different lengths – and this is why it is difficult to resist believing that the lines one sees really are of different lengths. (It is worth remarking, in confirmation of my classification of the two illusions, that in the case of the 'bent stick' illusion, the relevant *sense organ* – here, the eye – is stimulated in a manner *similar* to that in which it is stimulated in the non-illusory condition of seeing a stick which really is bent, because a similarly shaped retinal image is formed, whereas in the case of the Müller-Lyer illusion similarity of sensory stimulation is *not* involved – for, in the latter case, the lengths of the retinal images of the two lines are in fact equal and thus *differ* from the relative lengths of the images in the non-illusory condition, in which one correctly seems to see lines of different lengths.)

One final point of great importance is this: perceptual sensations are not themselves *objects of perception* (items that we see, hear or otherwise perceive). It was the mistake of most traditional 'sense datum' theorists to suppose precisely this. Rather, perceptual sensations are, as I have said, features of the perceptual experiences which we typically (but not exclusively) enjoy when we perceive the genuine objects of perception (items such as tables and trees). In view of my stance on this issue I can fairly claim to be a 'direct realist' (since it is no part of a sensible direct realism to deny that we perceive objects by virtue of enjoying perceptual experiences of them).[13] I should perhaps also remark here – if it is not sufficiently obvious already – that perceptual sensations constitute a wholly *non-conceptual* component of perceptual experience; whereas the question of whether the intentional or 'representational' content of perceptual experience itself has a non-conceptual component is altogether more controversial.[14]

---

[13] Although I align myself with 'direct realism' inasmuch as I deny that the 'immediate' objects of perception are mental items ('sense data'), I do not in fact believe that we see 'external' objects like tables and chairs 'directly', because I consider that our retinal images are items that we *do* see, even in the normal circumstances of vision, and that it is only *because* we see them that we also see 'distal' objects such as tables and trees. See further my 'What Do We See Directly?', *American Philosophical Quarterly* 23 (1986), pp. 277–85, and also section 3 below.

[14] One philosopher who thinks it does is Christopher Peacocke: see his 'Scenarios, Concepts and Perception', in T. Crane (ed.), *The Contents of Experience: Essays on Perception* (Cambridge: Cambridge University Press, 1992).

3. A CAUSAL THEORY OF PERCEPTION

To *perceive* an object, I said earlier, is to have a perceptual experience which is appropriately causally related to the object perceived. It seems to me that any remotely plausible philosophical theory of perception must be a 'causal' theory to the extent that it accepts this much as true.[15] But to say this much is still not to say a great deal: we need to specify in far more detail the nature of the 'appropriate' causal relation in question. At the same time, however, as philosophers we must be wary not to trespass upon the proper territory of physiology and empirical psychology by engaging in armchair pseudo-science, but limit ourselves to articulating the causal notions embedded in the very concept of perception.

It is surely a conceptual requirement that perception be a *possible* (not necessarily an *actual*) source of knowledge or belief about the object perceived. When one perceives an object, I suggest, one's perceptual experience must be causally related to certain properties of that object in such a fashion that one is thereby enabled to form a fairly reliable judgement as to what those properties are.[16] (It doesn't follow, of course, that one must actually *make* such a judgement; and even if one does, I am not denying that one's possession of certain 'background information' will play an important part in determining the judgement one arrives at.) And the properties in question will on that account qualify as *perceptible* properties of the object perceived – perceptible, that is, to that percipient in those circumstances. The question which immediately arises, then, is this: *what features*, exactly, of the percipient's perceptual experience should we take to be thus causally dependent upon the perceived object's perceptible properties – and what is the precise nature of this causal dependency?

In order to focus matters, I shall concentrate on the case of vision (but I believe that the account which follows may be extended in appropriately modified forms to the other sense modalities). According to my proposal, then, one *sees* an object if and only if one's visual experience is directly causally dependent on certain prop-

---

[15] See further the *locus classicus* for modern causal theories of perception, H. P. Grice, 'The Causal Theory of Perception', *Proceedings of the Aristotelian Society*, supp. vol. 35 (1961), pp. 121-52.

[16] Observe that although the account which follows invokes a connection between perceiving and knowing, it would be incorrect to describe it as treating perception itself as an epistemic state. I discuss this point in more detail below.

erties of that object in such a fashion that one is thereby enabled (with the aid of certain background knowledge, maybe) to form a fairly reliable judgement as to what those properties are. These properties will then qualify as *visible* (to the observer) properties of the object that is seen. As it stands, the proposal is somewhat schematic, and details need to be filled in at various places. This I shall do in due course. But first certain possible queries and objections of a more general nature need to be addressed.

One objection might be that it is circular to define seeing in terms of visual experience. But that would only be so if I also proposed to define visual experience in terms of seeing, which I do not. I do not, for instance, want to define a visual experience as one caused by stimulation of the natural organ of sight, the eye, by light. A perceptual experience qualifies as a *visual* experience purely by virtue of its intrinsic phenomenal or qualitative character (and thus by virtue of the kind of *sensations* in involves) – or so I would claim. It is true that such experiences are normally caused by light impinging on the retina of the eye, but they can also apparently be caused by direct stimulation of certain parts of the cortex, as the well-known findings of Wilder Penfield indicate.[17] It is not inconceivable that a congenitally blind person (one whose eyes or optic nerves were damaged beyond repair) should be capable of enjoying such experiences and have sight conferred upon him artificially by being fitted with a prosthetic device. The device would not necessarily have to be sensitive to light in the spectral range to which the natural eye is sensitive: indeed, there is no reason in principle why it should not be sensitive to some form of energy other than electromagnetic radiation. So what qualifies an experience as visual has nothing to do with its causal provenance (at any stage earlier than the cortex, at least). Qualitative character is what counts – and I shall say more about it later. (I shall, however, return to the question of circularity in section 6 below, where a rather more challenging form of the objection will be addressed.)

A second objection might be that in insisting that seeing involves having visual experiences I am ignoring the phenomenon of so-called 'blindsight'.[18] Blindsight subjects, in whom the striate cortex has been

[17] See W. Penfield and L. Roberts, *Speech and Brain Mechanisms* (Princeton: Princeton University Press, 1959), pp. 51ff.

[18] See L. Weiskrantz, *Blindsight: A Case Study and Implications*, upon which my description and interpretation of the phenomenon is heavily dependent.

(wholly or partially) destroyed by injury, disease or surgical intervention, are capable of discriminating the locations of light stimuli and
even of distinguishing elementary differences of shape or form in
them, but without the benefit of enjoying visual experiences of any
sort (at least in that part of the visual field corresponding to the
damaged part of the cortex). It is significant, however, that the subjects
themselves resolutely *deny* that they see the stimuli in question, and
have to be asked to 'guess' their locations and shapes. Even after
learning that their 'guesses' are highly accurate (though they are less
so than the visual judgements of normal subjects), they still deny that
they *see*, and continue to think of themselves as just 'guessing'. I think
that they are right to deny this, and hence that the phenomenon of
blindsight actually confirms my definition. Seeing *does* require having
visual experiences. Note too that my definition requires that the subject be enabled to form a fairly reliable *judgement* as to the relevant
properties of the seen object: so that the blindsight subject is dis-
qualified as a seer not only by virtue of lacking the appropriate experiences, but also because his discriminations apparently have to take the
form of 'guesses' rather than judgements. I shall return to the issue of
blindsight later, in an attempt to explain why sense perception is
indispensable for creatures genuinely capable of belief or judgement.

Another general issue I should address concerns the extent to which
my definition makes seeing an *epistemic* process. First of all, it will be
observed that it does not follow from my definition that if a person
sees an object he must thereby acquire knowledge (or even belief)
about it. And this is how it should be: for it is clear that very often one
sees objects of whose very existence one is quite ignorant at the time
of seeing them. Thus it can happen that at the time of being presented
with an array of visible objects one fails to notice certain of them, but
that one is able to recollect their presence at a later time. This requires
that one must indeed have *seen* them at the earlier time – for one
cannot recollect what one has not experienced. However, on the
other hand, my definition of seeing is not wholly *non*-epistemic, for
it recognizes that seeing should at least provide a *possible* means of
gaining knowledge about the object that is seen – though it allows,
too, that the realization of that possibility may depend crucially upon
the subject's store of background knowledge. Someone who knows
nothing about telescopes may *see* a distant galaxy when peering
through the eyepiece of a telescope, but the experience will not

issue in any reliable judgement concerning that celestial object, as it would in the case of an astronomer's observation.

But now it may be objected that the clause concerning background knowledge in my definition is too lenient, in that it forces me to say that ordinary folk *see* their own retinal images whenever they are looking at their everyday surroundings – for, certainly, anyone with a specialized knowledge of physiological optics can form fairly reliable judgements concerning properties of his retinal images on the basis of the visual experiences he enjoys in such ordinary situations.[19] This is the 'problem of the proximal stimulus'. The 'problem', supposedly, is to characterize seeing in such a way that only 'distal' stimuli – things like tables and trees, and presumably also distant galaxies – qualify as objects that are *seen*, and *not* things like retinal images and patterns of neural activity in the retina or cortex (unless, that is, they themselves happen to occur as distal stimuli, as when an ophthalmologist investigates another person's eye). But *why not* things like these? As far as I can see, no good reason can be given for excluding them as *bona fide* objects of vision, and the mere fact that ordinary folk would not *say* that they see such objects is just a symptom of their fully excusable ignorance. Perhaps the supposed problem arises from a tacit assumption that objects of vision compete with one another for that status: that if one were always seeing one's own retinal images, one would thereby be prevented from ever seeing one's own everyday surroundings (almost as though the retinal images would 'get in the way'). But that is absurd: when one sees a televised football match, one sees the images on the television screen *as well as* seeing the players, though normally one's attention is focused on the latter. What is perhaps true is that objects of vision compete for *our attention*, so that we cannot *attend* to our retinal images while also attending to our everyday surroundings. But that, if true, is a fact about attention, rather than a fact about vision as such.

Incidentally, when I stipulate that in seeing an object one's visual experiences should *enable* one to form fairly reliable judgements about certain properties of the seen object, I do not mean to suggest that one must form those judgements (when one does) as a result of *inferring* them from judgements about one's visual experiences (though nor do I wish to deny that this may happen on occasion). The seer need not

---

[19] I readily embrace this consequence in my 'What Do We See Directly?', pp. 279-81.

form any judgements about his visual experiences, even when he does form judgements about the seen object 'on the basis of' those experiences. At most the seer needs to be recognitionally sensitive to relevant features of his visual experiences, in the sense that he is capable of noticing or discriminating the presence or absence of these features. I shall come back to this issue later.

I shall now turn to the task of filling in some more details in what I admitted as being a somewhat schematic account of visual perception. One notion which particularly needs expansion is that of *direct causal dependency*. According to my definition, when a person sees an object, his visual experiences must be 'directly causally dependent' upon certain of that object's properties. The key idea here is that vision involves a certain kind of *responsiveness* to its objects: it is not enough that there merely be *some* sort of causal dependency between visual experiences and things seen. A simple example of the kind of responsiveness I have in mind would be this: when a magnet is passed over a pile of iron filings, the filings *respond* to its movement by the changing pattern which they form. Similarly, the television images produced in a 'live' broadcast *respond* to changes in the televised objects – for example, to the movements of players on a football field. When a video-recording of the match is played, the images on the screen are still *causally dependent* upon the original movements of the players – but not 'directly' so, as in the 'live' broadcast: what is missing is precisely the element of *responsiveness*. Giving an explicit definition of this special kind of causal dependency is no easy matter, and I do not wish to commit myself to a specific proposal here.[20] But it seems

[20] According to an account I currently favour, 'responsiveness' is a causal relation between certain properties P possessed by an object a at a time t_1 and certain properties Q possessed by another object b at an earlier time t_0. The time-lag $(t_1 - t_0)$ can, in principle, be made as large as we please. (There must be *some* time-lag, since a causal influence can only be propagated at a finite velocity.) What is required for 'responsiveness', I think, is that there should exist a continuous causal process originating in the Q at t_0 and terminating in the P at t_1 of such a nature that for any intermediate time t_n there is an object c possessing properties R at t_n, where (i) b's possession of Q at t_0 causes (via the process) c to possess R at t_n and (ii) c's possession of R at t_n causes (via the process) a to possess P at t_1. Whereas a 'live' broadcast meets this condition, a recorded one does not, because, although properties of the television images in a recorded broadcast are indeed *effects* of properties of the televised objects, the *time* at which the television images are produced in a recorded broadcast is not determined by a continuous causal process originating in the televised objects, but rather by some quite independent causal process involving a decision of the television company. I am indebted to Jerome Pelletier for stimulating me to clarify my understanding of responsiveness, with the above result.

clear that it is this special kind of dependency that is involved in sense perception. This, indeed, is why it is admissible, in my view, to say that one literally *sees* the match in the case of the 'live' broadcast, but not in the case of the video-recording. (Compare hearing someone over the telephone and hearing a recording of their voice.) Note, incidentally, that what disqualifies the video-recording is *not* the time-lag between the events on the field and what appears on the screen – for even with a 'live' broadcast there will be a small time-lag, which could in principle be made as large as we liked (by reflecting the radio waves from a suitably distant object).

The next aspect of my account of visual perception which needs elaboration has to do with the *effects* upon visual experience that seeing involves. I say nothing explicitly about these in my definition, and advisedly so – for I think it would be wrong to try to build an explicit account of them into such a definition. What I do say is that visual experiences have to be affected by certain properties of the seen object *in such a fashion* that the observer is thereby enabled to form a fairly reliable judgement as to what those properties are. Even so, I can and should try to say what would qualify an effect upon visual experience as apt for the role which it is here called upon to play. Two questions in particular arise: first, *what* features of visual experience need to be affected by an object if one is to see it, and second, *how* do these features need to be affected? My answer to the first question is that it is features of the *phenomenal or qualitative character* of visual experience that need to be affected, and my answer to the second question is that these features need to be affected in a way which *depends systematically* upon properties of the seen object.

One reason for my first answer is that if effects upon visual experience are to enable the observer to *form judgements* about properties of the seen object, those effects must be ones of which the observer is, or at least *can* be, *conscious* or *aware*: and it is precisely the phenomenal or qualitative features of visual experiences of which their subjects are aware. (Recall that blindsight subjects feel unable to make perceptual judgements – as opposed to 'guesses' – concerning light stimuli precisely because they lack any visual phenomenal awareness in the relevant portions of their visual fields.) Another way of putting my answer to the first question is to say that the features of visual experience that need to be affected by an object if one is to see it are its *sensuous* features (see section 2 above). And thus I suggest that it is our *visual sensations* that are causally dependent upon the visible properties of seen objects, and that it is their being thus dependent that enables us (no doubt with the aid of certain background information) to form fairly reliable judgements as to what those visible properties are when we see the objects possessing them. What ultimately motivates my suggestion is simply this. We have remarked already that it is the character of our visual sensations which grounds our talk of how things 'look' or (visually) 'appear' in this or that set of circumstances. But, furthermore, it is precisely on the basis of *how things look* to us when we see them that we are able to form visual judgements concerning their visible properties. I don't mean to suggest, here, that whenever one forms a visual judgement to the effect that a certain seen object possesses a certain visible property, one necessarily arrives at this judgement *by inference* from a prior judgement concerning how that object looks – though one *may* do so. (Certainly, it is only rarely that one *consciously* engages in such inferences, and whether or not one ever engages in them *unconsciously* is more a matter for empirical psychological investigation than for philosophical argument.) All I am saying is that it is only *because* things look thus and so to us in visual perception that we are able to form fairly reliable visual judgements concerning their visible properties: their looking thus and so is a *causally necessary condition* of our being able to form such judgements, not necessarily a *premise* from which we infer them. To put it another (a 'counterfactual') way: if the things we see *didn't* present various different (visual) appearances or looks to us in various different circumstances, in a manner causally dependent upon their visible properties, we *wouldn't* be able to form reliable visual judgements concerning those properties in the way that we do.[21]

Now let me turn to my second question and my answer to this. Here the question was *how* the relevant features of visual experience need to be affected, and my answer was that they need to be affected in a *systematic* way by visible properties of the seen object. The reason for my second answer is that only *systematic* dependencies between

---

[21] Here again the phenomenon of 'blindsight' might be raised in objection. But the 'judgements' of its victims are more in the nature of happy guesses than genuine judgements, and are in any case limited to verdicts on relatively crude stimuli such as the orientation of light sources rather than exhibiting anything as sophisticated as object-recognition. For further discussion, see section 4 below.

such properties of seen objects and qualitative features of visual experience will enable the observer to form *fairly reliable* judgements concerning those properties. What is a 'systematic' dependency, though? In general, it will I suggest be some sort of *functional* dependency, in the mathematical sense of the term – the sort of dependency we find, for instance, between ambient temperature and the height of a mercury column in a thermometer.[22] (Note that what makes a thermometer a fairly *reliable* source of information about ambient temperature is precisely that its behaviour is governed by such a functional dependency, subject to the satisfaction of certain background constraints.) I should stress, however, that many of the relationships of functional dependency we may expect to find exhibited in visual perception will be a good deal more complex, mathematically, than this simple analogy might suggest: some of them, for instance, will involve rates of change, or even rates of rates of change, in qualitative features, and hence will require expression in the form of differential equations (perhaps even partial differential equations).

Now, if features of the qualitative character of visual experience are to enter into such relationships of functional dependency, they must of course be susceptible to continuous variation in appropriate ways, or along appropriate dimensions. But I think it is clear that they *are*. Thus the *colour* features of our visual experience vary continuously along the three independent dimensions of brightness (or intensity), hue and saturation. However, *chromatic* colour features are not essential to visual experience, as the possibility of colour-blindness demonstrates, and as the normally sighted can confirm for themselves by the use of filters (or, indeed, just by watching black-and-white television). What *are* essential, though, are the features of *extensity* that are always to be found in visual experience.[23] These features also exhibit continuous variation along independent dimensions – in fact, along two such dimensions. A complication arises however inasmuch as we cannot in this case plausibly speak of these as *natural* dimensions as we can in the case of colour variation. What we *can* say though is that the extensive features of visual experience exhibit a two-dimensional or surface-like topology – a claim which can be supported by

[22] Cf. Roderick M. Chisholm, *Perceiving: A Philosophical Study* (Ithaca: Cornell University Press, 1957), pp. 148-9.
[23] I borrow the term 'extensity' from James Ward's *Psychological Principles* (Cambridge: Cambridge University Press, 1918): see pp. 78f, 116f.

evidence of a phenomenological character which I have marshalled elsewhere.[24] It is of course possible to *select* two orthogonal 'directions' as 'axes' for this topological manifold, labelling them perhaps 'altitude' and 'azimuth', but such a selection would be more or less arbitrary in that many other coordinate systems would serve equally well (including, for instance, systems of polar coordinates).

A further crucial property of the qualitative character of visual experience is this. At any given moment at which a subject is undergoing visual experience, the manifold of *extensive* features of visual experience is manifested in its entirety (unless, indeed, part of the visual field is 'missing', as in the case of some blindsight subjects). By contrast, only a small and fairly arbitrary selection of the *colour* features of visual experience need be manifested at any one time. It is, at least in part, this fact about visual experience which leads us to regard it as the pre-eminently *spatial* mode of experience – in fact, for the sighted it provides the very paradigm of the idea of space or extension. But it is important to realize that this is merely an accident of our psychology and physiology. The 'extensive' features of visual experience are, in reality, no *more* inherently 'spatial' in character than are the colour features, paradoxical though this may sound. Each set of features constitutes a manifold exhibiting a particular structure, a structure which can be mapped onto that of a certain abstract mathematical space with certain distinctive topological properties (in the case of the colour features, a solid cylinder). Analogously, the state of an ensemble of physical particles can conveniently be described in terms of an

---

[24] See my 'The Topology of Visual Appearance', *Erkenntnis* 25 (1986), pp. 271-4. In that paper I demonstrate that if x and y are any two objects which visually *appear* (in the phenomenal sense) to be separated, then it is possible to position a thin loop of wire, A, and a length of flexible wire, B, in such a fashion that if the two ends of B visually *appear* to touch x and y respectively, then B must visually *appear* to intersect A. This fact about the phenomenology of visual perception (which holds for both monocular and binocular vision) corresponds precisely with the following theorem of the topology of two-dimensional surfaces: if x and y are any two separate points on a surface, then it must be possible to draw a closed curve A on the surface in such a fashion that any open curve B on the surface whose end-points coincide with x and y must intersect A. There is thus a perfectly clear sense in which the topology of visual appearance (in the phenomenal sense of 'appearance') is *two-dimensional*, that is, a perfectly clear sense in which the spatial properties which objects visually *appear* to have obey a two-dimensional geometry. Given the way in which facts about the visual appearance of spatial properties correspond with facts about the extensive features of visual experience, as established elsewhere in this chapter, we can use the foregoing conclusion in defence of the claim that the latter features themselves exhibit a two-dimensional topology.

n-dimensional 'phase space'. If we think of the features of visual extensity as somehow more genuinely *spatial* than such features as the momenta of particles in such an ensemble or the colour features of visual experience, this is partly just because when we *imagine* space we represent it to ourselves visually (if we are sighted, at least) – and we tend to do so precisely because visual experience is distinctive in making available to the subject's consciousness a *simultaneously* presented manifold of spatially structured features, namely, the extensive ones. (It is this that sustains our talk of the 'visual field'.)

It should be remarked, however, that another reason why we think of the extensive features of visual experience as somehow more genuinely 'spatial' than other features is that it is these features of visual experience which form the basis of our visual judgements concerning the spatial properties of the physical objects that we see. Yet, of course, a manifold of physical objects is itself *spatial* only by virtue of its structural isomorphism with a certain abstract topological structure, even if it is true that mankind's first scientific knowledge of such abstract structures – embodied in the axioms and theorems of Euclidean geometry – arose from our interest in measuring and comparing the sizes and shapes of physical objects. We shouldn't think of the likeness between the two-dimensional manifold of visual extensity and a two-dimensional physical surface as going anywhere beyond a purely formal structural isomorphism.

Of course, ordinary folk will not describe the qualitative or phenomenal characteristics of their visual experience in the technical terms of 'brightness', 'hue', 'saturation', 'extensity', and so forth. But it would be wrong to suppose that they are therefore not equipped to describe them *at all* (much less that they are incapable of noticing and recognizing them, and indeed with considerable precision). As I explained in section 2 above, in practice what we do to communicate our awareness of these qualitative characteristics of visual experience is to employ constructions involving certain senses of words like 'look' and 'appear'. The senses in question are the *non-epistemic* or *phenomenal* ones: not, thus, the sort of sense that is typically at work in a statement like 'That man appears to be waving at us', but rather the sort of sense that is found in such statements as 'That round plate appears elliptical from this angle' and 'That red surface looks yellow in this light'. The point about such statements is that although they are ostensibly statements about properties of the *objects* of visual experience (plates, surfaces, and so on), in fact what they achieve is to communicate in an oblique fashion information concerning the qualitative character of a subject's visual experience. There is much more to be said on this issue – and some of it has been said already in the previous section – but it would involve a deviation from the main thrust of this chapter to go into the matter in any further detail here. All I would urge at present is that the language of visual appearances affords a means of describing the qualitative character of visual experience quite as effective, in its own way, as that provided by the more austere and technical language of dimensions of qualitative variation.[25]

It may be objected at this point – if not long before – that I am indulging in the 'myth of sense data'. Well, yes and no. If 'sense data' are construed as being private objects of introspection whose properties are incorrigibly known by their subject, I want no truck with them. But insofar as sense datum theorists are or were attempting to talk about qualitative features of visual experience, I concur with them in thinking that there *is* something to talk about – something of vital importance in the philosophy of perception. However, the debate which still goes on between sense datum theorists and 'adverbial' theorists of sensation I feel to be in some ways an idle one. The adverbialists are surely right in rejecting an 'act/object' account of sensation – right to avoid 'reifying' sense data as visual objects possessing visible qualities of shape and colour. But the sense datum theorists are right in supposing, for instance, that spatial *adjectives* can be legitimately employed to describe certain aspects of the qualitative character of visual experience. For instance, it is perfectly legitimate to say that the manifold of extensive features of my current visual experience is such that a certain rectangular region of it exhibits a certain uniformity of hue. This no more requires us to 'reify' this region as a private object of introspection than the description of a certain region of 'phase space' as possessing some geometrical property requires us to reify that region as a peculiar kind of quasi-physical object existing over and above the ensemble of physical particles with their properties of position and momentum.

Now that we have to hand means of describing the qualitative features of visual experience – whether in the austere terms of dimen-

[25] For an exemplification of this, see again my 'The Topology of Visual Appearance'.

sions of qualitative variation or in the more homely terms of the language of visual 'appearances' – we are in a position to corroborate my suggestion that when one *sees* an object, certain of its properties stand in relationships of functional dependency to certain qualitative features of one's visual experience: relationships which, furthermore, enable one to form fairly reliable judgements as to what those properties of the seen object are, given that one possesses appropriate background knowledge. Take, then, as a typical example, a case in which a normally sighted subject sees a rigid material object possessing a certain shape – for instance, a flat, circular dinner plate. Typically, the subject may hold the plate in front of him, turning it this way and that as he fixes his gaze on it. During the course of such an exercise – assuming that the subject's eyes are open and the plate is suitably illuminated – the subject will enjoy a sequence of visual experiences whose qualitative character varies systematically with changes in the orientation of the plate relative to the subject's line of sight. For instance, as he tips the face of the plate more and more away from a vertical plane orthogonal to his line of sight, it will 'appear' more and more eccentrically elliptical (a fact which could be described more austerely in terms of changes and constancies in the dimensions of variation of visual qualitative features, the relevant changes being in certain aspects of visual extensity).

The functional relationships that govern such systematic covariations are given by the laws of projective geometry – or, more familiarly, by the so-called laws of perspective. Provided that the subject has a working knowledge of these laws (and what I mean by this will emerge later), and provided that he is entitled to certain general assumptions concerning his physical environment (such as that most of the physical objects he is likely to encounter are relatively rigid and stable), such a sequence of visual experiences equips him to form the fairly reliable – and in this case correct – judgement that the object which confronts him is flat and circular in shape. (I shall say more about these provisos later, and try to justify the claim that they may be satisfied in a wide range of circumstances.)

It is worth remarking here that, given the assumption of rigidity, the laws of perspective are in fact remarkably unambiguous in their implications for the shape of seen objects. As David Marr has pointed out, it is a mathematically provable fact that just three different views of four mutually fixed points suffice to determine their geometrical relationships up to a reflection.[26] In fact, I venture to affirm that the laws of perspective constitute our *main* basis for three-dimensional space-perception. Stereopsis is a relatively unimportant additional luxury, as is demonstrated by the fact that subjects possessing only monocular vision from birth have no difficulty in attaining to perfectly adequate three-dimensional space-perception. (Here I should remark, incidentally, that although stereopsis clearly does make a difference to the qualitative character of visual experience, it does not do so by adding a third dimension to visual extensity.[27]) However, it must be stressed that *motion parallax* is a vital ingredient in the point I am making: a single 'snapshot' view grossly underdetermines the geometrical properties and relations of an array of visible objects, but once motion in the observer and/or objects is introduced, visual experience specifies its environmental objects geometrically to a remarkably high degree of accuracy. (To convince oneself of this, one need only survey the passing scene from a moving railway carriage.) It is perhaps also appropriate at this point to reiterate my earlier remark that the functional dependencies in visual perception include relationships between rates of change, or even between rates of rates of change, in qualitative features and properties of seen objects, so that, for instance, the *motions* and *accelerations* of seen objects must be included amongst their visible properties.

It may be recalled, incidentally, that the sort of functional causal dependency which we have been discussing admits of a variable *time-lag* between cause and effect; and this, of course, is why we can see distant stars even long after they have ceased to exist, and also why we may *hear* a man hammering a stake some moments later than we *see* him. (A thermometer reading similarly lags slightly behind the changes in temperature that it records.) Another point worth stressing is that the functions involved in such causal relationships may not only be functions of more than one independent variable, but also need not always provide one-to-one correlations – that is to say, they may be functions which sometimes take the same value for different arguments. This helps to explain a good many perceptual illusions (especially what I have called 'sensory' ones). Thus, returning once more to our dinner plate example, the shape which the plate (visually)

---

[26] See David Marr, *Vision* (New York: Freeman, 1982), p. 209.
[27] See further my 'The Topology of Visual Appearance', p. 274.

appears to have, or 'looks', is in fact not just a function of its orientation to the line of sight, but rather a function of both this *and* its 'real' shape (though we have naturally been assuming that it remains constantly circular). But the function in question in general provides only a many-one correlation, which is why two plates with different orientations and shapes may nonetheless both *look* the same shape. And it is, of course, partly because different things may sometimes appear the same that we sometimes fall victim to errors of perceptual judgement – the straight stick half-immersed in water looks (somewhat) like a bent stick out of water, and on that account we may on occasion actually *judge* it to be bent. (It is to allow for such errors that I stipulate only that perception should be a 'fairly' reliable source of information concerning the objects perceived; this only requires that the functions involved should not *too often* take the same values for different arguments – though I shall remain deliberately vague as to what constitutes 'too often'.) This is perhaps also the place to observe that it is through appeal to the necessity for suitable functional dependencies in perception that genuine perception can be distinguished from various fanciful examples of so-called 'veridical hallucination' with which philosophers have entertained us in recent years.[28]

I should just emphasize that according to my version of the causal theory of perception, the causation in perception operates on our perceptual sensations, not – or at least not directly – on our perceptual *beliefs* or *judgements*.[29] (Nor, indeed, does it operate directly upon the intentional objects or representational contents of our perceptual experiences: we are not directly caused, by the objects we perceive, to have perceptual experiences *with such-and-such intentional objects*, only to have perceptual experiences *with such-and-such sensuous features*.) By my account, then, perceiving is not as such a matter of being caused, by the object perceived, to have (or even to be inclined to have) certain beliefs about that object. On my view, indeed, one may perceive an object and not have (or even be inclined to have) *any* beliefs about it – say, because one firmly believes (erroneously) that

---

[28] See, e.g., David Lewis, 'Veridical Hallucination and Prosthetic Vision', *Australasian Journal of Philosophy* 58 (1980), pp. 239-49.

[29] Contrast D. M. Armstrong, *Perception and the Physical World* (London: Routledge and Kegan Paul, 1961), pp. 105ff. I raise serious difficulties for belief-acquisition theories of perception in section 4 below.

one is hallucinating.[30] At the same time, I have emphasized that there *are* important connections, implicit in the very concept of perception, between our perceptual sensations (and thus how things appear to us) and our perceptual judgements, and some of these connections may be causal rather than inferential.

This is perhaps the place to point out that the theory I have just outlined deserves to be called a *representative* theory of perception, precisely inasmuch as it insists upon the obtaining of certain functional dependencies between the sensuous or qualitative features of perceptual experiences and the perceptible properties of perceived objects – for the meeting of this requirement entitles us to say that those sensuous features serve to *represent* those properties to the perceiver (much in the way in which, say, contour lines on a map represent variations of height in a stretch of terrain, or lengths of mercury in a thermometer represent different ambient temperatures.) Such 'representation' carries, of course, no implication whatsoever of *resemblance*, at least of the sort appealed to in some more traditional 'representative' theories of perception, and consequently the present theory is not vulnerable to familiar criticisms on that score. (At most one is entitled to speak of relationships of *structural isomorphism* between experiential and physical features, not of 'resemblance' in any sense which implies that one thing must 'look like' another if it is to resemble it.)

I must briefly deal with one final issue before I close this section of the chapter. Many of those who are sympathetic to the notion of sensory experience and accept its vital role in any adequate account of sense perception may none the less feel that, in emphasizing the *phenomenal* or *qualitative* character or 'content' of visual experience, I have been neglecting the other and perhaps more important kind of experiential content, namely, *intentional* or *representational* content. When one enjoys a visual experience, one does not just enjoy a state of qualitative awareness, one enjoys a state which represents – or, better, which *presents* – the world as being thus-and-so in one's

---

[30] This is consistent with my saying – as we shall see in section 6 – that to have a perceptual experience with a certain *intentional* object is to have an experience *of the sort* that one would typically enjoy when, because of the experiential state one is in, one is inclined to believe that one is perceiving an object of an appropriate kind; my only point at present is that being caused to have certain beliefs, or even certain inclinations to believe, is not *constitutively* involved in what it is to perceive an object on a particular occasion.

vicinity. In general, one's visual experience will present the world as containing certain objects with certain properties standing in certain spatial relationships both to one another and to one's own location in physical space. For example, a visual experience might present the world as containing a red cow to the left of a green bush directly ahead of and a little below the point at which one is standing (normally, of course, it would present much more than *just* this).

Now I by no means wish to belittle the importance of such facts about visual experience. In particular, I do not wish to assign this sort of intentional content exclusively to the *judgements* or *beliefs* that we may form on the basis of our visual experiences, rather than to the visual experiences themselves. Even so, I would urge that the task of explaining why visual (and other sensory) experiences have this sort of intentional content is closely akin to the task of explaining how we are able to form perceptual judgements concerning objects in our environment, and hence that to this extent the intentional content of visual experience belongs to the *explanandum* rather than to the *explanans* of a theory of visual perception. In order to explain what it is to *see* an object, it will not do just to take as given the intentional content of visual experiences invoked in the explanation, since that the visual experiences involved in seeing an object should be capable of carrying appropriate intentional content is part of what needs to be explained. My own opinion, thus, is that such intentional content as a visual experience has must ultimately be grounded in its phenomenal or qualitative content – though explaining the nature of the 'grounding' relation involved here is a task of no small magnitude. I shall try to make some headway with this problem in the last section of this chapter.

4. PERCEPTION, EXPERIENCE AND BELIEF

I think I have said enough, for the time being, in explanation and defence of my account of what it *is* to perceive something by (visual) sense, though more will emerge in due course. The next question I wish to address is whether sense perception is – as indeed I consider it to be – indispensable for creatures capable like ourselves of genuine judgement and belief. For if it is not, then it is I suggest a subject of relatively little philosophical significance, however interesting it may be from a psychological point of view.

Consider once more the phenomenon of 'blindsight'. It appears that the discriminatory capacities of blindsight subjects are in fact fairly rudimentary, albeit quite accurate as far as they go. Such subjects can for instance discriminate, with a fair degree of precision, the direction of a light stimulus, and can distinguish an 'X' shape from an 'O' shape. But they cannot, it seems, register the presence or absence of a specified kind of physical object, such as a table, in the 'blind' regions of their visual fields. However, it is not difficult to conceive of a blindsight subject who *could* do this – who could 'guess', with a high degree of accuracy, what sorts of physical objects were located at various places in his immediate environment, without benefit of visual experience of any sort (by a causal mechanism involving the eye, and without the aid of other sensory cues). But can we intelligibly extend this thought-experiment to conceive of a subject who, *from birth*, was deprived of *all* modes of sense perception and yet possessed instead blindsight (of the sophisticated sort just hypothesized) and perhaps also 'deafhearing', 'numbtouch' and so forth as well? I think it is clear that we cannot. For consider again the less extreme hypothesis of the 'sophisticated' blindsight subject who, we suppose, enjoys other modes of sense perception and formerly enjoyed normal visual perception. We have no difficulty in supposing that he could at least *entertain the thought* that a table, say, was located at such-and-such a distance and direction from him, and hence that he could 'guess' this and turn out to be right. But the reason why we have no difficulty in supposing this is that we have no difficulty in understanding how such a subject could possess the *concept* of a table: for we can assume that he knows what tables *look* like, or at least what they *feel* like. (For the same reason, we can assume that he possesses some concept of what it is for an object to occupy a position in physical space relative to himself.) But we can't assume this in the more extreme case: indeed, in that case we have to assume that the subject has *no idea* what a table, or indeed any other physical object, *looks* like, *feels* like, *sounds* like, or *tastes* like – in short, how it *appears* to any sense. And that means, I suggest, that we cannot intelligibly attribute to such a subject any physical concept, nor, hence, any thought involving physical concepts. This still perhaps leaves open the possibility that such a subject might possess purely abstract concepts, though it is strongly arguable that these in fact require a substratum of physical concepts. And if that is so the lesson would appear to be that genuine thought of any sort –

and hence genuine belief and judgement – is only possible for a being endowed with sense perception. The point is hardly a new one, I confess, since it may be summarized in the Kantian slogan 'thoughts without content are empty'.

One of the obvious implications of this conclusion is that it is impossible to endow a computer with genuine cognitive states without equipping it with suitable sense modalities. This is not to deny that an ordinary computer may contain information-bearing states. But genuinely *cognitive* states like belief are not just informational states, because cognitive states have conceptual content and structure, which mere informational states do not. The pattern of rings in a tree trunk is an information-bearing state – it carries information about the tree's age, amongst other things. But there is all the difference in the world between such a state and a *belief* that the tree is such-and-such a number of years old. It is true that books, and other written records, carry information in a richer, conceptually articulated sense, inasmuch as the sentences which they contain have compositionally structured semantic content assignable to them; but, of course, such content is only derivative, depending as it does on the capacity of intelligent beings with genuine cognitive states to interpret what is written. Accordingly, such sentences provide no adequate model for the cognitive states of intelligent beings. Sentences in a 'brain code', analogous to the machine code of a computer, cannot then provide an adequate basis for the conceptually articulated cognitive states that we find in human beings – and again I would urge that what such a purely computational account of human cognition crucially neglects is the internal relation between conceptual content and the qualitative character of sensory experience. (A detailed account of that relation is, however, a mammoth task which goes far beyond the ambit of this chapter.) To possess any physical concepts at all a being must know how at least some physical objects appear to at least one sense modality. This does not, I hasten to point out, rule out possessing concepts of *unobservable* physical objects, though it does rule out the possibility of a being for whom *no* physical objects were conceived of as observable.

So one reason why a being genuinely capable of belief and judgement must have a capacity for sense perception is that without this it could possess no states with conceptual content. But another reason can be given too, and this is that without a capacity for sense perception a being has no adequate basis upon which to *correct* its beliefs and judgements – and having an ability to do this is partly constitutive of having an ability to believe and judge at all. In order to appreciate this point, imagine that in addition to our ordinary senses a subject were endowed with an 'extra-sensory' faculty rather like the 'sophisticated' kind of blindsight hypothesized a moment ago, but differing from it in that the deliverances of this faculty would take not the form of 'guesses' but rather of *beliefs* – beliefs to the effect that objects of such-and-such sorts were located in such-and-such places in the subject's vicinity. Thus, on a particular occasion, the subject might suddenly find himself acquiring a belief that a red wooden table was standing in the corner of the room, even though he had detected no such object there by sense (either because he hadn't looked in that direction, or because the light was out, or whatever). We can further suppose, if we like, that the deliverances of this faculty are very often correct. We cannot, however, suppose them to be *infallible*, without invoking supernatural powers.

Now the question we must address is this: what are we presuming when we describe the deliverances of this faculty as *beliefs* that the subject acquires? At the very least, I suggest, we are presuming that the subject is capable of taking a critical stance towards them: that he has at least some sort of idea of what would constitute evidence for or against the deliverances, and hence how he might go about confirming or disconfirming them. In a word, to qualify as genuine beliefs the deliverances must be open to *correction* by the subject. (Of course I don't mean that he must be able to tell, infallibly, whether or not they are correct, only that he should have available some rational strategy for trying to detect errors in them. Incidentally, if this seems to rule out the possibility of animal belief – and I am by no means sure that it does, at least for the higher mammals – then recall that we can still attribute *informational* states to them which fall short of belief.) Now, of course, in the case hypothesized none of this is problematical: for the subject in that case can check the deliverances of the special faculty against the evidence of his senses – he can, for instance, go and *look* for a red table in the corner of the room. It is true that this is not the *only* means he has of weeding out erroneous deliverances of the faculty, since he may be able to weed out some because they conflict with other well-entrenched beliefs that he already has. For instance, if the faculty prompts him to believe that a round square table stands in the corner of the room, he may reject its deliverance because it conflicts with his logical beliefs; if it prompts him to believe that his Aunt Jemima is standing in the corner, when he firmly believes that she is dead, then likewise the deliverance of the faculty may be overridden. However, it is clear that these alternative means of checking the deliverances of the faculty can only play a secondary role to that played by sense perception (and here we should note that when the subject does correct the deliverances of the faculty by appealing to already well-entrenched beliefs of his, many of these will originally have been acquired through sense perception in any case). So we see that it is only in virtue of possessing capacities for sense perception that a subject could genuinely acquire beliefs in the *non*-sensory manner which the faculty involves: and hence we see that it is incoherent to suppose that there could be a being *all* of whose capacities for sense perception were replaced by faculties such as the one hypothesized.

The lesson is, once again, a not unfamiliar one, since it is the basic thought underlying all traditional empiricist epistemologies – namely, that the acquisition of belief must make contact at some point with sensory experience. It will not do, then, to regard perception *merely* as a mode of belief-acquisition, since this precisely leaves out the crucial contribution of *experience*.

An objection which might be raised here is that it cannot be experience itself, but at most only our beliefs about our experience, that provide a basis for correcting other beliefs of ours: so that the process of checking and adjusting our corpus of beliefs must after all be one which takes place wholly from *within* that (constantly changing) corpus. Beliefs, on this view, can only be corrected in the light of *other beliefs*, albeit often in the light of beliefs *about our experience*. But I don't accept this, not least because I don't consider that we need to have, or in general do have, the sorts of belief about our experience which this proposal would require us to. When, for instance, I check my belief that there is a red table in the corner of the room by going and having a look, *is* it the case that I must *form a belief that I see a red table there* in order to satisfy myself that my original belief was correct? Surely not: I am satisfied simply provided I enjoy the requisite sort of visual experience. (I don't even have to *believe* that I am having such an experience, much less that in virtue of having it I am seeing a red table.) The assumption behind the objection that I am dismissing would appear to be that beliefs can only be confirmed or corrected by *processes of inference from other beliefs*, but I can see no good grounds for regarding this assumption as true. However, I am now verging on some large and difficult questions of epistemology, which I cannot address within the ambit of the present chapter.

One question which I should perhaps address at this point, though, is the question of why it is that in *actual* cases of blindsight, in contrast to our hypothesized case of the subject with the special extra-sensory faculty, the subject's discriminations issue in 'guesses' rather than judgements or beliefs. Couldn't the blindsight subject learn to trust his ability to discriminate stimuli to the extent that his natural response was indeed one of belief? Perhaps so – rather as someone whose 'hunches' about horse race winners were constantly borne out might eventually cease to have 'hunches' and just acquire straight-forward *beliefs* about future winners. But the trouble I suppose is that the blindsight subject has no adequate conception of *what it is* that he has to learn to trust. Compare the case of someone who has had his vision restored after being blind (in the normal sense) since infancy: he may indeed have to learn to trust his new-found mode of experience. But then at least he is *aware* of what it is that he has to trust as providing a basis for belief. The blindsight subject's problem, how-ever, is that he lacks all awareness of the provenance of his 'guesses', and has no means of determining (internally, at any rate) whether a given 'guess' issues from his blindsight faculty or not. It is not as though a special feeling comes on when the faculty is working, to tell him that it is in operation (as I suspect we imagine happens in the case of the horse race predictor). And this I think should caution us not to take the hypothesized case of the extra-sensory faculty too seriously after all: I suspect that, as described, it is probably of doubtful coherence even if we do grant the subject ordinary modes of sense perception as well. If so, however, this just serves to emphasize all the more how vital genuine sense perception is to the process of belief-acquisition.

5. THE COMPUTATIONAL APPROACH TO PERCEPTION: A CRITIQUE

At this point I want to digress a little in order to make some critical remarks about modern computational approaches to perception, again with special emphasis on visual perception – though in the course of doing this I shall also complete some unfinished business concerning my own theory. Perhaps the best, and best known, representative of the computational approach is the late David Marr, whose work surely transcends all other in this field in its originality, sophistication and methodological awareness. My complaint is that the goal which theorists such as Marr set themselves, though highly relevant to the technology of artificial remote-sensing and kindred matters, is not at bottom the right goal for one concerned to understand the nature of human visual cognition (not that I think that their work has no relevance at all to the latter issue, I hasten to add). In essence, the goal which such theorists set themselves is one of discovering how a (largely geometrical) description of the three-dimensional physical environment can be computed from information encoded in two-dimensional optical images produced by the focusing of light scattered from surfaces in that environment.[31] There is some attempt to constrain the choice of computational algorithms for this task by what is known about the neurophysiology of the human eye and brain, but in general the level of 'implementation' (as Marr calls it) is kept fairly firmly in the background.[32] I have no particular complaint about that, but what I do object to as importantly misguided is that the computational approach treats visual experiences (if indeed it deigns to mention them at all) as effectively just epiphenomenal. An admirably explicit admission of this is made by Steven Pinker, who writes that subjective experience

is noncontroversially epiphenomenal if one subscribes to the computational theory of the mind in general. In no computational theory of a mental process does subjective experience *per se* play a causal role . . . subjective experience, if it is considered at all, is assumed to be a correlate of . . . processing.[33]

As I remarked a moment ago, the objective which the computational approach sets itself is one that *is* highly relevant to the problem of designing artificial remote-sensing devices, and this in itself brings out one reason why that approach may be expected to throw less light on human visual cognition than its proponents hope. The point is that in designing such a device one would of course not attempt to endow

[31] See, e.g., Marr, *Vision*, pp. 36ff.
[32] See Marr, *Vision*, pp. 24ff.
[33] Steven Pinker, 'Visual Cognition: An Introduction', in S. Pinker (ed.), *Visual Cognition* (Cambridge, MA: MIT Press, 1985), p. 38.

it with *general intelligence* as a means to enabling it to accomplish its design goals, partly because so little is understood about the nature of general intelligence but also because this would be a strategy of over-kill and massively wasteful of computational resources. So for practical purposes the problem of designing such a device has to be seen as that of programming a fundamentally *unintelligent* machine to compute three-dimensional environmental descriptions from two-dimensional optical images. That is a complex problem, of course, as Marr's work makes clear. For instance, one needs to find efficient algorithms to detect 'salient' features such as edges, terminations and perhaps texture gradients in the optical array of light intensities, and then further algorithms to compute the angles and distances of physical surfaces from such data, accommodating along the way problems arising from the occlusion of some of these surfaces by others, variations in the ambient illumination, the presence of shadows, and so forth. And even that is only a beginning along the road to a fully three-dimensional object-centred description of the physical environment.

But, I would urge, the complexity of the computational problem involved here arises not least from the fact that there is in this case no possibility of calling on the resources of *general intelligence*, and indeed nothing like visual *experience* for general intelligence to operate upon. An artificial remote-sensing device has to generate environmental descriptions from optical inputs quite *unintelligently*, and of course that is a laborious and complicated task for it (or, more properly, for its designer). But human perceivers, it seems safe to affirm, do *not* operate in this way. We have and use the benefits of *visual experience and general intelligence* to acquire knowledge of our visible surroundings. As I see it, the task which early stages of the human visual processing system has to perform is to deliver to us visual experiences which fairly faithfully reproduce salient aspects of the geometrical stucture of the retinal image (I ignore, for simplicity's sake, the complications of stereopsis and chromatic colour vision, neither of which is essential for visual perception). That is certainly no small information processing task. But thereafter general intelligence can be brought into play, as we shall see.

It surely cannot be dismissed as irrelevant to human visual cognition that we *do* in fact enjoy visual experiences whose qualitative characters display to a striking degree a fundamental isomorphism with the geometrical structures of the retinal images which give rise to those experiences. For instance, if there is a small rectangularly shaped region of relatively uniform light intensity in one quadrant of the retinal image, this will normally translate into a similarly shaped and correspondingly located region of relatively uniform intensity in the extensive space of visual experience enjoyed by the subject – more or less, at any rate. (We should not, incidentally, be misled here by myths about the alleged poverty of the retinal image: the human eye is in fact a remarkably fine optical instrument with a high degree of resolution and little refractive distortion or blur in the normal circumstances of vision.[34])

Now, *why* do we (unlike blindsight subjects and artificial remote-sensing devices) enjoy visual experiences thus related to our retinal images? Not in order to allow us to acquire knowledge of the properties of those retinal images, to be sure (though we *can* put our experience to this use if we are so minded, provided we possess the appropriate background knowledge which, however, ordinary folk generally lack). Nor do we plausibly enjoy them purely as epiphenomena of neural processing in the optical pathways of the brain (an 'explanation' of the last resort). The answer, I suggest, is that what this state of affairs equips us to do is precisely to acquire a knowledge of the three-dimensional layout of surfaces surrounding us. And the reason why it so equips us is that that layout is fairly accurately specified (at least, once motion parallax is introduced) by the geometrical structure of the retinal image in conjunction with the laws of perspective (subject, once again, to certain rigidity assumptions). That is to say, by making the geometrical structure of the retinal image available to general intelligence in the form of conscious visual experience, the visual system renders a knowledge of the geometry of our physical environment possible for us in virtue of our implicit grasp of certain principles of projective geometry.

It is worth remarking here that recognition of the above-mentioned power of the retinal image to specify its environmental causes was one of J. J. Gibson's major contributions to the understanding of visual perception in his earlier work, particularly in his book *The Perception of the Visual World*. What was, however, peculiar about his position then and subsequently was that he was reluctant to acknowledge the need

[34] See J. J. Gibson, *The Perception of the Visual World* (Boston: Houghton Mifflin, 1950), pp. 112, 116.

for the information encoded in the optical array at the retinal surface to be made available to consciousness in the form of visual experiences. To the limited extent that he allows talk of the qualitative character of visual experience at all, in terms of what he calls the 'visual field', he is usually at pains to play down its cognitive significance. Workers in the computational paradigm, such as David Marr, have taken Gibson to task for failing to appreciate how much processing of the retinal image is needed to make its information usefully available to the percipient,[35] though they too markedly downplay the significance of visual experience, as we have already seen from Pinker's remarks. I shall return to this curious agreement between opponents a little later.

However, to make the answer I gave a moment ago begin to seem acceptable, I must now explain the sense in which we can be said to possess an implicit knowledge of the laws of perspective and how that knowledge may be presumed to be deployed in the process of visual cognition. In the first place, then, I do not think that a possession of such knowledge *in the form I suppose it to take* should be regarded as particularly taxing intellectually for creatures with our level of general intelligence. I have thus no hesitation in attributing such knowledge to quite young infants. Of course, I am *not* supposing that we all implicitly grasp certain principles of projective geometry in the form in which those principles would be expressed in textbooks of analytic geometry. Rather, our implicit grasp of those principles manifests itself in our ability to recognize what a wide variety of three-dimensional objects *look like* from a wide variety of points of view: that a pyramidal object looks thus-and-so at such-and-such an angle, and so forth. I am not even supposing that we have an ability to *describe* all these objects and how they look, merely that we are recognitionally sensitive to these facts. And this is a capacity which I believe we all do possess from infancy (indeed, it may quite conceivably be to some degree innate).[36] Some of us, it is true, can *utilize* this geometrical knowledge in more ways than most folk can: for instance, artists and draftsmen can use it to *depict* how an object looks, as well as to *recognize* it – though even they cannot state explicitly, in mathematical terms, the

---

[35] See Marr, *Vision*, pp. 29f.

[36] For findings which could be taken to support this view, see T. G. R. Bower, *The Rational Infant: Learning in Infancy* (New York: Freeman, 1989), pp. 9ff.

precise projective relationships concerned, much less compute specific numerical values for the quantities involved. But in the ordinary process of visual perception the knowledge in question is deployed purely at a recognitional level, to motivate judgements about the spatial properties and relations of surrounding objects. No elaborate process of *inference from judgements* about the qualitative character of visual experiences and the laws of perspective need be invoked here, however, and only a gross intellectualist bias could make one suppose this necessary.

I should add that I take a very similar stance towards the role of rigidity assumptions in visual cognition. These too need not constitute judgements on the part of the subject but operate, rather, on an unreflective level in normal circumstances. Likewise they may well have some innate basis, and don't need to be acquired from experience – indeed *can't* be to the extent that they guide us in the formation of the perceptual judgements that we make on the basis of experience. As to their precise content, this is a complex matter and partly one for empirical psychological research, though what is at least clear is that visual perception would simply be impossible in a world in which physical objects exhibited very much less stability of form than they actually do.

An objection which may be raised against the approach to visual cognition that I am advocating is that it is just a cheat – that it has 'all the advantages of theft over honest toil'. The complaint would be, then, that I am somehow just assuming as given most of what needs to be explained. I don't agree. I don't, in particular, think that there is any vicious circularity involved in my characterizing our implicit knowledge of the laws of perspective in terms of our capacity to recognize how variously shaped objects *look* from various points of view. For I do not regard that capacity as involving perceptual knowledge about a class of *visible properties* of physical objects, their 'looks' (recall my earlier remarks about the communicative purposes of the language of visual appearances). Rather, what this recognitional capacity reflects is an implicit grasp of the laws of functional dependency between the geometrical properties of visible objects and the extensive features of visual experience – and these laws, as we have seen, are precisely the laws of perspective. (Incidentally, it is true enough that if physical space were not locally Euclidean and light did not travel in straight lines, then an object of a given shape would not necessarily look how it actually does from a given angle. But this just reflects the fact that the laws of perspective are not wholly *a priori* principles of pure projective geometry.)

Of course, what my approach *does* assume is general human intelligence – a big mystery, to be sure – but it is no business of a theory of *visual perception* to give an account of general intelligence.[37] Indeed, as I see it, the problem with the computational approach is that it seeks to throw light on human visual cognition *without* invoking general intelligence. As I remarked earlier, that is indeed a sensible strategy if one's goal is to design an artificial remote-sensing device: but that is not what the human visual system *is* (even allowing for the fact that it is natural rather than artificial). For the plain fact is that *we* use our visual experience and general intelligence in arriving at judgements concerning our visible surroundings, whereas a remote-sensing device possesses neither (and is additionally incapable of making judgements in any case). Of course, these last remarks do not apply to blindsight subjects, who have no visual experiences upon which to turn their general intelligence. Hence it is at least conceivable that visual discrimination in their case *does* operate as it might in an artificial remote-sensing device (moreover, such subjects, as we have seen, do *not* make visual *judgements*). It has in fact often been hypothesized that we have *two* visual systems, only one of which survives in the blindsight subject.[38] But then my thesis is that the other, and dominant, visual system is the one which requires to be understood in the way I propose.

But perhaps it will be objected now that 'general intelligence' *cannot* play anything like the role I take it to in processes of visual cognition, because to suppose that it does is to overlook the extent to which perceptual processes are 'modular', and so 'informationally encapsulated' or 'cognitively impenetrable'.[39] It may be urged that evidence

---

[37] As will be evident, I do not believe that a purely computational account of human intelligence is possible – in holding which opinion I am in agreement with a wide range of authors, including J. R. Lucas, John Searle and Roger Penrose. I sympathize with many of their arguments, but the issue is too large for me to engage with it here on my own account. See, however, my remarks on computers and cognition in section 4 above.

[38] See Weiskrantz, *Blindsight*, p. 162.

[39] See Jerry A. Fodor, *The Modularity of Mind* (Cambridge, MA: MIT Press, 1983), pp. 47ff, and Zenon W. Pylyshyn, *Computation and Cognition* (Cambridge, MA: MIT Press, 1984), pp. 214f, 269.

of this is provided, for example, by studies of the various forms of visual agnosia[40] – conditions in which subjects suffering from lesions in specific areas of the visual cortex display quite specific disorders of visual recognition, such as prosopagnosia (the inability to recognize familiar faces by sight). For the subjects in question do not, by and large, suffer from any general intellectual impairment.[41]

However, I am not convinced that this sort of objection to my approach is valid. First of all, it appears that many types of visual agnosia involve lesions at locations in the cortex (for instance, in the occipital lobes) at which information from the left and right halves of the retinas is still being processed separately,[42] and hence at a stage prior to the production of unified whole-field visual experience.[43] And my proposals only concern what happens *after* the production of such experience. Visual agnosia may, then, be a consequence of the visual system's failure to present the subject with visual experiences whose qualitative content is fully determinate and clearly organized at both local and global levels. On this view, the ability to recognize faces may be specifically affected just because it requires a particularly fine sensitivity to the overall organization of detailed features, and not because there is a specific 'face-recognition module' in the human visual system which can be selectively affected by damage to dedicated neural circuits. The introspective reports of visually agnosic subjects would seem to confirm this diagnosis. They say, for instance, 'I can see the whole face – the bit I am looking at . . . is quite clear . . . but everything else is . . . as though there was a thin layer all over it or as though it was out of focus'.[44]

---

[40] See, e.g., Glyn W. Humphreys and M. Jane Riddoch, *To See But Not To See: A Case Study of Visual Agnosia* (London: Lawrence Erlbaum Associates, 1987).

[41] Fodor makes precisely this point in *The Modularity of Mind*, p. 99.

[42] This certainly seems to be true of the case studied in Humphreys and Riddoch, *To See But Not To See*: see p. 30, where the patient is described as suffering from 'extensive brain damage in both occipital lobes'.

[43] Unification would appear to take place in the infero-temporal cortex, which lies 'several synapses beyond the striate cortex' (the latter being in the occipital lobe): see Lawrence Weiskrantz, 'Some Contributions of Neuropsychology of Vision and Memory to the Problem of Consciousness', in A. J. Marcel and E. Bisiach (eds.), *Consciousness in Contemporary Science* (Oxford: Clarendon Press, 1988), pp. 196-7. It was in the temporal lobe that Penfield's previously mentioned electrical stimulations of the cortex elicited vivid visual experiences. By contrast, stimulation of the striate cortex only gives rise to reports of scattered 'phosphenes': see Weiskrantz, *Blindsight*, p. 171.

[44] Quoted in Humphreys and Riddoch, *To See But Not To See*, p. 87.

In any case, there is considerable evidence, both direct and indirect, that perceptual systems in humans are *not* in fact all that strongly 'encapsulated' or 'cognitively impenetrable'. For example, although we are strongly habituated to interpreting our visual experience in terms of three-dimensional scenes, we can (*pace* Fodor[45]) very easily switch to a 'flat', 'pictorial' interpretation, given sufficient motivation and a little practice. Again, there is the evidence provided by experiments with inverting spectacles and other devices for displacing the retinal images systematically. These experiments show that human subjects (unlike, be it noted, less intelligent creatures such as birds and reptiles) are able to adapt remarkably well to such inversions, and indicate that the adaptations do not involve any basic reorganization of early visual processing but rather a cognitive adjustment on the part of the subject to his visual experience.[46] This conflicts with the suggestion, characteristic of the 'modular' view, that visual recognitional processes are substantially 'hard wired', or possess a relatively fixed neural architecture.[47]

As a final example, there is the evidence provided by experiments with 'tactile visual substitution systems' (TVSS), which enable even congenitally blind adult subjects to achieve three-dimensional quasi-visual perception of objects in their immediate environment, in the course of a training period of the order of three weeks.[48] If different perceptual systems like touch and vision were strongly 'encapsulated', it is hard to see how such rapid adaptation of one, so as to confer on it characteristics of the other, could be achieved through exploratory learning. In view of their complete novelty in a tactile employment, the 3D geometrical recognitional capacities developed and exploited by congenitally blind TVSS users are evidently not capacities that are specific to the domain of tactilely presented information.[49] Nor, in

[45] See Fodor, *The Modularity of Mind*, p. 54.

[46] See R. L. Gregory, *Eye and Brain: The Psychology of Seeing* (London: Weidenfeld and Nicolson, 1972), pp. 204ff.

[47] See Fodor, *The Modularity of Mind*, p. 98, and Pylyshyn, *Computation and Cognition*, pp. 215, 269.

[48] See further P. Bach-y-Rita, *Sensory Substitution* (New York: Academic Press, 1972) and G. Guarniero, 'Experience of Tactile Vision', *Perception* 3 (1974), pp. 101-4. For discussion of some of the implications, see M. J. Morgan, *Molyneux's Question: Vision, Touch and the Philosophy of Perception* (Cambridge: Cambridge University Press, 1977), pp. 197ff. For discussion of analogous experiments using auditory substitutes for vision with congenitally blind infants, see Bower, *The Rational Infant*, pp. 26ff.

[49] 'Domain specificity' is, according to the 'modular' view, one of the leading characteristics of perceptual systems: see Fodor, *The Modularity of Mind*, pp. 47ff.

view of their rapid development, can they plausibly be associated with a fixed neural architecture. They would appear, in fact, to be essentially the *same* capacities as those that normally sighted subjects deploy in recognizing objective shape from perspectival changes – whence we may reasonably conclude that in the normally sighted too these capacities are not 'hardwired' components of the visual system. (This does not, however, preclude the possibility – which I tentatively endorsed earlier – that the tacit geometrical knowledge involved here may have some innate basis: for I am only concerned to challenge the suggestion that this sort of knowledge is 'encapsulated' in specific perceptual processing modules, as opposed to being an endowment of general intelligence.)

In sum, it emerges that human beings are able to respond remarkably flexibly to their sensory stimulations, and that their perceptual recognitional capacities can be substantially developed and modified, even in adulthood, through intelligent adaptation to changes in the format of these stimulations. If I am right, it is only because we can be *aware* of such changes, by virtue of possessing conscious experience, that we find such adaptation possible. The advantage over less intelligent creatures which such adaptability confers on us is easy to appreciate, and helps to make an evolutionary explanation of the emergence of consciousness quite thinkable. More to the point, though, the clear implication is that, in human beings at least, general intelligence does indeed have an important role to play in processes of perceptual recognition – a role which the often strongly *habitual* character of such processes should not be allowed to obscure. (Habits don't have to be stupid, nor need they be unamenable to intelligent modification.)

At this point let me return briefly to my earlier observation that one major respect in which advocates of the computational approach to visual perception and advocates of J. J. Gibson's 'ecological' approach are in agreement, despite their many differences, is precisely in their playing down of the role of *conscious visual experience* in visual perception. The focus of both of these schools is on the question of how the mind-brain can extract environmental information from the light energies encountered by the eye. And that is of course also my concern, at least in part. But the point is that neither of these schools considers as a solution to this problem the possibility that what the human visual system does is to supply the subject with qualitatively structured visual experiences from whose character the subject can extract environmental knowledge by the intelligent (albeit habituated) deployment of a body of implicitly grasped principles, such as those principles of projective geometry a grasp of which we manifest (according to my claim) in our perspectival recognitional abilities.[50]

Why, however, is there this concurrence in downplaying visual experience? Partly, no doubt, it reflects a continuing hostility amongst psychologists to subjectivity and introspective awareness, which are exclusively associated (I think mistakenly) with a supposedly forbidden Cartesian paradigm of the mind. And in the case of the computational school there is the additional consideration that no one has the slightest idea how to set about *designing* something to be a recipient of visual experiences, within the computational paradigm. Of course, it is not news that 'qualia' and consciousness pose problems for a functionalist conception of the mind, but it is worth emphasizing the point that this is no 'mere' philosophical or metaphysical difficulty, but impinges directly upon the viability of computational explanations of specific human cognitive capacities, like visual perception. Nor does the fact that I myself have little to offer by way of an explanation for the phenomenon of consciousness, and more particularly for the genesis of qualitative states of visual awareness, constitute the basis of a legitimate objection to my own approach to visual perception: for at least I do justice to the inescapable fact that such states *occur* and play a vital role in the process of seeing. Better this than to try to explain visual perception *without* reference to visual experiences. For that is to adopt the wrong *explanandum*, and at best offers the prospect of an explanation of blindsight.

[50] Of course, the computational approach *does* invoke something like tacit knowledge of projective geometry (and likewise of rigidity constraints) in its account of visual cognition, so that my opposition to it is by no means unqualified but is focused rather on the questions of where that knowledge resides within our cognitive economy (e.g., whether it is 'encapsulated') and how it is deployed (e.g., whether we exercise it in forming judgements on the basis of the qualitative character of visual experiences). Clearly, there is scope for much fuller exploration than I have undertaken here into the overall structure of our cognitive economy and the place within it, and relations between, various *different* sets of organizing principles, such as principles of projective geometry and principles of gestalt formation. That principles of the latter kind have a key role to play in visual cognition – for instance, in face recognition – in addition to the role played by geometrical principles, seems evident, but I have as yet no adequately worked-out theory of how these two kinds of principle might interact (nor am I even sure to what extent this is a proper task for a philosopher, as opposed to an empirical psychologist).

One final objection to my emphasis on the role of visual experiences in visual perception might, however, be this: if, as I say, visual experiences possess qualitative or phenomenal characteristics exhibiting a structural isomorphism with certain geometrical properties of the retinal images which give rise to them, how does it *help* for us to have visual experiences *in addition to* retinal images? In order to extract environmental information from *experiences*, won't we need to process *them* in very much the same way in which retinal images are supposed to be processed by early stages of the visual system? Won't we, for instance, have to possess some way of detecting edges, terminations, texture gradients and so on *in the qualitative array of experiential features* constitutive of a visual experience? No, we won't, for this is to overlook one of the crucial differences between visual experiences and retinal images, namely, that the former are constituents of consciousness whereas the latter are just a species of physical object (in the broadest sense of the term). We do not have to *detect* structure in our visual experiences, for what they are is precisely *structured states of awareness*. Visual experiences are not objects of visual perception – items that we *see*. By contrast, retinal images are indeed precisely this, by my account.[51] They are, as I say, physical objects (in the broad sense), being patterns of electromagnetic energy-distribution with location and dimensions in physical space. Their crucial role in the process of human visual perception arises from the fact that they encode highly specific information about properties of the environmental objects that are of direct concern to us. Visual experience makes this information available to us by more or less replicating relevant features of the retinal image in the structural organization of phenomenal awareness, which general intelligence then enables us to decode by exploiting our implicit grasp of such principles as the laws of perspective. That, at any rate, is the story that I have tried to tell so far in this chapter. If it has at times the air of (what some would regard as) old-fashioned empiricism, that is not something which I find in the least embarrassing.

---

[51] See further my 'What Do We See Directly?', pp. 279-81.

6. SEEMING TO PERCEIVE AND THE INTENTIONAL
CONTENT OF PERCEPTION

To sum up my overall position so far: when one *perceives* an object, one has a perceptual experience involving certain perceptual sensations (and hence qualitative characteristics) which are causally dependent in a functional way upon certain properties of the object perceived, so facilitating a fairly reliable judgement as to what those properties are. But – to return to a worry first raised in section 3 above – a kind of circularity seems to threaten here, inasmuch as I have used the very word 'perceptual' (twice) in explaining what it is to perceive. What we require to avert this threat are non-circular accounts of (1) what it is for an experience to be a *perceptual* experience, and (2) what sorts of sensations qualify as *perceptual* sensations.

Taking the latter, and easier, task first: we may say that *any* range of sensations *could* qualify as perceptual sensations provided they exhibited a sufficiently fine-grained variability to enter into functional relationships of the sort we have described.[52] The sense-organs, so-called, are distinguished precisely by this feature of the sensations to which they give rise. Thus *pain* sensations could, it seems, never play the role of perceptual sensations simply because they are too coarse to be employed in conveying the sort of detailed information about the environment that genuinely perceptual processes would require them to. Quite simply, we are insufficiently discriminating in our sensitivity to pain. (In rather the same way, a 'thermometer' which discriminated only between, say, boiling point and freezing point would scarcely deserve the name.) A connected point is that perceptual sensations should not be at all *intense*, since an intense sensation will attract the subject's attention and therefore distract it from the *object* perceived, so defeating the very purpose of perception. Thus a very bright light dazzles us, to such an extent that our attention is distracted from the light and drawn solely to the intense and disagreeable sensation in our eye; in such circumstances, it seems proper to say, we no longer *see* the light – we can't see it precisely because we are dazzled by it.

---

[52] Thus recall the 'tactile visual substitution systems' (TVSS) described in section 5, giving blind persons a crude kind of surrogate vision by means of devices designed to stimulate variable patterns of skin sensations on the subjects' backs.

What now remains is for us to explain precisely what it is for an experience to be a *perceptual* experience. Many of the elements of such an explanation have already been developed in the preceding sections. One point that we have dwelt on at sufficient length is that perceptual experiences involve perceptual sensations, that is, possess sensuous features of appropriate kinds. Another is that perceptual experiences are *intentional* (or 'representational') states – they are 'object-directed'. We expressed this (in section 1) by saying that a perceptual experience is always an experience 'as of' perceiving such-and-such an object, or, equivalently, that having a perceptual experience is always a matter of *seeming to perceive* something of some sort. But now circularity again seems to threaten: for I want to explain *perceiving* in terms of having a perceptual experience that is appropriately causally related to a (real) object, and at the same time explain what a *perceptual* experience is in terms of seeming to *perceive*. Thus it plainly wouldn't be satisfactory just to say that seeming to perceive is being in an experiential state of the sort one typically enjoys when one is perceiving something: this is (perhaps) *true*, but uninformative if one intends to analyse perceiving in terms of seeming to perceive.

Now, a first step towards averting this threat of circularity is to be made by recognizing a certain important truth about the concept of perception. This is that we do *and must* learn that we perceive things *prior* to learning that in perceiving we enjoy experiences of a characteristic sort – experiences which we could enjoy even in the absence of perceiving anything. This, indeed, helps to explain the unreflective appeal of naïve realism. (Incidentally, when I say that we must learn that we *perceive* things, I don't mean to suggest that we must actually learn to use a higher-level cross-modal term like 'perceive' itself: we must learn, rather, that we *see, hear, feel, smell, taste* things – we needn't necessarily learn that these are all modes of 'perceiving' things.) In the order of the *genesis* of our perceptual concepts, the notion of perceiving has priority over the notion of perceptual experience – though in the order of the *analysis* of these concepts, the reverse is true. This means, paradoxical though it may superficially appear, that we must learn *that* we perceive things before we can fully understand *what* perceiving is.

The relevance of these remarks to our circularity problem is just this. 'Seeming to perceive' is *not* a matter of seeming to have a perceptual experience which is appropriately causally related to a (real) object – even though having such an experience is what perceiving *is*. Perception does not *seem* ('from the inside') to be a causal transaction between oneself and the object(s) one perceives, though philosophical analysis reveals that this is just what it is (and, again, this helps to explain why naïve realism, despite its falsehood, is intuitively appealing). So what then *is* 'seeming to perceive'? To a first approximation we might say that it is, quite simply, being in an experiential state of the sort one typically enjoys when, because of the experiential state one is in, *one is inclined to believe that one is perceiving something*.[53] (Here the 'because' indicates a causal relationship, not an inferential one; and we need this causal condition because someone surely *could* believe that he was perceiving something through, say, hypnosis or drug-treatment, quite independently of his experiential state.[54]) This general formula can, I suggest, be adapted to capture more specific cases: thus we may say that seeming to see a snake is being in an experiential state of the sort one typically enjoys when, because of the experiential state one is in, one is inclined to believe that one is seeing a snake. In this formula (in both its general and its specific forms), I say only a state *of this sort* and 'typically' because, as I have tried to make clear already, I don't want to say that someone enjoying a perceptual experience *must in fact* be inclined to believe that he is perceiving something – for he may, for example, be convinced that he is hallucinating. (Notice, however, that only someone who has already learned to distinguish between perceiving and having perceptual experiences could be in this condition for *this* reason, that is, by reason of being convinced that he is hallucinating.) Again, in the more specific case, someone who has a visual experience as of seeing a snake need not *on this occasion* be at all inclined to believe that he is seeing a snake: he may be quite sure that he is in fact seeing a stick, and yet sees it 'as' a snake – that's what he seems to see. My proposal is merely that what gives his visual experience this character is the fact that it is relevantly similar to other actual

---

[53] I should stress, incidentally, that the state of believing something is not itself an experiential state; so there is no problem here of distinguishing between a perceptual belief and the perceptual experience which gives rise to it.

[54] There is indeed a bizarre clinical condition (anosognosia, or Anton's syndrome) in which subjects believe that they can see even though they are functionally blind: see, e.g., E. Bisiach, 'The (Haunted) Brain and Consciousness', in A. J. Marcel & E. Bisiach (eds.), *Consciousness in Contemporary Science*.

or possible experiences of his which *do* (or would) incline him to believe that he is seeing a snake.

Now, provided we realize that someone can *believe that he is perceiving something* without thereby attributing to himself that state of causal relatedness to an object which philosophical analysis reveals perception to be, we can see that there need be no vicious circularity in analysing perceiving in terms of seeming to perceive – even where this is, as just proposed, taken to mean being in an experiential state of the sort one typically enjoys when, because of the experiential state one is in, one is inclined to believe that one is *perceiving* something. (The point is that someone can understand this analysis of seeming to perceive prior to understanding the analysis of perceiving advanced in this chapter.) At the same time, one can now understand why there should be a strong temptation to suppose that 'perceive' in fact has two distinct senses: a sense in which it may be used to report our unreflective and un-philosophical beliefs that we are perceiving things – beliefs which even young children may possess – and a sense in which scientists and philosophers use it in describing the cognitive transactions of human beings with their environment. (If you like: a sense in which the *first person* use of the verb has semantic priority, and a sense in which the *third person* use of the verb has semantic priority.) But, as I have tried to explain, I don't think we should allow ourselves to succumb to this temptation, since I believe that it stems from confusion over the distinction between the analysis and the genesis of concepts.

I described the foregoing proposal regarding 'seeming to perceive' as being only a first approximation. This is because it appears that we should be prepared sometimes to ascribe perceptual experiences even to individuals – young infants, say, and perhaps even certain animals – who have not yet learned, or indeed may never learn, that they perceive things. For if such an individual enjoys perceptual experiences, then when it does so it is plainly *not* in an experiential state of the sort it typically enjoys when, because of the experiential state it is in, it is inclined to believe that it is perceiving something – because it is, *ex hypothesi*, altogether incapable of forming such a belief. (Nor will it shed much light on the matter, I think, to 'go counterfactual', and talk, say, about an individual being in an experiential state of the sort it typically enjoys when, because of the experiential state it is in, it *would* be inclined to believe that it was perceiving something *if* it were capable of forming such a belief.) However, what we surely *can* insist on is that it would be improper to ascribe perceptual experiences to individuals incapable of forming beliefs about objects *at all*, including beliefs about the location of those objects in their environment. (How could an individual enjoy object-directed experiential states if it were incapable of forming beliefs about objects?) This may encourage us to try to modify the previous proposal by saying, instead, something to the effect that seeming to perceive is being in an experiential state of the sort one typically enjoys when, because of the experiential state one is in, one is inclined to believe that an object of some sort is located in some part of one's environment. Unfortunately, as it stands, this clearly won't do, because it fails to distinguish between perceptual experiences and (and least some) experiences of *remembering*. Perhaps the obvious way to overcome this objection would be to invoke again the already defended claim that *perceptual* experiences directly involve *sensation*, leading us thus to say that seeming to perceive is being in a *sensational* experiential state of the sort one typically enjoys when, because of the experiential state one is in, one is inclined to believe that an object of some sort is located in some part of one's environment.[55] (Notice, by the way, that this proposed analysis of 'seeming to perceive' eliminates the threat of circularity very much more directly than did the previous one, though it is debatable to what extent this should be seen as a consideration in its favour.)

However, I am by no means convinced that even this last analysis will ultimately do, at least on its own. One reason for my dissatisfaction is that, although I want to say that perceptual experiences can be enjoyed not only by those who have learned that they perceive things but also by those who are merely capable of forming beliefs about objects in their environment, I consider that the *character* of perceptual experience shifts radically once an individual learns that it is a perceiver. The advance in knowledge brings with it, as it were, a change in perspective – or, rather, a change *to* a perspective. The perceiver acquires a 'point of view': not just in a physical, geometrical sense –

---

[55] Observe that, in accordance with this suggestion, seeming to *see* may be distinguished from (for instance) seeming to *hear* by virtue of the character of the sensations involved. This presupposes – what I believe to be true – that the involvement of certain characteristic sensations is essential to a mode of sense-perception's being the particular mode that it is (for instance, sight). (I would therefore deny that the kind of tactile substitute for vision described in section 5 is genuinely a kind of *vision*, lacking as it does the appropriate sensuous character.)

in that sense he always had one – but rather in a subjective sense, inasmuch as perceived objects have now come to be perceived precisely *as* objects perceived, that is, as *objects of perception*. Perhaps, then, we should allow that *both* of the accounts of 'seeming to perceive' advanced above are satisfactory within their appropriate spheres. However, whatever decision we may ultimately come to on this issue (and I don't mean to rule out further refinements to either analysis), I believe we have done enough already to show that the threat of circularity raised earlier can certainly be disarmed, one way or another: there is, it emerges, no serious barrier to analysing perceiving in terms of seeming to perceive.

A final point is this. We now have to hand the ingredients of an account of the relationship between the intentional and the sensuous or qualitative contents of a perceptual experience, which will enable us to see in what sense the former kind of content is grounded in the latter. Consider, for instance, a visual experience as of seeing a snake, where the 'as of' clause specifies its intentional content (or part of it, at least). By my (original) account of seeming to perceive, to say that the experience has this intentional content is to say that it is an experience of the sort one typically enjoys when, because of the experiential state one is in, one is inclined to believe that one is seeing a snake. However, what it *is* about such an experience in virtue of which it inclines one to believe this is precisely that its *sensuous* character resembles that of previous visual experiences which one has learnt to be indicative of the presence of objects with the characteristic visible properties of snakes – such learning being precisely a matter of coming to know what snakes *look like*. (My second account of seeming to perceive brings no relevant difference to bear here.) Thus we see that the intentional content of a perceptual experience is determined by its sensuous content *only relative to a particular history of perceptual learning*, and consequently that the intentional content of a perceptual experience, unlike its sensuous content, is not intrinsic to it, in the sense that its possession of just that content is a non-contingent feature of the experience. Clearly, there is a great deal more that can and should be said about how the intentional contents of perceptual experiences are related to learned facts about how objects 'look' or 'appear', and are thus 'grounded' in the sensuous or qualitative features of those experiences – but I hope that I have said enough to indicate the broad outlines of the sort of approach to this problem that I favour.

5

Action

Persons or selves do not merely *perceive* their world – they also *act* upon it intentionally. Indeed, the self's capacities for perception and action are inseparably intertwined, even if these capacities may be exercised independently on some occasions. For example, a person incapable of voluntary self-movement cannot spontaneously generate the kind of motion parallax which, as we saw in the previous chapter, is vital to extracting information about the spatial structure of his environment from the light energies encountered by his eyes. And a person incapable of self-perception is deprived of the information feedback necessary for executing fine-grained movements of her limbs. In this chapter I shall be arguing that there must exist a class of mental acts corresponding to the traditional notion of a *volition* or *act of will*, and that any human action properly described as *voluntary* must involve the occurrence of at least one such mental act. Volitions, I maintain, play an indispensable causal role in the genesis of voluntary bodily movement, a role for which mental states like belief and desire are constitutionally unsuited, even though states of the latter sort are indeed normally to be included amongst the causal antecedents of volitions. Volitions are different from states like belief and desire not only in respect of their distinctive causal role, but also in respect of their distinctive intentional content, which, as we shall see, always has an ineliminably self-referential character.

1. AGENTS AND ACTIONS

Let me begin by introducing some basic terminology and explaining the theoretical framework I mean to deploy. In what follows I shall, at least to start with, be using the terms *agent* and *action* in very broad senses. An agent, in this sense, may be any sort of enduring object (or

140

'continuant') capable of entering into causal relationships with other such objects. It need not, thus, be a person or an animal, though persons and animals *are* agents in my broad sense, and most of what I have to say will concern them. By an *action sentence* I mean a sentence of the form '*a* is F*ing*' (in the present tense case), where '*a*' names an agent and '*F*' is a verb or verb-phrase describing some sort of *activity*, in the broadest sense of that term, whereby it betokens a change (or indeed a non-change) either in the agent itself or in some object causally affected by it. For instance, '*a* is falling', '*a* is breathing' and '*a* is opening the window' are all action sentences, in my terminology. An *action* (or *act*), correspondingly, is something whose occurrence is necessary for the truth of an action sentence, and may be referred to by a noun-phrase of the form '*a*'s F*ing*'. So, for example, *a*'s falling, *a*'s breathing and *a*'s opening the window are all actions.

Very often action sentences submit to a *causal* analysis. That is to say, an action sentence of the form '*a* Fed' (to use the past tense case) may very often be analysed as entailing a sentence of the form '*a* caused *x* to G', where '*x*' names an object and '*G*' again describes an activity. For instance, 'Smith opened the window' may be analysed as entailing 'Smith caused the window to open' and 'Smith killed Jones' may be analysed as entailing 'Smith caused Jones to die'. (Observe that I do not claim that 'Smith killed Jones' is *logically equivalent to* 'Smith caused Jones to die' − a claim which has been much disputed of late.[1] However, this is not because I am convinced that there is no such equivalence, but only because the weaker claim made above is all that I need for my current purposes.)

Consider now a sentence of the form '*a* caused *x* to F'. We can, it seems, always ask *how a* caused *x* to F, and be entitled to expect that an answer will at least in principle be forthcoming. And the answer will be of the form 'by G*ing*' or, more fully, '*a* caused *x* to F by G*ing*'. The 'how' and the 'by' invoked here we may call the 'how' and the 'by' of *causal means* (to distinguish them from certain other 'hows' and 'bys' which need not presently concern us). Now, where we have such an answer to the how-question, two possibilities arise concerning the further action sentence '*a* Ged' (the sentence which reports an action *by* doing which *a* caused *x* to F). Either '*a* Ged' will submit to a causal

<hr/>

[1] See, e.g., Judith Jarvis Thomson, *Acts and Other Events* (Ithaca: Cornell University Press, 1977), p. 128.

analysis, or it will not. Suppose it *will not*. Then I contend that '*a* caused *x* to *F* by G*ing*' entails '*a*'s G*ing* caused *x*'s F*ing*'. Suppose, alternatively, that '*a* G*ed*' *will* submit to a causal analysis, as entailing, say, '*a* caused *y* to *H*'. Then I contend that '*a* caused *x* to *F* by G*ing*' entails '*a* caused *y* to *H* and *y*'s H*ing* caused *x*'s F*ing*'.

Some examples will help to make these contentions clearer and more persuasive. Consider first, then, the action sentence 'Smith caused Jones to fall'. Suppose we ask *how* Smith caused Jones to fall and the answer returned is 'Smith caused Jones to fall by colliding with him'. Now, 'Smith collided with Jones', it seems clear, is *not* causally analysable. And accordingly I propose that 'Smith caused Jones to fall by colliding with him' entails 'Smith's colliding with Jones caused Jones's falling'. Next consider the action sentence 'Smith caused the light to go on' and suppose we again ask *how*, receiving this time the answer 'Smith caused the light to go on by turning the switch'. This time, 'Smith turned the switch', unlike 'Smith collided with Jones', *is* causally analysable, entailing as it does 'Smith caused the switch to turn'. So what I want to say here is that 'Smith caused the light to go on by turning the switch' entails 'Smith caused the switch to turn and the switch's turning caused the light's going on'.

Suppose I am right in what I have said so far (and I have, to be fair, glossed over some subtleties which are not pertinent to the general thrust of my argument). Then the following important result may be deduced. All causal action sentences in which the name of an *agent* appears as the grammatical subject of the verb 'to cause' depend for their truth upon the truth of causal sentences in which noun-phrases solely referring to *actions* appear as grammatical subjects of this verb. Sentences of the first type are ones of the form '*a* caused *x* to *F* (by G*ing*)' and sentences of the second type are ones of the form '*a*'s G*ing* caused *x*'s F*ing*' (or are conjunctions of such sentences). Let us call the two types of causal sentence *agent-causal* and *action-causal* sentences respectively. Then our interesting result is that all agent-causal sentences depend for their truth upon the truth of action-causal sentences. (Whether this means that agent-causal sentences are in principle altogether eliminable in favour of action-causal sentences is another question, though I am inclined to think that they are.)

The proof of this result is simple enough, given my earlier contentions. For suppose we have an agent-causal sentence of the form '*a* caused *x* to *F*' and that in answer to the how-question this is expanded as '*a* caused *x* to *F* by G*ing*'. Then if '*a* G*ed*' is *not* causally analysable we immediately have the consequence that our original agent-causal sentence depends for its truth upon the truth of the action-causal sentence '*a*'s G*ing* caused *x*'s F*ing*'. If on the other hand '*a* G*ed*' *is* causally analysable, say as '*a* caused *y* to *H*', then we have the consequence that our original agent-causal sentence depends for its truth upon the truth of the causal sentence '*a* caused *y* to *H* and *y*'s H*ing* caused *x*'s F*ing*', which is partly agent-causal and partly action-causal. But now the same considerations may be applied to the agent-causal part, '*a* caused *y* to *H*', which has exactly the same form as our original agent-causal sentence, '*a* caused *x* to *F*'. Hence, on pain of an infinite regress which would certainly appear to be vicious, that original agent-causal sentence must ultimately depend for its truth upon the truth of some *purely* action-causal sentence (one which will be conjunctive in form). Moreover, the grammatical subject of the first conjunct of that sentence will necessarily be a noun-phrase referring to an action of *a*'s which is *not causally analysable*. I shall call this action the *original* action of the causal chain of actions terminating in *x*'s F*ing* (though there is no presumption here that the 'original' action is itself *uncaused*, nor even that it in any sense 'initiates' the subsequent chain of actions). Thus, if the agent-causal sentence '*a* caused *x* to *F*' is ultimately dependent for its truth upon the truth of the action-causal sentence '*a*'s G*ing* caused *y*'s H*ing* and *y*'s H*ing* caused *x*'s F*ing*', then *a*'s G*ing* is what I would call the 'original' action of the causal chain of actions terminating in *x*'s F*ing*. And *a*'s G*ing* will be an action of *a*'s that is not causally analysable.

2. BODILY MOVEMENTS AND BODILY MOTIONS

So far I have not, officially, been concerned exclusively with human agents and actions, but from now on I shall concentrate on these. Assuming – as seems reasonable unless we are given good grounds to think otherwise – that human actions provide no exception to the general conclusions reached so far, it is clear that at least *some* human actions must fail to be causally analysable – in particular, those that are 'original' in causal chains of human action. Evidently, then, these original actions cannot be *bodily movements* of any sort, if by bodily movements we are talking of human agents' *movings of their bodies*: for all such actions *are* causally analysable. For instance, 'Smith raised his arm' is analysable as entailing 'Smith caused his arm to rise'. Of course, there is *another* sense of 'bodily movement' in which it denotes not a moving by an agent of his body, but simply a movement of his body – and to avoid ambiguity and confusion I shall call this a *bodily motion*, reserving the term 'bodily movement' exclusively for agents' movings of their bodies. A bodily motion in this sense is an action which is *not* causally analysable. For instance, the action sentence 'Smith trembled', as it is normally used, reports a bodily motion. Only in exceptional circumstances would this sentence be used to report a bodily movement, when it would be causally analysable as entailing 'Smith caused himself to tremble'.

Now, the peculiarity of human agents (and of some animal agents, I assume) is that they can perform *voluntary* actions. And in the case of voluntary actions it is sufficiently clear that the 'original' actions of the causal chains involved must be *mental* acts of some sort (and *not*, say, items such as mere bodily motions). The reason why I say this is simply that the possession of a mind is so obviously the distinguishing feature of the sort of agent that is capable of engaging in voluntary action, while some actual *exercise* of that mind's capacities must equally evidently be what makes the difference, in any particular case, between a voluntary action and an action that might just as well have been attributable to an agent altogether devoid of a mind. These distinctive mental acts we shall shortly identify as *volitions*. But before we reach that point, I need to comment briefly on the view of some philosophers that certain bodily movements are 'basic' in the sense that in the case of such movements there is *no* answer to the question of *how*, or by doing what, they are done.[2] For if this view were correct, it would totally undermine the volitional theory that I wish to defend.

Consider again the action sentence 'Smith raised his arm', which is causally analysable as entailing 'Smith caused his arm to rise'. And suppose we ask *how* Smith did this. I expect an answer of the form 'Smith caused his arm to rise by *F*ing', entailing in turn the action sentence 'Smith *F*ed'. But the philosophers of whom I speak seem to think that very often there is *no* such answer to a question such as

---

[2] See, e.g., Arthur C. Danto, 'Basic Actions', *American Philosophical Quarterly* 2 (1965), pp. 141-8.

this, and that then the arm-raising is what they call a 'basic' action. At other times they *would* allow an answer, such as 'by tugging on a rope attached to his arm via a pulley'. But in all *normal* cases of arm-raising, they would say, there is simply *no* answer to a question such as 'By doing *what* did Smith raise his arm?' However, this creates a considerable difficulty, for it then appears that there must be agent-causal sentences which do not depend for their truth upon the truth of action-causal sentences – although only, it seems, where human and perhaps animal agents and voluntary actions are concerned. This makes for unnecessary mystery, suggesting as it does the operation, in certain cases of human and animal action, of a *kind* of causation not to be found in the realm of inanimate things. A naturalistic view of animate beings certainly cannot tolerate such a suggestion. (I should perhaps add, however, that I do not dispute that there *is* something special about 'normal' cases of voluntary bodily movement, which justifiably motivates the description of such actions as 'basic' – I merely dispute the view of 'basicness' adverted to above. An alternative view will be proposed later.)

3. VOLUNTARY ACTIONS AND VOLITIONS

I asserted a little while ago that in the case of voluntary human actions, it is clear that the actions which are 'original' in causal chains of human action must be *mental* acts of some sort. That is to say, if *a*'s causing *x* to *F* was a *voluntary* action of *a*'s, then it appears that the causal chain of action terminating in *x*'s *F*ing must have had as its original action a certain sort of mental act of *a*'s. Such a mental act will, of course, not be causally analysable. Plainly, though, we cannot assume that just *any* sort of causally unanalysable mental act which is original in a causal chain of human action would suffice to render that chain of action voluntary. The sort of mental act which *would* suffice I shall call – by definition, in effect – a *volition*, or *willing*, or *act of will*. I am contending, thus, that what distinguishes voluntary from involuntary human actions is the *kind* of mental origin they involve, and I am further assuming that there is some *single* kind of original mental acts which are characteristically involved in all chains of voluntary human action.

(This is a view of voluntary action which, while held in some disrepute in recent decades, has a venerable history.[3]) And the assumption that I am making seems a reasonable hypothesis, in the absence of countervailing argument. (Later I shall offer a positive defence of it.) But if it is correct, then there is no question but that *there are* volitions or acts of will, since undoubtedly human agents do sometimes voluntarily cause things to happen. All that remains, then, is to try to characterize volitions more closely.

Suppose, then, that *a* caused *x* to *F*, and did so voluntarily. Then by my account this means that the sentence '*a* caused *x* to *F*' depends for its truth upon the truth of some sentence of the form '*a*'s Ging caused . . . *x*'s Fing', where the gap may or may not (but almost always will) be capable of containing further noun-phrases referring to intermediate steps in a causal chain of actions, and where '*a*'s Ging' denotes what we have decided to call a *volition*. Thus in such a case the ultimate answer to the question of *how a* caused *x* to *F* is 'by willing'. But by willing *what*? It is clear that the mental activity of willing, if it is to play the causal role we have assigned it in voluntary human action, must always have an intentional object: willing must always be willing *something*. But *what* is it that the agent wills, when by so willing he voluntarily causes something to happen? Two principal possibilities suggest themselves.[4] One is that the agent wills *something to do something* – for instance, wills *x* to *F*. The other is that the agent wills *to cause something to do something* – for instance, wills to cause *x* to *F*. (Some would prefer to say that willing is a propositional attitude, that is, a matter of willing *that such-and-such be the case*.[5] But for a number of reasons, which need not be gone into just now, I find this proposal

[3] See, in particular, John Locke, *An Essay Concerning Human Understanding*, bk. II, ch. XXI, sect. 5. I discuss Locke's theory in my 'Necessity and the Will in Locke's Theory of Action', *History of Philosophy Quarterly* 3 (1986), pp. 149-63 and in my *Locke on Human Understanding* (London: Routledge, 1995), ch. 6. Volitionism is now enjoying a revival amongst a minority of action-theorists: see further Lawrence E. Davis, *Theory of Action* (Englewood Cliffs, NJ: Prentice-Hall, 1979), ch. 1 and Carl Ginet, *On Action* (Cambridge: Cambridge University Press, 1990), ch. 2. Ginet arrives at his position through a train of reasoning somewhat similar to mine in sections 1 and 2 above: see his *On Action*, pp. 4ff.

[4] Cf. H. A. Prichard, 'Acting, Willing, Desiring', in his *Moral Obligation* (Oxford: Clarendon Press, 1949). I disagree with Prichard's answer to the question, however.

[5] See, e.g., Hugh McCann, 'Volition and Basic Action', *Philosophical Review* 83 (1974), pp. 451-73, especially p. 468 and Ginet, *On Action*, pp. 31-2.

unacceptable. I shall return to the issue later.) Which of these two possible accounts should we prefer?

In order to settle this question, let us consider a relatively simple case of an agent *a*'s voluntarily causing a motion of his own body, for example, causing his arm to rise. And suppose, for the sake of simplicity, that he does this 'in the normal way', rather than as in the rope and pulley example (so that his action is what many philosophers would call a 'basic' action). On my view, the ultimate answer in such a case to the question of *how a* caused his arm to rise is that he did it *by willing*. And now our further question is by willing *what*? In such a case, the two rival hypotheses supply the following two answers respectively: (1) by willing *his arm to rise*, and (2) by willing *to cause his arm to rise*.[6] My own opinion is that the former answer is quite untenable. One simply cannot, I believe, 'will' one's arm to rise any more than one can 'will' a table across the room to move. Indeed, I think it is this erroneous view of the intentional objects of acts of will that has, as much as anything, brought into such ill repute the belief that such acts exist at all. For if willing *were* like this it would apparently be purely a matter of *a posteriori* discovery that some acts of will happened to be causally efficacious and others not, and this seems incomprehensible. Can it really be supposed that I just *discover* (by trial and error?) that if I will my arm to move, it does move, but that if I will the table to move, it does not?[7] Surely not: this would make willing too much like mere wishing. (Whether or not our wishes come true is not in general up to us.) I believe, on the contrary, that the very concept of an act of will must be of a kind of mental activity that is (normally) efficacious with respect to its own intentional content (see section 6 below) – and that this feature of willing is much easier to accommodate within the alternative account mentioned earlier, precisely because that account incorporates an intention to *cause* a specific effect into the very content of an act of will and thereby secures a constitutive connection between what it *is* to will and the expectation that an act of will should be causally efficacious in the relevant way. (This is

---

[6] I would be happy to treat (2) as equivalent to 'by willing *to raise his arm*' – but, as I mentioned in section 1, this sort of putative equivalence has been disputed by some philosophers of action, so I shall not insist on it here.

[7] To suppose that this sort of thing could be discovered by *trial* and error is manifestly absurd, at least if generalized to embrace all acts of will – for 'trial' itself implies the performance of voluntary action. Yet what other method of discovery could there be, if what is to be discovered is merely an empirical truth?

not to say that I think that an act of will realizes its own intentional content by virtue of a logical or conceptual necessity – a view which some opponents of volitionism have attempted to foist upon it – for this would be incompatible with the *causal* role of such acts, as well as being utterly mysterious.)

Having rejected what I like to call the 'magical' account of willing, my view is, then, that when *a* voluntarily causes his arm to rise 'in the normal way', he causes his arm to rise *by willing to cause it to rise*, so that, in this sort of case, we may say that *a*'s willing to cause his arm to rise causes his arm to rise. But if this is so, then it turns out that we haven't, after all, yet fully specified the intentional content of *a*'s act of will. For if what *a* wills is *to cause his arm to rise*, then earlier considerations of ours require that *a* must, at least implicitly, will *to cause his arm to rise by Fing* (for some appropriate *F*), and that, in fact, *F*ing in such a ('basic') case must be none other than *willing*. That is to say, a fuller specification of the (perhaps only implicit) content of *a*'s act of will must have it that *a* wills *to cause his arm to rise by willing* – the point being that, as was explained earlier, we are always entitled to expect an answer to the question of *how* an act of causing is (to be) done, and in this case 'by willing' seems to be the only answer that is ultimately acceptable. After all, it is barely comprehensible that *a* should, in such a case, will to cause his arm to rise by doing anything *other* than willing. (Even in the rope and pulley case, where *a* wills to cause his arm to rise by tugging on the rope, there is *something* that he wills to cause by willing: thus here he wills to cause his *other* hand to move *by willing*. Of course, I don't mean to suggest that ordinary, philosophically untutored human agents necessarily *think* of themselves as 'willing to cause things by willing' – that is, think of the contents of their volitions under this sort of description.)

Now, however, another difficulty looms. I have just argued that when *a* voluntarily causes his arm to rise 'in the normal way', he must cause it to rise by willing *to cause it to rise by willing*. But then the question again arises, with respect to the willing mentioned in the specification of the content of *a*'s act of will, as to what *its* content is – for all willing, we have agreed, is willing *something*. An infinite regress seemingly threatens: we appear to be in danger of having to say that *a* causes his arm to rise by willing to cause his arm to rise by willing to cause his arm to rise by willing . . . and so on *ad infinitum*. But in fact I don't believe that there is a serious difficulty here. The lesson to be drawn from the threatened regress is that a's act of will must be, in respect of its content, *self-referential.*[8] What we must say is that when a voluntarily causes his arm to rise 'in the normal way', he causes it to rise by willing *to cause it to rise by performing THAT act of will*, where 'THAT' refers to the very act of will whose content is being specified. (Henceforth, I shall reserve the capitalized form, 'THAT', exclusively for this sort of self-referential use.) In this way, we respect both the demand that the content of a's act of will should be *fully* specifiable and the demand that its content should specify *willing* as the means by which the arm is to be caused to rise.

One phenomenon that this self-referential characterization of willing seems to illuminate is our feeling that when, after a period of deliberation and hesitation, we suddenly go ahead and *do* something, we reached a 'point of no return' in our deliberations, at which action immediately and irrevocably followed: we sometimes call such points 'moments of decision', and use metaphors such as tipping a balance or releasing a spring to describe them. This is quite understandable on the account of willing advanced above: for once I *do* perform the mental act of willing to cause something to happen by performing THAT very act of will, there is no holding back. Provided my neural mechanisms are functioning normally, the willed action is already underway, that is, the causing is already in process of occurring – for if it were not, the willing would *already* have failed to realize its intentional content, which would imply some defect of neural functioning (since willing is by its very nature normally causally efficacious). I often can, it is true, subsequently will to reverse matters, and thus *undo* voluntarily something that I have voluntarily begun to do: but undoing what has begun to be done is quite different from withholding from doing, and moreover *feels* quite different. The alternative account of willing rejected earlier cannot, it seems, properly accommodate these facts.[9] For if, say when I raise my arm voluntarily, all

---

[8] Other recent authors have similarly contended that *intentions* are self-referential: see, e.g., John R. Searle, *Intentionality* (Cambridge: Cambridge University Press, 1983), ch. 3. See also Ginet, *On Action*, pp. 35-6, where the claim is made for both volitions and intentions.

[9] Similarly, it is at most this other account which succumbs to the objection raised by G. E. M. Anscombe in her 'Will and Emotion', in R. M. Chisholm & R. Haller (eds.), *Die Philosophie Franz Brentanos* (Amsterdam: Rodopi, 1978), pp. 145f. Anscombe remarks:

that I will is *my arm to rise a short time hence*, it is not at all obvious why this act of will may not be immediately countermanded and the arm-raising withheld. Performing an act of will should *commit* the agent to realizing (or at least to *beginning* to realize) the content of his willing, or else it is not even clear how willing can be causally sufficient (in the circumstances) for its intended effect. For willing cannot be sufficient if the absence of a countermanding act of will is necessary.

4. BASIC AND NON-BASIC VOLUNTARY ACTIONS

I should make it clear that the foregoing account of volitional content strictly applies only in the case of voluntary actions which would standardly be called 'basic', such as raising one's arm 'in the normal way'. But this now provides us with the material for an account of *basicness* (or, more precisely, of *basic voluntary causing*) which has considerable advantages over the account rejected earlier. According to that earlier account, *a* caused *x* to *F* – for example, caused his arm to rise – as a basic (voluntary) action only if *a* caused *x* to *F* but *not* by doing anything else (where the 'by' is the 'by' of causal means). I reject this because – for one thing – I want to say that even where *a* voluntarily caused his arm to rise 'in the normal way', he did it *by* doing such things as causing the muscles in his shoulder and back to contract (even if *a* may not have been *aware* that this was how he did it). But, more fundamentally, of course, I reject it because I also want to say that in such a case *a* caused his arm to rise not least *by willing*. (There is, incidentally, no inconsistency in saying *both* of these things – that he did it *both* by causing his muscles to contract *and* by willing. For he *also* caused his muscles to contract *by willing* – though not by willing *to cause them to contract*, but only by willing *to cause his arm to rise*. And the 'by' of causal means is transitive.)

However, what *is* special about voluntarily raising one's arm 'in the normal way' is that in such a case the bodily movement in question is made *the direct object of one's volition*: in such a case, as we have seen, one causes one's arm to rise precisely by willing *to cause one's arm to rise* (by

'That an act is voluntary doesn't mean that it is preceded by an act of will . . . In proof of this, consider how, whatever inner event precedes an act, one can still ask *if it* [i.e., the act] *was voluntary when it occurred.*' But if the 'inner event' is willing as I have characterized it, and *does* cause the intended effect as specified in the content of that willing, then this question is *not* genuinely still open.

performing THAT act of will). And *this* is why the action is properly described as 'basic'. By contrast, consider a non-basic voluntary action such as causing a ball to move. One cannot (I think) cause a ball to move precisely by willing *to cause it to move* (by performing THAT act of will). Rather, one's volition must be directed upon a bodily movement of one's own body, albeit in the knowledge or belief that the bodily motion so brought about will cause motion in the ball. So, typically, one might cause a ball to move by willing *to cause one's foot to move into contact with the ball* (by performing THAT act of will).

Thus we may offer the following as a definition of basic voluntary causing:

a voluntarily caused *x* to *F basically* (or as a basic action) if and only if *a* caused *x* to *F* by willing to cause *x* to *F* by performing THAT act of will.

Instances of *non*-basic voluntary causing will fall into two categories. First, there are familiar cases such as the one just discussed of causing a ball to move, in which *a* causes *x* to *F* voluntarily by voluntarily causing something *y* to *G* as a basic action – for example, he voluntarily causes a ball to move by voluntarily causing his foot to move into contact with the ball as a basic action. Here *a*'s willing causes *y*'s Ging which causes *x*'s Fing. Secondly, there are more esoteric cases like the one mentioned earlier concerning the causation of muscle contractions, in which *a* causes *x* to *F* voluntarily by willing to cause something *y* to *G* and where, typically, *x*'s Fing will be an intermediate cause of *y*'s Ging – for example, he voluntarily causes his shoulder and back muscles to contract by willing to cause his arm to rise, and the contraction of his shoulder and back muscles causes the rising of his arm. For in such a case I see no reason to deny that *a* causes his shoulder and back muscles to contract *voluntarily*, even though he may be unaware that he is doing so. (A voluntary action need not be *intentional*, even though an intentional action must be voluntary.[10]) These, then, are cases in which, typically, *a*'s willing causes *x*'s Fing which causes *y*'s Ging.

I repeat, then, that what is peculiar to basic voluntary actions is that they are made the direct object of the agent's will – and for the most part such actions are limited in practice to the agent's movement of

---

[10] For more on the distinction between voluntariness and intentionality, see my 'An Analysis of Intentionality', *Philosophical Quarterly* 30 (1980), pp. 294-304.

various parts of his own body 'in the normal way'. We may appropriately say of such actions that they are done 'at will'. One may raise one's arm or kick one's foot 'at will' (unless one is disabled or impeded), but cannot in general do such things as contract one's shoulder muscles or move a ball 'at will'. I say 'in general' because it must be recognized that an agent can with practice *extend* his repertoire of basic actions (thus infants have to learn to walk and talk 'at will'), and so it would be dangerous to attempt to lay down *a priori* limits to the range of basic actions. Some people can indeed learn to do such things as control their heart-beat 'at will', and one might equally wish to ascribe to a competent typist an ability to type the word THE 'at will'. But although there may not be specific *a priori* limits, limits there certainly must be, for we are not God and do not, *pace* Descartes, have an infinite or boundless will.

We can understand now, while still rejecting, the alternative account of basicness discussed earlier. The reason why one may be tempted to *say* that where *a* voluntarily caused *x* to *F* as a basic action he did not do it *by* doing anything else is simply that no other action will in such a case *enter into the content of a's volition* as constituting a causal means to the end of bringing about *x*'s *F*ing (apart, of course, from that very act of volition itself). But this is just to say that *a* need not *will* to do something else by doing which he may cause *x* to *F*: it is not to imply that he need not in fact *do* any such further thing.

5. IN DEFENCE OF VOLITIONS

It is now time to answer some familiar objections to the kind of account of voluntary action that I have just offered. One particularly well-known objection, due to Gilbert Ryle, is that such an account is driven into an infinite regress of willings (a different sort of regress, however, from the one which we earlier evaded by recognizing the self-referential character of volitional content).[11] The argument is that if only those actions are voluntary that originate in an act of will, then we need to ask whether acts of will themselves are voluntary or not, which presents the following dilemma. If they are not, then it is hard to see how they can serve to make the actions which originate in them

[11] See Gilbert Ryle, *The Concept of Mind* (London: Hutchinson, 1949), pp. 65f.

voluntary (because we normally regard the consequences of involuntary actions as being themselves involuntary). On the other hand, if it
is said that acts of will *are* voluntary, then by the volitional theorist's
own lights this will apparently have to mean that acts of will themselves originate in *other* acts of will, these in yet others, and so on *ad
infinitum*.

My own response to this objection – in which I differ from some
other volitionists[12] – is to accept quite happily that acts of will are *not*
themselves voluntary and to deny that the first horn of the alleged
dilemma presents a genuine difficulty. Here it should be recalled that I
effectively *define* 'willing' as that kind of mental activity which is
characteristically 'original' in those causal chains of human action
which we would ordinarily describe as voluntary. (This does indeed
presuppose – though as far as I can see quite unproblematically – that
we can very often recognize actions as being voluntary other than by
means of identifying their causal origins.) So there is no mystery as to
why 'willed' causings should be voluntary, particularly since our
further characterization of the causal and intentional features of volitions has, I hope, gone some way towards explaining their suitability
for the theoretical role that has been assigned to them. The fact that
other sorts of involuntary human activities, such as twitches and blinks,
do *not* render voluntary the causal chains of action which issue from
them is quite irrelevant. (Here I should perhaps emphasize that I am
not concerned to try to define or explicate *what we ordinarily mean* in
describing an action as 'voluntary'. What I am interested in is the
question of what *in fact* makes a voluntary action voluntary, and this
in my view unquestionably has to do with the special nature of its
causal provenance.)

One reason why I am quite happy to deny that acts of will are
voluntary is that by my account, it will be recalled, such acts are
necessarily not causally analysable, and I am only prepared to regard
as voluntary those actions that *are* causally analysable. (Willing is not
itself a matter of causing something to happen – in the way that killing
is a matter of causing death – even though *by* willing one may, and
typically does, cause something to happen.) But I should add that
while I have denied that willing can be voluntary, I do not mean to
rule out *a priori* the possibility that an agent might *voluntarily cause*

---

[12] See, e.g., McCann, 'Volition and Basic Action', p. 472.

himself to perform a certain act of will. In the simplest case, this would occur if the agent were to cause himself to will to do something by willing to cause himself so to will by performing THAT act of will. In such a case, the voluntary causing of volition would of course be 'basic' – though in fact I very much doubt whether it is possible even in principle for an agent to cause himself to *will* 'at will', any more than it appears that he can cause himself to *believe* 'at will'.[13] If one can voluntarily cause volitions in oneself, one can I think only do this in a roundabout way – for instance, by voluntarily conjuring up thoughts of certain attractive or desirable prospects (as a weight-watcher may invoke the image of a desirably slender future self in order to prompt a volition to resist eating a cream cake). Thus we see that a volitional theory of the sort that I am advancing need not represent agents as being the perfect slaves of their wills, since it may allow that they can have a measure of voluntary control over some of the operations of the will itself.

Another time-worn objection to volitions is that we are, supposedly, quite ignorant of their existence – and this is put down to their being the mere inventions of the overspeculative philosophical imagination.[14] To this I have a twofold reply. First, we are *not* in fact universally oblivious of our volitions (though most of us, of course, will not recognize them by that name). Second, there are very good reasons why too conscious an awareness of our volitions would impede us in the performance of voluntary actions. On the first point, I should say that we *are* sometimes made aware of our volitions, especially in circumstances in which, contrary to our expectations, we fail in the attempt to perform some voluntary action. Thus there is the famous example of the patient cited by William James who, lacking kinaesthetic sensations in his arm, was surprised to be told that he had failed to raise it when instructed to do so, the arm being (unbeknownst to him) kept under restraint.[15] The patient was evidently conscious of having done *something* but not, obviously, of having raised his arm – since he failed to do this. What I would say,

---

[13] Cf. Bernard Williams, 'Deciding to Believe', in his *Problems of the Self* (Cambridge: Cambridge University Press, 1973).

[14] See, e.g., Ryle, *The Concept of Mind*, pp. 63ff.

[15] See William James, *Principles of Psychology* (New York: Henry Holt & Co., 1890), vol. 2, p. 490. This is the famous case of Landry's patient.

of course, is that he was conscious of *willing* to raise his arm – what else? Furthermore, the fact that when we *are* made aware of our volitions our perception of them is often only confused and indistinct (as this patient's evidently was) should be unsurprising to anyone who has abandoned the Cartesian view of the mind as peculiarly transparent to itself. Here I might add that although nothing quite equivalent to my use of the term 'volition' seems to exist in ordinary language, the vocabulary of *trying* comes close to capturing its sense – a point to which I shall return.

As for the second point made above – that too conscious an awareness of our volitions would impede us in the performance of voluntary actions – this is just a corollary of a more general observation, that too conscious an awareness of *any* of the actions *by* doing which we do some further thing intentionally (of which willing is of course one) tends to impede us in the performance of that further intended action. For instance, a competent typist who attends to the movements of his fingers tends to make more errors than one who does not. (An analogous response may be made in defence of the universal presence of visual sensations in visual perception despite our general obliviousness of them: see chapter 4, section 2 above.)

One last objection that I shall mention concerns the *number* of willings or volitions we execute in the course of performing some train of voluntary action. Thus Ryle asks, with heavy sarcasm, how many acts of will one executes in, say, reciting 'Little Miss Muffet' backwards.[16] Now, the first thing to say about this objection is that volitions are not in any way peculiar amongst actions in raising problems of enumeration and, by implication, of individuation. One might equally well ask, with as little expectation of receiving an obvious and uncontentious reply, how many *utterances* one executes in reciting 'Little Miss Muffet' backwards – but this does not, or should not, engender scepticism about the existence of utterances.

At another level, however, the enumeration question does raise some important, though in no way embarrassing, issues about volitions and voluntary action. In particular, it raises the question of whether complete action-routines or only the components of such routines can constitute the intentional objects of volitions. For instance, when a competent typist types the sentence 'The cat sat on the mat', should

[16] See Ryle, *The Concept of Mind*, p. 64.

we suppose that he simply has a volition to type that sentence, or should we suppose rather that he first has a volition to type 'The', then a volition to type 'cat', and so forth? (I stipulate that the typist is a 'competent' one because it seems clear that in the case of a novice the typing even of each letter will be a non-basic voluntary action: recall our earlier discussion.) I do not consider that this is a question that can be settled conclusively without recourse to empirical psychological evidence: either hypothesis seems tenable, *a priori*. What is clear, however, is that not *every* component action of *every* action-routine can individually be the intentional object of some volition of the agent. (After all, even so 'simple' an action as raising one's arm 'in the normal way' involves many component actions.) What also seems clear is that as competence in performing an action-routine improves with practice, fewer of its components or sub-routines need individually to be made the intentional objects of volitions of the agent. If this implies that someone well-rehearsed in reciting 'Little Miss Muffet' backwards executes *fewer volitions* in reciting it than someone not so well-rehearsed – as it may well do – then I do not regard this as a consequence which a volitionist need feel embarrassed about accepting. The only reason, I suspect, why the enumeration question may *appear* at first to present an embarrassing difficulty for the volitionist is that it is tacitly being supposed that the volitionist is committed to regarding introspective awareness of one's own volitions as a transparent and infallible source of all that one ever needs to know about them – in short, it is being supposed that the volitionist must adhere to the Cartesian conception of the mind. For since introspection provides no conclusive answer to the enumeration question, it is then inferred that acts of will as the volitionist supposedly conceives of them cannot really exist.[17]

---

[17] There is no conflict between my remarks here and my adherence, in chapter 7 below, to the claim that the self as agent necessarily knows, of any current action which it is consciously performing, that *it itself* is the agent of that action. One can know that one is the author of a complex train of action while remaining unclear as to precisely which components of that action are the objects of one's volition – especially when the action has become more or less habitual.

6. BELIEF, DESIRE AND WILL

I shall conclude with some remarks concerning the place of volitions within the taxonomy of mental states and processes. One question which immediately arises is why we should suppose that volitions exist *in addition to* more familiar mental phenomena such as beliefs and desires: that is to say, why can't we suppose that the mental causes of voluntary human actions are beliefs or desires or combinations of the two, rather than members of a distinctive species of mental act? Part of the answer lies in the fact that these causes must indeed have the status of *acts* – as our earlier analysis showed – whereas beliefs and desires are *states*. To this it might be replied that while states are admittedly items of the wrong category to constitute the causes we seek, *events* are not, and that the *onset* of belief or desire is the sort of event which might very well play the causal role which we have assigned to volitions.[18] Is it not gratuitous to postulate the existence of volition *in addition to* the onset of belief or desire?

My answer to this draws on two related points which have been touched on already. One is that volition (or whatever is to play the causal role which I have assigned to volition) is not a propositional attitude. The other is that volition is a species of mental act which is by its very nature (normally) causally efficacious with respect to its own intentional content. The mental causes of voluntary human action need to meet both of these demands, and the onsets of belief and desire meet neither. In terms of old-fashioned 'faculty' psychology, we may summarize the matter by saying that the mental causes we seek must be located neither in the cognitive nor in the appetitive faculty of the mind, but in a distinct *conative* faculty. Indeed, as other volitionists have emphasized, there is an intimate relationship (though not, I think, an identity) between the concepts of *willing* and *trying*.

The link between willing and trying has an immediate bearing on the first of the two points just mentioned. It is highly significant that whereas we believe *that* such-and-such is the case and desire or wish *that* such-and-such be the case, we do not *try* that such-and-such is or be the case but rather always simply try *to do* something.[19] And the same applies to willing. Indeed, if either trying or willing *were* a

---

[18] Cf. Donald Davidson, *Essays on Actions and Events* (Oxford: Clarendon Press, 1980), p. 12.

[19] Cf. Colin McGinn, *The Character of Mind* (Oxford: Oxford University Press, 1982), p. 91.

propositional attitude, it is hard to see how tryings or willings could be attributed to agents – such as animals and perhaps infants – lacking a reflexive conception of themselves, since reflexive reference to the agent would apparently have to figure in the propositional content of the attitude. That is to say, the agent would have to try or will that *he himself* do something, and this would require him to have a reflexive conception of himself.[20] But because trying or willing is in fact always merely trying or willing *to do* something, its intentional content is always representable by an infinitival verb-phrase rather than by a complete sentence containing a grammatical subject making reference to the agent. Reference to the agent is indeed necessarily otiose, since one cannot, logically, try or will to do someone else's actions.

Here it may be remarked against me that one may not only *try* to do something but also *desire* to do something. However, I have no wish to divorce desire altogether from action, nor to deny that desire is one of the causal determinants of action. I am happy to allow, indeed, that volition is partly determined by desire (and also partly by belief). But desire is not, as trying and willing are, *essentially and exclusively* directed upon action. That is why it is significant that whereas desire may take as its intentional object not only the performance of some action but also the truth of some proposition or the realization of some state of affairs, trying and willing are always and only trying and willing *to do*.

The second point made a moment ago was that the mental processes required to play the role we have assigned to volitions must be ones which are, by their very nature, (normally) causally efficacious with respect to their own intentional contents. This is related to my earlier contention that we cannot intelligibly be supposed, quite generally, merely to discover *a posteriori* the causal relationships which obtain between our volitions and their intended effects (though Hume seems to have supposed something of this sort).[21] I am not denying that a volition to raise one's arm, say, *may* fail on any given

[20] On such reflexive conceptions of the self, see chapter 7 below.
[21] This is not to gainsay my remark, in chapter 3 above, that causal relations are not *in general* knowable *a priori*, in the manner of logico-mathematical relations: so my opposition to Hume on this point is quite limited and specific. Moreover, I do not claim that we can know *a priori* anything about *how* our volitions give rise to their intended effects nor, hence, that the causal mechanisms involved must be be peculiarly 'intelligible' or 'transparent'.

occasion to produce its intended effect, the rising of one's arm (whether through hindrance or through neural malfunctioning). Nor am I denying that it might in principle be possible, through neurosurgical intervention, to arrange that a person's volitions to raise his arm brought about instead movements in his foot – though I do consider that this situation could only obtain temporarily and would be fairly rapidly rectified by a psychological adjustment analogous to that experienced by subjects wearing inverting spectacles.[22] Nor, yet again, am I denying that an agent may expand his voluntary behavioural repertoire – and, more especially, the range of actions which he can perform 'at will' – through experiment and practice. What I *am* saying is that, at least in the case of basic actions, there is an especially intimate relationship between our volitions and our knowledge of their normal effects which implies that such knowledge cannot be supposed to be acquired by the agent merely empirically, because its possession is a prerequisite of the agent's very capacity to engage in voluntary action at all. Only because one knows that willing to cause one's arm to rise normally *does* cause one's arm to rise can one *attempt* to raise one's arm voluntarily by willing to do so.[23] For one cannot intelligibly be said to attempt to do something without having some preconception of how one might reasonably hope to accomplish that thing by making the attempt. Thus one cannot so much as *have* a volition to raise one's arm, say, in the absence of knowledge of the effect that it will typically cause, the rising of one's arm. Hence, since even a newborn infant must be capable of doing *something* voluntarily, if it is ever to learn how to do anything else, at least some of our volitional repertoire and associated causal knowledge must be innate, not acquired. Directly related to these

---

[22] Cf. Ginet, *On Action*, pp. 43-4.

[23] Might it not be enough merely to *believe* (perhaps erroneously) that willing to cause one's arm to rise normally causes one's arm to rise? After all, may not a person whose body, unbeknownst to himself, consists solely of a brain in a vat, *attempt* to raise his arm? I am not inclined to assimilate such a case to one of an amputee suffering from a persistent phantom limb illusion, but in the latter case it seems legitimate to say that the agent's knowledge of what the 'normal' effects of his willing would be is *not* compromised by his unfortunate condition (he still *does* know that willing to cause his limb to move 'normally' causes it to move). As for the envatted person, however, it simply is not clear to me whether or not he can be in the right kind of cognitive state to be able to endeavour to 'raise his (non-existent) arm'. The question deserves further exploration.

[24] See, e.g., G. E. M. Anscombe, *Intention* (Oxford: Basil Blackwell, 1963), pp. 13f.

facts, I should add, is the phenomenon of our 'non-observational knowledge' of our own intentional actions which has been discussed by numerous philosophers of action.[24] We know what we have done not (or not only) because we observe or sense it, but because we have *willed* to do it, and know that willing normally brings about its intended effect.

Now, given that this is how matters must stand with regard to the mental processes whose causal role we have invoked volitions to fill, it is clear that nothing akin to the *onset of desire* could occupy that role in their stead. For there is *not* in general any especially intimate relationship between the onset of desires and a knowledge of the effects to which desires give rise. It is not the case, for instance, that one could not so much as *have* a desire to drink a cup of tea, or even to raise one's arm, without knowing that the onset of such a desire typically and normally contributes causally to the production of the desired state of affairs – for, of course, it doesn't. Desire is *not*, by its very nature, normally productive of its own object. Volition – or anything capable of occupying the role that we have assigned to it – is and must be.

Of course, saying this by no means prevents me from allowing that volitions themselves are, typically, partly caused by appropriate combinations of desire and belief – for this certainly doesn't imply that I might as well by-pass volitions and directly invoke such combinations of desire and belief (or the onsets thereof) as the mental causes of chains of voluntary action. That would be like arguing that when the combination of a spark and the presence of gas causes an explosion, which in turn causes a building to collapse, one might as well ignore the role of the explosion. The immediate or proximate cause of collapse – and equally of voluntary action – must be an event of an appropriate sort to occupy that causal role. Only volitions more or less as I have characterized them could occupy the relevant causal role in the case of voluntary action.

One minor question remains outstanding. It may be asked why, given the similarity between willing and trying that I have emphasized above, I do not simply *identify* willing with trying. My answer is that I do indeed regard any particular willing as a trying, but don't consider that the term 'trying' denotes any unitary *kind* of act, in the way that 'willing' does and must. Trying, quite generally, is a matter of doing something in the hope and expectation of achieving some end: thus, for instance, casting a fly in the hope and expectation of catching a fish constitutes *trying to catch a fish*. Since all willing is, by its very essence, doing something in the hope and expectation of achieving some end, all willing is trying. But it is not the case that all trying is willing (even though it is true that all trying *involves* willing). For instance, casting a fly in the hope and expectation of catching a fish is trying, but it is not willing (though it involves willing). However, we can see, by this account, that the relationship between willing and trying, though not one of identity, is close enough to explain the absence from ordinary language of any special term for volition as I have tried to characterize it: whereas the philosophical psychologist has need of such a term, the layman can say all he needs to say about volition in the vocabulary of trying.[25]

---

[25] This paragraph anticipates my answer to the recent claim of Frederick Adams and Alfred R. Mele that 'there is no need to incorporate volition – construed as something other than intending, trying, sensory feedback, or a combination thereof – into one's theory of action. One can get by quite well with more familiar notions': see their 'The Intention/ Volition Debate', *Canadian Journal of Philosophy* 22 (1992), pp. 323-37 (quotation taken from p. 337). For lay purposes one can indeed do this – but 'trying', being a generic notion, is unsuited to the theoretical role of characterizing a specific stage in the aetiology of voluntary action, unlike 'willing'. What constitutes 'trying' can, in different conversational contexts, vary enormously – though in most contexts what constitutes it is simply some variety of voluntary action (for instance, casting a fly), so that in these contexts the notion of trying actually presupposes (and hence cannot help to explain) the notion of voluntary action. As for the idea that the 'familiar' notion of *intention* can supplant that of volition, I would point out that while *prospective* intentions are indeed familiar enough, they are *not* suitable rivals for volitions, whereas so-called *intentions-in-action* are probably just volitions under another name, with no greater claim to 'familiarity': see further chapter 6 of my *Locke on Human Understanding*.

6

Language, thought and imagination

Our abilities to perceive and act are clearly ones which we share with
at least some of the animals, even if they possess them in less sophisticated forms than we do. But our higher cognitive capacities – for
language, speculative thought and reflexive self-knowledge – may
very well be exclusive to ourselves. Even so, I believe these higher
capacities to be intimately related to our abilities to perceive and act,
in many ways being extensions of those abilities. In this chapter I shall
examine the relationship between our capacities for language and
thought and our capacity for sense-perception, which I consider to
be mediated by our powers of *imagination* – a view which I share with
John Locke but not, I think, with many modern philosophers of
mind.

If there is one theory of language which almost all modern philosophers have been united in repudiating, usually with contempt, it is
the *ideational* theory – in essence, Locke's theory.[1] The fundamental
theses of the theory are these: (1) that the primary end of language is
the communication of thought, (2) that thinking at its most basic
consists in 'having ideas' – that is, is fundamentally *imaginative* in nature
– and (3) that words acquire their power to express thoughts by being
made, through custom and convention, to represent or signify 'ideas'
in the minds of those who use them. I think it would be correct to say
that the current philosophical opposition to this theory stems

---

[1] There have been a few more sympathetic treatments of Locke's theory of language in
recent times, notably: Norman Kretzmann, 'The Main Thesis of Locke's Semantic
Theory', *Philosophical Review* 77 (1968), pp. 175-96; Ian Hacking, *Why Does Language
Matter to Philosophy?* (Cambridge: Cambridge University Press, 1975), pp. 43ff; and E. J.
Ashworth, 'Locke on Language', *Canadian Journal of Philosophy* 14 (1984), pp. 45-73. I am
particularly indebted to Hacking's brief but illuminating remarks. I discuss Locke's views
on language more generally in chapter 7 of my *Locke on Human Understanding* (London:
Routledge, 1995).

ultimately from the work of Frege and Wittgenstein – from the former's quite general hostility to 'psychologism' in semantics and logical theory and from the latter's rejection of appeals to 'inner' or 'private' mental processes in the explanation of linguistic behaviour. But my contention is that such philosophers as Locke were not so absurdly and wildly mistaken in their accounts of language as present-day orthodoxy would have us believe. Modern arguments against ideational theories of linguistic signification are, I believe, often directed at figures of straw. Certainly, I see the ideational approach as correct in regarding the faculty of imagination as being crucially involved in our ability to use and comprehend language.

1. IDEATIONISM AND LOCKE'S THEORY OF LANGUAGE

Before looking in some detail at what Locke himself says, I shall state briefly and in very general terms what I see as being the basic philosophical problem of language and how the ideational theory purports to solve it. The basic problem I take to be this: how is it that we can use words – which in themselves are merely arbitrary sounds or visible marks – to speak about things in the world? That is, how do words and sentences acquire *semantic* properties like reference, meaning and truth? The answer of the ideational theory is that words acquire such semantic properties in virtue of being used by speakers to express and communicate their thoughts about things in the world. That is, words come to be 'about' things in the world by being made, through custom and convention, to represent our thoughts about those things. But if such an answer is not to be vacuous, it must plainly be denied that thought itself is essentially linguistic. Which, of course, is precisely what the theory does deny. The ideationist may concede that thought is *sometimes* linguistic – that on some or many occasions we may 'think in words' – but must and does insist that there is a fundamental level of thought at which it is not linguistic but *imaginative* in nature: a level at which we 'think in ideas'.

The great advantage of the ideational view of thought is that there is, apparently, no comparable problem or mystery as to how processes of *imagination* can be 'about' things in the world, because such processes are clearly akin to, and in respect of their content ultimately derivative from, processes of *sense-perception* – and the latter, it seems clear, are quite *naturally* 'about' things in the world, in stark contrast with the way in which linguistic utterances are only *conventionally* 'about' such things. It would be wrong, of course, to suppose that there is no problem *at all* as to how processes of imagination can be 'about' things in the world. (We might call this the problem of the *intentionality of imagination*.) The point, however, is that the prospects for a solution to this problem from an ideationist viewpoint are much more promising than are the prospects for a solution to the problem of how *words* can be 'about' things in the world from a viewpoint which opposes ideationism. And this has to do with the fact just alluded to, that the connection between imagination and its objects is natural rather than conventional in character. A slightly cryptic way of putting the point would be to say that the things which we are primarily equipped by nature to think about are things which – however they may be 'in themselves' – are *for us* essentially *perceptibilia*, that is, possible objects of perception. Consequently, they are also essentially *imaginable* for us, and so *thinkable* for us, according to the ideationist's view of thought. Another way of putting the point, which draws upon some of the conclusions of chapter 4 (section 4), is to say that our ability to *conceive* of physical objects of various sorts is intimately tied to our knowledge of how such objects 'appear' to one or more of our sense modalities (for example, how they 'look') – so that in thinking of such objects we necessarily draw upon recognitional capacities whose primary field of deployment lies in sense-perception.

In order to understand the ideational theory of language properly, however, it is important not to confuse two quite distinct, but inter-related, levels on which it operates. Only on one of these levels should it be seen as offering an account of linguistic *meaning* – a semantic theory – in anything like the modern sense. By a 'semantic theory' I mean a theory of those *word-to-world* relations which confer upon linguistic entities such properties as reference, extension and truth.[2] Historically, proponents of the ideational approach did not in fact busy themselves much with this level, because they were much more concerned to present an account of linguistic *expression* – that is, a theory of those *word-to-thought* relations which confer upon

---

[2] If such a theory is to accommodate *intension* as well as *extension*, it perhaps needs to appeal more widely to word-to-(possible) worlds relations, but this does not materially affect the point I am making. For the possible-worlds approach to semantics, see Richard Montague, *Formal Philosophy*, ed. R. H. Thomason (New Haven: Yale University Press, 1974).

linguistic entities a power to convey one speaker's thoughts to another. Clearly, though, a theory of word-to-thought relations can be combined with a theory of *thought-to-world* relations – a theory of *cognition* – to produce a theory of word-to-world relations: and that this is the correct route to semantic theory is implicit in the ideational approach, even if its historical proponents were not much concerned to chart that route in detail themselves. But, it seems to me, many modern critics of the ideational approach criticize its account of *linguistic expression* as though it were intended to be an account of *linguistic meaning*, with the result that the ideational approach is represented in so preposterous a guise that it is hard to see how such eminent philosophers as Locke and Hobbes could have entertained it at all.[3]

It is vital to appreciate that the ideational theory of language is *not* maintaining, absurdly, that the words or sentences which we utter *refer to* or are made *true or false* by the thoughts we use them to express: that is, the theory is not offering a subjective – indeed, almost solipsistic – theory of *meaning*. The explanation for this common misinterpretation, I surmise, is that it arises precisely from the disparity of interests between the historical proponents of ideationism and their modern critics: the critics, being primarily interested in semantic theory themselves, assume that when the ideationists speak at such length about words 'signifying' ideas they, too, must be advancing a semantic thesis, and find confirmation for this assumption in the fact that little else in the way of explicit semantic theory appears in the writings which they

---

[3] This is the verdict, too, of Ian Hacking, in his *Why does Language Matter to Philosophy?*, ch. 5, and in a milder form of E. J. Ashworth, in her 'Locke on Language' and '"Do Words Signify Ideas or Things?" The Scholastic Sources of Locke's Theory of Language', *Journal of the History of Philosophy* 19 (1981), pp. 299-326. This 'revised' reading of Locke has been challenged recently by Michael Losonsky, in his 'Locke on Meaning and Signification', in G. A. J. Rogers (ed.), *Locke's Philosophy: Content and Context* (Oxford: Clarendon Press, 1994). I would stress two points in response to Losonsky. First, I by no means wish to deny that Locke has the *resources* for a theory of linguistic meaning in the modern sense and readily concede that he does develop some elements of such a theory – but, secondly, I would still insist that Locke's account of the '*primary* signification' (my emphasis) of words is *not*, and is not *intended* by him to be, a theory of meaning in this sense, but is rather a theory of expression and communication. (Incidentally, it seems to me irrelevant whether or not Locke himself ever uses the words 'signification' and 'meaning' interchangeably, since what is at issue is whether his theory of signification is a theory of meaning *in the modern sense*.)

criticize – not realising that this absence is due to the ideationists' relative lack of interest in semantic theory altogether.

It is time now that we began to examine Locke's own account of language, as he presents it in the first two chapters of book III of the *Essay Concerning Human Understanding.*[4] Chapter I opens with these words:

God having designed Man for a sociable Creature, made him not only with an inclination, and under a necessity to have fellowship with those of his own kind; but furnished him also with Language, which was to be the great Instrument, and common Tye of society. *Man* therefore had by Nature his Organs so fashioned, as to be *fit to frame articulate Sounds*, which we call Words. But this was not enough to produce Language; for Parrots, and several other Birds, will be taught to make articulate Sounds distinct enough, which yet, by no means, are capable of Language. (III, I, 1)

We may question, of course, the allegedly divine origin of man's linguistic ability, as we may also question the teleological explanation offered by Locke for man's ability to produce articulate sounds. We may suppose that creatures capable of language will just employ whatever species of physical signs or symbols they find most convenient, which in the case of human beings happen to be vocal. However, parrots, as Locke points out, can also make these same sounds: so what do parrots lack which renders them incapable of speech? Locke answers as follows:

Besides articulate Sounds . . . it was farther necessary, that [Man] should be *able to use these Sounds, as Signs of internal Conceptions*; and to make them stand as marks for the *Ideas* within his own Mind, whereby they might be known to others, and the Thoughts of Men's Minds be conveyed from one to another. (III, I, 2)

So what parrots lack is *thought*. They cannot speak because they have no thoughts to convey by speech; or, at least, their utterances are certainly not used by them to *express* thoughts, even if they have any – and this is why their utterances do not constitute speech. Plainly, though, Locke's presumption here is that human thought itself is *not*

---

[4] All quotations from the *Essay* are taken from the Clarendon edition, edited by P. H. Nidditch (Oxford: Clarendon Press, 1975). For the benefit of readers using other editions, I identify the locations of these passages by book, chapter and section, thus: '(III, II, 1)'.

essentially linguistic, but on the contrary *imaginative* – it consists of 'ideas'. If thought itself were conceived of as essentially involving speech – whether overtly or covertly, in the form of 'silent soliloquy' – then, as I have already emphasized, a theory such as Locke's would just be vacuous. For, clearly, if, as Locke wants to say, what makes an utterance speech as opposed to mere babble is that it is expressive of *thought*, and yet thought itself essentially involved the use of words, then we should need some further criterion to distinguish between words that are used 'thoughtfully' from those that are not.

Now, the suggestion that at the most fundamental level we 'think in ideas' can easily be made to seem preposterous by unsympathetic critics: for instance, by misrepresenting 'ideas' as being *images* – ghostly pictures floating before the mind's eye. However, there is in fact little reason to suppose that even Locke himself subscribed to this naïve conception of ideas, and certainly it is in no way essential to an ideationist theory of thought.[5] We shall return to this issue in a moment, but first of all I want to emphasize again the close kinship between imagination and *perception*. Speaking loosely, it might almost be said that imagination is a kind of surrogate perception – that to exercise one's imagination is to rehearse or anticipate actual or possible episodes of perceptual experience, though with a degree of voluntary control that is characteristically absent from perception itself. (In perception one can direct one's attention at will, but has very little voluntary control over *what* is perceived once one's attention has been fixed.) Imagination, like perception, may be classified by reference to its sensory modes and thus we have visual, auditory and tactile imagination, just as we have these forms of perception. Unsurprisingly, there is neuropsychological and neurophysiological evidence that many of the same areas of the cortex are typically engaged in imagination as in perception.[6] A great deal more can no doubt be said about imagination and its relation to perception, but these observations may suffice to highlight the intimacy of that relation.

---

[5] See further my *Locke on Human Understanding*, ch. 3, and compare John W. Yolton, *Locke and the Compass of Human Understanding* (Cambridge: Cambridge University Press, 1970), p. 134: 'I see no evidence in the *Essay* that Locke thought of ideas as entities'.
[6] See, for example, Stephen M. Kosslyn, 'Mental Imagery', in Daniel N. Osherson *et al.* (eds.), *Visual Cognition and Action* (Cambridge, MA: MIT Press, 1990), pp. 78–9.

What is particularly important for our present purposes is the fact that very often one may *understand* a situation simply in *perceiving* it, and that this kind of non-discursive or intuitive understanding carries across to imagination. For example, in observing a road accident one may register in a holistic fashion what is happening before one's eyes: one's understanding of the situation isn't the product of a sequential articulation of the scene in thought, and certainly isn't a matter of describing to oneself what is happening *sotto voce*. But then, in the same way, one may *imagine* just such a road accident, and here again the kind of understanding involved is intuitive or non-discursive. What one is then doing is precisely 'thinking in ideas' rather than in words. But such thought is certainly not a matter of being confronted with anything that one could helpfully call 'images'. Images or pictures, after all, require interpretation in order to be understood, whereas what I am saying about imaginative thought is that the understanding involved in it is integral to the imaginative process itself and not superimposed upon it by a further act of thinking. Obviously, in view of this it is unfortunate that we call imagination what we do – since it *doesn't* involve the presentation of 'images'. The name, no doubt, is the result of a bad theory – and this is why I prefer to speak sometimes of 'ideation' instead.

2. SOME MODERN PREJUDICES AND MISCONCEPTIONS

One reason why many modern philosophers tend to underrate the scope and versatility of imaginative thought is that they succumb to the prejudices of literacy, which lead them to exaggerate the importance of discursive thinking. Illiterate and inarticulate people often complain that they understand some matter perfectly clearly but are unable to express this understanding adequately in speech – they can't, they claim, put what they think 'into words'. Linguistic philosophers have tended to dismiss such claims with the argument that the only satisfactory test of whether or not someone really *does* understand a certain matter is precisely whether or not he can clearly *state* what he means in language: if he can't, the presumption must be that he was only under the illusion of understanding clearly. Here we see the prejudices of literacy at work. Because philosophers are usually highly articulate themselves, they find that lack of clarity in their own thought is generally reflected in unclear articulation – and by extension they tend to regard the rest of humanity in the same light. But the argument that I have just referred to – that clear articulation is the only satisfactory criterion of clear thought – is plainly mistaken. For clear thought and understanding may be manifested in *non*-verbal behaviour quite as well as in speech and writing.

Those philosophers who are sceptical regarding the possibilities of thought without language might do well to reflect on the famous passage in William James's *Principles of Psychology*, in which the childhood reminiscences of a deaf-mute are recorded:[7]

Some two or three years before my initiation into the rudiments of written language, . . . I began to ask myself the question: *How came the world into being?* When this question occurred to my mind, I set myself to thinking it over a long time. My curiosity was awakened as to what was the origin of human life in its first appearance upon the earth . . . and also the cause of the existence of the earth, sun, moon, and stars.

If they are to be trusted, these memories are testimony to a capacity for non-discursive thinking even about matters of a fairly abstruse character, quite far removed from the concrete circumstances of everyday experience. This child, it seems, was perfectly capable of thinking non-verbally about the abstract and the general as well as about the concrete and the particular. (Incidentally, it is curious and perhaps instructive to observe how awkwardly Wittgenstein deals with James's passage in paragraph 342 of the *Philosophical Investigations*.)

Locke himself has the beginnings of an answer to those who suppose language to be an inherently superior vehicle for abstract and general thought, when he remarks that

[T]hose [Words], which are made use of to stand for Actions and Notions quite removed from sense, *have their rise from thence, and from obvious sensible* Ideas *are transferred to more abstruse significations,* and made to stand for *Ideas* that come not under the cognizance of our senses; *v.g.* to *Imagine, Apprehend,*

---

[7] William James, *Principles of Psychology* (New York: Henry Holt & Co., 1890), vol. I, pp. 266ff: the few lines I quote here are drawn from a very much longer passage. For further discussion, see: H. G. Furth, *Thinking without Language* (London: Collier-Macmillan, 1966); M. M. Lewis, *Language and Personality in Deaf Children* (Slough: National Foundation for Educational Research in England and Wales, 1968), pp. 44ff; and, especially, Richard F. Cromer, *Language and Thought in Normal and Handicapped Children* (Oxford: Basil Blackwell, 1991), pp. 1ff.

Comprehend, Adhere, Conceive, Instil, Disgust, Disturbance, Tranquillity, etc. are all Words taken from the Operations of sensible Things. (III, I, 5)

What Locke is suggesting here is that etymology betrays the fact that the language which we use to discuss more 'abstruse' subjects has largely developed through the use of metaphors and similes grounded in our intuitive understanding of concrete, perceptible things. But if the scope of language can be extended in this way, so too can that of imaginative thought itself (indeed, according to an ideationist like Locke, the two developments go hand-in-hand). We should never underestimate the importance of imaginative models and metaphors in our understanding of even the most abstract and sophisticated subjects. Consider, for instance, the heuristic value of graphs and diagrams in mathematics and logic, and the historical role of visual and even physical models in the development of scientific theories of atomic and molecular structure.

Of course, it must be allowed that in an area like that of mathematical thinking, most of us depend very largely upon a learned ability to manipulate symbols according to formal rules. But it need not be claimed on behalf of the ideational theory that *whatever* can be thought in language can equally be thought 'in ideas'. One may readily concede, for instance, that a creature altogether lacking language could hardly have the thought that tomorrow is Tuesday. It is quite enough that the ideational theory can rebut the charge that imaginative thought is, by its very nature, limited to the concrete and the particular, or to the here and now. At the same time, however, we shouldn't allow ourselves to be deceived by the familiarity of words and the facility with which we can use them into overestimating the extent to which ordinary language provides a vehicle for clear and determinate thought. Locke and his contemporaries were much more acutely aware than many modern philosophers are of the deficiencies and abuses of words: the thought which language clothes is often much less splendid than its attire.

Quite commonly, nowadays, the ideational theory of language is represented as proposing that speakers and auditors are constantly engaged in processes of *translation* from ideas to words and from words to ideas – and is often criticized precisely on this account. But this is a distortion, because it imposes a quasi-linguistic model upon ideational thought – as though 'ideas' occupied a wordlike role in a 'language of thought'. Modern philosophers of mind such as Jerry Fodor have, of course, quite explicitly adopted a 'language of thought' hypothesis and, along with it, a theory of natural language comprehension which represents speakers as translating into and out of 'Mentalese'.[8] But, however appropriate such a translational model might be for Fodor, it is clearly inappropriate for Locke. The point is that 'Mentalese' is at least language-like in having, putatively, quasi-lexical symbolic elements which combine to form sentence-like syntactic structures. But in describing ideational thinking as 'non-discursive' I am precisely denying that it exhibits anything that could meaningfully be called 'syntactic structure'. And, lacking such structure, it cannot really be put into any relation of *translation* to linguistic utterances. 'Being a translation of' is a relation which holds between two language-like representations when they share the same *meaning* – that is, when they possess the same *semantic* properties. But, as we have already seen, according to the ideational approach it is vital not to confuse *semantic* (word-to-world) relations with *cognitive* (thought-to-world) relations. Consequently, it would be quite contrary to the precepts of ideationism to treat the *expressive* relation between thought and language as though it were a relation of *translation*. Indeed, the ideationist must regard the Fodorian 'language of thought' hypothesis and its attendant account of natural language comprehension as being guilty of confusion on precisely this score.

Another point which needs to be emphasized on behalf of ideationism is that its proponents can quite consistently allow that a good deal of our thinking, even when it concerns matters which *could* be thought about non-discursively, is done 'in words' – that is, in words of ordinary natural languages like English and French. Such thinking often consists, in fact, in *imagined discourse*, and thus still involves 'having ideas', albeit (auditory) ideas *of words*. But the ideationist will add that what makes such discursive thought thought about an *extra-linguistic subject matter*, rather than just thought about *words*, is that the person engaging in it has a capacity to use these words to express non-discursive, imaginative thoughts about that very subject matter.

When we think purely 'in words' we are, as Berkeley would put it, 'regarding only the signs' – but what gives life to these signs, on the ideationist view, is precisely our capacity to use them at will to express

---

[8] See Jerry A. Fodor, *The Language of Thought* (Hassocks: Harvester Press, 1976).

our *ideas*. Hence, on this view, when a speaker uses words, whether overtly or in 'inner speech', without knowing what non-verbal ideas they may serve to express, he uses them insignificantly – unless, of course, the words (or symbols) are indispensable for thought about the subject matter in question, as in mathematics. In this, as in many other respects, Berkeley's sophisticated version of the ideational theory represents an advance on Locke's original rather sketchy and primitive account.[9] (Berkeley, as is well known, did not regard the ideational approach as appropriate to all aspects of language use: in particular, he saw its limited applicability to mathematical language and rightly emphasized the performative and emotive dimensions of our use of words – but the core of his theory is still clearly ideational in character.)

3. THE PROBLEM OF PRIVACY AND ITS SOLUTION

I come now to what many would regard as being the fatal difficulty of the ideational theory: the problem of *privacy*. In chapter II of book III of the *Essay*, Locke writes as follows:

Man, though he have great variety of Thoughts, and such, from which others, as well as himself, might receive Profit and Delight; yet they are all within his own Breast, invisible, and hidden from others, nor can of themselves be made to appear. The Comfort, and Advantage of Society, not being to be had without Communication of Thoughts, it was necessary, that Man should find out some external sensible Signs, whereby those invisible *Ideas*, which his thoughts are made up of, might be made known to others . . . The use Men have of these Marks, being either to record their own Thoughts for the Assistance of their own Memory; or as it were, to bring out their *Ideas*, and lay them before the view of others: *Words, in their primary or immediate Signification, stand for nothing, but the* Ideas *in the Mind of him that uses them.* (III, II, 1-2)

Now, Locke would obviously see no absurdity in the notion of a *private* language (for instance, one used purely 'for the Assistance of [a man's] Memory'). But his insistence that words 'primarily' signify ideas 'in the Mind of him that uses them' lays him open to the charge that he makes *all* language irredeemably private – a charge which is

---

[9] See, especially, Berkeley's *Alciphron; Or, the Minute Philosopher* (1732), Dialogue VII, the opening sections.

scarcely undermined by his rather lamely remarking, a little later, that '[U]nless a Man's Words excite the same *Ideas* in the Hearer, which he makes them stand for in speaking, he does not speak intelligibly' (III, II, 8). On his view, it may seem, men have their *words* in common but may for all we know assign them very different meanings, so that the same word in the mouths of two different speakers of English may effectively be related in the same way as homophones of two different languages – which is as much as to say that what we call 'English' is not in reality a single language at all. The problem, of course, is this: how can one speaker, A, convey in words to another speaker, B, the ideas that are in his mind, if B can only ever attach to A's words ideas that are in his own mind?

At this point we need to appreciate that, although Locke's theory does indeed face a *prima facie* difficulty which requires some careful handling, the difficulty in question is not one which should be described in *semantic* terms. The question of whether or not two speakers speak the *same language* is a semantic question – a question of whether or not the words which they utter stand in the same word-to-world relations – whereas the difficulty which Locke's theory faces concerns, rather, the word-to-thought relations (the *expressive* relations) of different speakers. Indeed, Locke himself, by implication, rejects the suggestion that speakers who use the same words to express different ideas should for that reason alone be deemed to be speaking different languages, when he criticises what he takes to be the common supposition that a speaker's words can be signs of ideas in another person's mind:

[Men] *suppose their Words to be Marks of the* Ideas *in the Minds also of other Men, with whom they communicate*: For else [they suppose] they should talk in vain, and could not be understood, if the Sounds they applied to one *Idea*, were such, as by the Hearer, were applied to another, which [they suppose] is to speak two Languages. But in this, Men stand not usually to examine, whether the *Idea* they, and those they discourse with have in their Minds, be the same: But think it enough, that they use the Word, as they imagine, in the common Acceptation of that Language; in which case they suppose, that the *Idea*, they make it a Sign of, is precisely the same. (III, II, 4)

As I have acknowledged, Locke is still faced with a *prima facie* difficulty, albeit one concerning the expression and communication of thought by means of language rather than one concerning semantics, or the meanings of words in a common language. The problem is that we have, and apparently *can* have, no interpersonal standard of comparison between the 'ideas' of different speakers, by which we can determine whether the ideas expressed by one speaker's use of certain words are the same as or different from those expressed by another's use of them, even when the speakers are indisputably talking the same language. One might be inclined to respond to this problem on Locke's behalf by urging that, since human beings are made in much the same mould, they will, in all probability, receive similar ideas of sense-perception in similar perceptual situations, so that there will be conformity amongst their ideas in thinking too. But, quite apart from the fact that this response is purely speculative, it threatens to undermine the whole basis of Locke's account of language and thought by raising the suspicion that, in fact, it really *doesn't matter* what 'ideas', if any, speakers associate with words, nor whether there is any conformity or resemblance between the 'ideas' of different speakers.

The point can be made vivid by reference to the notorious 'inverted spectrum' problem: for all we know, it seems, *A*'s idea of red might resemble *B*'s idea of green and vice versa, and yet since this would not be reflected in any detectable difference between *A*'s and *B*'s uses of the terms 'red' and 'green' to describe things, their ability to communicate successfully with one another using colour terminology would not be in the least disrupted. If it is then urged that, in view of the physiological similarities between *A*'s and *B*'s visual systems, it is unlikely that their ideas of red really do differ in this way, it may be replied that since it apparently doesn't matter *whether or not* such a resemblance obtains, to propose that it does serves no useful purpose. And from this it seems but a short step to conclude that all appeal to 'ideas' in one's account of the communication of thought by language – and hence, by extension, in one's theory of thought itself – is idle and vacuous. However, as we shall see, this 'short step' is in fact nothing less than a giant leap, and a quite unsupported one.

The first thing to note at this point is that Locke himself was fully aware of the inverted spectrum problem – indeed, he seems to have discovered it – and yet was not at all disconcerted by it. Here is what he says:

Neither would it carry any Imputation of *Falshood* to our simple *Ideas, if* . . . it were so ordered, That *the same Object should produce in several Men's Minds different* Ideas at the same time; *v.g.* if the *Idea*, that a *Violet* produced in one Man's Mind by his Eyes, were the same as that a *Marigold* produced in another Man's, and *vice versa*. For since this could never be known . . . neither the *Ideas* . . . nor the Names, would be at all confounded. (II, XXXII, 15)

Clearly, Locke's verdict on the inverted spectrum problem is that, indeed, it would not hinder the communication of thought by language if such inversions occurred, but that this by no means implies that ideas are not the very stuff of human thinking. The conclusion must be that, charitably intepreted, Locke is *not* committed to the view that successful communication of thought by language requires the *replication* in the hearer's mind of ideas present in the speaker's mind. This is not to say that the ideas of speaker and hearer need bear *no particular relation at all* to one another in order for communication between them to be successful. As we shall see, their ideas *do* need to be appropriately related, but – and this is the crucial point – the relation in question is one which can be known to obtain without appeal to any sort of intersubjective comparison between those ideas themselves.

In order to begin to get a grip on the desired relation, a simple example may help. Consider the case of two boys, Alf and Ben, who want to see a football match but cannot afford to pay for tickets to get into the stadium. They discover that if one of them stands on the other's shoulders he can see over the wall and describe the match to his friend – so they take it in turns to do this. Now suppose that Alf has first turn to watch. He will experience certain 'ideas' of sense-perception which he will then 'put into words'. Ben will hear these words and as a result enjoy certain 'ideas' of imagination as he envisages the scene taking place on the pitch. This seems to be the picture of linguistic communication that Locke is offering us, at a fairly primitive level – and it has a good deal of intuitive appeal. But now the question arises: what sort of ideas of imagination ought Ben to experience if Alf is to communicate satisfactorily to Ben his perceptions of what is going on inside the stadium?

At first one might suppose that what is required is that Ben's imaginings should somehow replicate Alf's first-hand experiences, so that Alf's description of the match enables Ben to visualise the match pretty much as Alf himself sees it. But this, as we are by now aware, is to impose a requirement of interpersonal similarity between

175

ideas whose satisfaction is impossible to verify. It seems, however, that a much less stringent requirement will secure all that is needed for successful communication between Alf and Ben: this is that Ben's imaginings should sufficiently resemble, not *Alf's* first-hand experiences, but rather the first-hand experiences that *Ben himself* would have had if he had been in Alf's place. Success in meeting this requirement is easy enough to corroborate: all that Ben needs to do is to swap places with Alf in order to confirm that the scene as he imagined it on the basis of Alf's description is consistent with what he now experiences at first hand.

We may draw from this example the following conclusion concerning the proper relationship between the ideas of speaker and hearer in a successful episode of linguistic communication, according to the ideational account. Rather than demand that a word used by the speaker, *A*, to signify a certain idea in his own mind should excite the *same* idea in the mind of the hearer, *B*, Locke ought to demand only that the word should excite what we may call a *corresponding* idea in *B*'s mind – where the criterion for such 'correspondence' is that *B*'s idea (of imagination) should resemble the idea (of perception) that *B* would have were he to confront an object which would excite in *A* the idea (of perception) which resembles that idea (of imagination) which *A*'s use of the word in question signifies. (Since this relation of correspondence between ideas is, to all intents and purposes, an equivalence relation, we might in fact say that it *does* constitute a kind of 'sameness' between the ideas of different subjects – and it is conceivable that it is just such a 'sameness' that Locke himself has vaguely in mind when he speaks, however incautiously, of speaker and hearer having the 'same' ideas in a successful episode of linguistic communication. The vocabulary of sameness and identity is, after all, notoriously slippery.)

It is not difficult to see how a correspondence between the ideas which a word signifies in the minds of different speakers within the same speech community could be set up through the process of passing language on from adult to child. Consider the archetypal situation so beloved of philosophers, in which an adult teacher draws a child's attention to various instances of some perceptible feature, perhaps by pointing to them, and utters the appropriate word – 'red', say. The (modified) Lockean story would then go as follows. In such a situation both teacher and learner enjoy certain ideas

176

of sense-perception and the learner, if he successfully identifies the perceptible feature pointed to by the teacher, comes to associate the word 'red' with the idea which he enjoys in perceiving that feature. When the learner subsequently attempts to use the word to describe a perceptible feature to the teacher, whether he is describing something he currently perceives or something he merely remembers or imagines, his implicit aim should be to excite in the mind of the teacher an idea of imagination which resembles that idea of perception which the teacher enjoyed in perceiving the perceptible feature which figured in the original learning situation. Success in this aim can be confirmed by the learner pointing to another exemplar of the perceptible feature he has in mind (has an idea of) – one which is visible to the teacher – and seeing whether the teacher agrees with the description of it as 'red'.

At no stage during this process need either the teacher or the learner make any assumptions concerning intersubjective similarities or differences between their respective ideas. The success of the process would be in no way hindered if the idea which the learner associated with the word 'red' resembled the idea which the teacher associated with the word 'green', and vice-versa. At the same time, it is clear that the role of ideas in this account of the learning process is by no means an idle one. Thus Locke can rebut the charge that the inverted spectrum problem demonstrates the vacuity of the appeal to ideas in a theory of thought and language. By the same token, he can defeat the accusation that the 'privacy' of ideas – if by this we mean that no one can really know what another's ideas are like – makes them worthless in an account of the workings of a public language.

4. ON HAVING SOMETHING 'IN MIND'

Critics of Locke's theory of language may concede, perhaps, that the strategy of the preceding section saves that theory from complete vacuity, but at the same time they may urge that the explanatory role which it confers upon 'ideas' is a superfluous one, in the sense that the phenomena which they are invoked to explain can be explained more economically without their aid. In the (modified) Lockean story of language learning told above, it was suggested that the learner comes to associate the word 'red' with *the idea* which he enjoys in perceiving a certain perceptible feature. But why, it may be asked, can't speakers learn to associate words *directly* with perceptible features, without the mediation of 'ideas'?

Well, in order to associate a word, such as 'red', with a certain perceptible feature, redness, one must be able to *think of both* in association with one another: the thought of one must call to mind the thought of the other. However, when I think of something I must think of it *in some way* – for instance, I might think of it *in words*. But, it seems clear, if one could only ever think 'in words', it would be impossible after all ever to associate words with non-verbal features, but at most only to associate words with other words. For in order to think of something 'in words', I must *already* have associated those words with the thing in question. So words cannot come to be associated with things unless there is some *other* way of thinking of things – and this other way, according to the ideationist, is the 'way of ideas'. And note here that the problem which faces the theory that we only ever think 'in words' does *not* repeat itself for the theory that, at the most primitive level, we think 'in ideas': for we don't need to *associate* our ideas with perceptible features in order to be able to think of those features by entertaining those ideas. As I remarked earlier, the connection between imagination and its objects is natural, in stark contrast with the conventional connection between word and object.

The following thought-experiment may help to drive home the foregoing conclusion. Suppose there were (*per impossibile*, as I believe) a race of beings capable of our full range of sense-perception but lacking all powers of imagination save an ability to call to mind various words and phrases, in the form of imagined sequences of spoken or written symbols. Then what would entitle us to say that their exercising this ability would ever constitute *thinking* ('in words') about extra-linguistic features of the world? Even if we allow (for the sake of argument) that these creatures could correctly apply words to name or describe perceptible features of the world *when they were actually confronted with those features*, in what sense could they be said to know what those words serve to name or describe when they were *not* confronted with the features in question? Lacking as the creatures supposedly do any *'ideas'* of these features, there is, I believe, no sense at all in which they could be said to possess such knowledge. I suppose it might be urged against me that their knowledge consists simply in a *disposition* to apply the words correctly in the presence of the features. However, the creatures' possession of such a disposition would not provide them with any *actual* conception of the features in their absence and so, I submit, could not in fact constitute the sort of knowledge we seek.

However, at this point someone might want to challenge my assumption that thought of something must always be, as I put it, thought of it *in some way* – whether 'in words' or 'in ideas'.[10] Why can't there be what we might call 'pure' thought of something? This is a deep and puzzling question, which I can only begin to get a grip on by asking what it is that a person *has in mind* when he thinks of something, such as the perceptible feature redness. In one sense, of course, what he has in mind is that very perceptible feature. But a perceptible feature can't *literally* be 'in one's mind': when one has redness 'in mind', one's mind is not itself red! But, surely, one's mind must be modified in *some* way such that it is in virtue of *that* modification that one has *redness* in mind as opposed, say, to *greenness*. Redness can only be 'in the mind' as a so-called *intentional* object – as something *thought of.* But what makes my thought of redness a thought of *redness* as opposed to a thought of *greenness*? It is obviously no answer to say that what makes my thought a thought of redness is that it has redness as its 'intentional object' – for the very notion of an intentional object has been introduced as the notion of *something that is thought of,* and so already presupposes an answer to the question of how a thought comes to be 'of' one thing rather than another. Now, the ideationist *does* have an answer to this question: his answer is that one may have *redness* 'in mind' by having an *idea* of redness, that is, by *imagining* something red. The mind *is* modified in different ways in thinking of different things: and these modifications – which the ideationist takes to be modifications of *consciousness* – consist in its having different ideas.

Some may be reminded at this point of a remark of Wittgenstein's which seems to bear upon this issue. At one point in the *Philosophical Investigations* he writes: 'What makes my image of him into an image

---

[10] It is worth noting that even the anti-psychologistic Frege writes: 'Although the thought does not belong to the contents of the thinker's consciousness yet something in his consciousness must be aimed at the thought.' See Gottlob Frege, 'The Thought: A Logical Inquiry', in P. F. Strawson (ed.), *Philosophical Logic* (Oxford: Oxford University Press, 1967), p. 35. How odd, though, to call *what is 'aimed at'* the 'thought', rather than calling the contents of the thinker's consciousness this!

[11] Ludwig Wittgenstein, *Philosophical Investigations*, trans. G. E. M. Anscombe (Oxford: Basil Blackwell, 1958), p. 177.

of *him*? Not its looking like him.'[11] Roderick Chisholm prefers to translate the German *Vorstellung* as 'idea' rather than 'image'.[12] But I would urge that the Anscombe translation at least brings out the fact that Wittgenstein's question only poses an immediate problem for an *imagist* view of ideas.[13] For only on that view can we talk at all straightforwardly about a *resemblance* (or lack of it) between an idea and its object. Having an idea of red isn't having a red idea! Rather, it is just *imagining* something red. But if it is now asked: 'What makes my imagining something red imagining something *red*?', I should answer by appealing once again to the kinship between *imagining* something red and *seeing* something red. That is to say, the relevant resemblance is between *acts*, not *objects*. And if it is then further asked: 'What makes my seeing something red seeing something *red*?', the obvious answer is that something red is the cause of my perceptual state.

By way of conclusion, I want to repeat with emphasis my warning against a facile acceptance of those tiresome modern criticisms of the ideational theory that are directed at crude or grossly distorted versions of it. The problem of negation provides an object lesson. Modern critics often laughingly dismiss the ideational theory as one which assigns a private image of redness as the meaning of the word 'red', a private image of a cat as the meaning of the word 'cat', and so on. Then the supposedly devastating blow is dealt: what, then, is the meaning of the word 'not'? Is it a private image of nothingness, or of absence, or is it rather the absence of a private image – in which case, *what* private image must be absent? Is the meaning of 'The cat is not on the mat' a private image of a mat with no cat on it? But how then does this differ from the private image of a mat with no dog on it? If the images are the same, the absurd implication is that 'The cat is not on the mat' and 'The dog is not on the mat' have the same meaning.[14]

We already know in part how to counter crude gibes like this. The ideational theory is not committed to an imagistic view of ideas, nor does it represent ideas as being the *meanings* of words. Furthermore, it

---

[12] See Roderick M. Chisholm, *The First Person* (Brighton: Harvester Press, 1981), p. 3.

[13] The full German version of Wittgenstein's remark is: 'Was macht meine Vorstellung von ihm zu einer Vorstellung von *ihm*? Nicht die Ähnlichkeit des Bildes.' The use here of the word *Bild* (= 'picture', 'image') seems to support Anscombe's translation.

[14] For a living example of criticism at this sort of level, see Daniel M. Taylor, *Explanation and Meaning* (Cambridge: Cambridge University Press, 1970), pp. 132ff, pp. 141ff

does not treat the relation between language and thought as one of *translation*, with individual words or phrases being paired off with individual ideas on a one-to-one basis. Consequently, the theory is simply not in the business of looking for some specific 'ingredient' of thought which plays the role of the word 'not' in language. At most the ideationist is committed to holding that, at least sometimes, a sentence containing a negative particle is used by a speaker to express a negative thought – and that thinkers are capable of imagining negative states of affairs. The latter claim seems entirely uncontroversial, because it would be very hard to deny that creatures altogether lacking language can nonetheless *perceive* negative states of affairs – for instance, that a dog can see that its dish is empty or that its master has gone. And if these states of affairs can be perceived, then they can also be *imagined*, at least by creatures with a capacity for imagination. (Whether *dogs* have such a capacity is another question, but human beings certainly do.) Moreover, the suggestion that human beings were simply *incapable* of entertaining negative thoughts before the inception of language is surely unsupportable: a creature so cognitively limited would simply be incapable of developing or learning language in the first place.[15] If anything, then, the problem of negation, rather than being a problem for ideationism, is a problem for its *opponents* – particularly those who are wedded to a strong version of the doctrine that thought requires language.[16]

---

[15] I take comfort from the fact that even so doughty a supporter of Frege and Wittgenstein as Michael Dummett is driven to the expedient of allowing languageless creatures to possess what he rather condescendingly calls 'proto-thoughts', partly in order to accommodate this sort of problem: see his *Origins of Analytical Philosophy* (London: Duckworth, 1993), chs. 12-13.

[16] For further reflections on the ideational theory of language and its merits, see my *Locke on Human Understanding*, ch. 7.

7

Self-knowledge

As I indicated in section 2 of chapter 1, I favour an analysis of the concept of selfhood which ties it to the possession of certain kinds of first-person knowledge, in particular *de re* knowledge of the identity of one's own conscious thoughts and experiences. Here I want to defend this analysis more fully. My defence of it will then lead me to explore the nature of *demonstrative reference* to one's own conscious thoughts and experiences. Such reference, I shall argue, is typically 'direct', in contrast to demonstrative reference to all physical objects, apart from those that are parts of one's own body in which one can localize sensations or which are directly subject to one's will. My conclusion will be that the semantic distinction between 'direct' and 'indirect' demonstrative reference helps to delineate the metaphysical boundary between oneself and the rest of the world. But, consistently with what I have argued for elsewhere in this book, I do not contend that one is to be *identified* with one's own body: indeed, I shall offer additional reasons for thinking that one can know *a priori* that no such identity can obtain.

1. SELFHOOD AND FIRST-PERSON KNOWLEDGE

The question 'What is the self?' may be understood in two different ways – as a request for the *meaning* of the term 'self', or as a request for an account of the *nature* of the self. Theories of the nature of the self may differ widely – some, for instance, regarding it as a substance and others not, with some of those that do regarding it as a material substance while others regard it as immaterial. But if these theories are not to talk past each other, they must at least agree about what they are supposed to be theories *of*: they must agree, that is, at least as to what is *meant* by the 'the self'. Accordingly, one would hope that

182

some account of the meaning of this term can be given which is neutral with respect to the various rival theories of the self's nature – a hope I shall try to fulfil. But I myself am not neutral regarding such theories, and shall argue that some are better able than others to explain certain characteristics of propositions expressed with the aid of that term and allied expressions.

What, then, do we mean by 'the self', or 'a self'? I should say at once that I do not take this to be a question of lexicography: what I am seeking is a philosophically helpful analysis of the concept of the self, not mere reportage on everyday usage of the term. With this in view, perhaps the obvious place to start is with the phenomenon of *first-person reference*. We might venture to say, thus, that by a *self* we mean a possible object of first-person reference: something that can refer to itself as 'I' – or, since we don't want to insist that a self be capable of articulating its thoughts in language, something capable of entertaining first-person thoughts. A self, then, is something that can think that *it iself* is thus and so – where the construction 'it itself' is to be understood (like Castañeda's reflexive pronoun 'he*') as a device for reporting in indirect speech thoughts which would appropriately be expressed by the thinker in the first person.[1] That is, if something is reported to think that it itself is thus and so, it is characterized as having a thought which it would be appropriate for it to express (in English) by saying '*I* am thus and so'. Of course, I do not want to imply that anything that utters a sentence capable of expressing a first-person thought is therefore a self: the computer that displays 'I am ready' on its screen is not on that account to be regarded as a self, because it is *not* thereby expressing the thought that it itself is ready, nor indeed any thought at all.

But there is arguably more to being a self than just being able to entertain first-person thoughts. Being a self plausibly implies possessing first-person knowledge about oneself. In particular, I suggest, being a self implies knowing, of certain thoughts, experiences and actions, that they are *one's own* – indeed, that they are exclusively one's own. That is to say, it is a logically necessary condition of selfhood that a self should know that it itself is the unique subject of certain thoughts and experiences and the unique agent of certain actions. Here I might add

---

[1] Cf. Hector-Neri Castañeda, "He": A Study in the Logic of Self-Consciousness', *Ratio* 8 (1966), pp. 130-57.

that while it will normally also be the case that a self knows that it itself is the unique possessor of a certain physical body, I do *not* consider that it is a logically necessary condition of selfhood that a self should know this (which is not to deny that physical embodiment may itself turn out to be a logically necessary condition of selfhood, though I myself am doubtful even of this). The reason why I do not insist on such bodily self-knowledge as a condition of selfhood is twofold. First, it is conceivable that two different selves might share a single body (as indeed some interpretations of brain-bisection cases propose), so that one cannot insist that a self should know that it itself is the *unique* possessor of any physical body. Secondly and more radically, however, it is possible for the self to exist in a condition – for instance, one of complete sensory deprivation – in which it may have no idea which, if any, physical body it possesses. (If physical embodiment *is* a logically necessary condition of selfhood, then, of course, such a sensorily deprived self may, if it has sufficient philosophical acumen, be able to know that it itself possesses *some body or other*, but it won't have identifying knowledge of that body.)

But let us now examine in more detail the kinds of self-knowledge that the self necessarily possesses. In particular, consider my claim that the self necessarily knows that it itself is the unique subject of certain thoughts and experiences. The obvious question to ask here is this: *which* thoughts and experiences are they of which the self necessarily knows that it itself is the unique subject? A seemingly equally obvious answer would be to say, quite simply: *its own*. But such an answer would be in one sense clearly false and in another sense merely trivially true, so that neither of these senses will do. To see that the answer is in one sense clearly false, consider whether the self necessarily knows that it itself is the subject of its own *unconscious* thoughts or *past* experiences. In one sense, plainly not. So perhaps we should amend the answer to say that the self necessarily knows that it itself is the unique subject of its own *present, conscious* thoughts and experiences. But now consider the sense in which both this and the original answer are just trivial. *Of course* I know that *I* (and I alone) am the subject of *my own* thoughts and experiences (whether or not they be present and conscious) – just as I know that *you* (and you alone) are the subject of *your own* thoughts and experiences. The way around this difficulty, however, is to distinguish between *de re* and *de dicto* knowledge of this sort. Taken *de dicto*, such knowledge claims are indeed unremarkable and thus not especially revelatory of oneself: they scarcely qualify as expressions of *self*-knowledge, since they arise purely from a general understanding of the principle of individuation of thoughts and experiences, that is, from a grasp of the fact that thoughts and experiences are individuated by their subjects (inasmuch as different subjects cannot, logically, have numerically the same thought or experience). The interesting and significant way to take the knowledge claims is, of course, to take them *de re*. I necessarily know, of any present conscious thought or experience that is my own, that I (and I alone) am the subject of that thought or experience. But then I *don't* of course necessarily know, of any of *your* present conscious thoughts or experiences, that you are their subject. So asymmetry between knowledge of self and knowledge of others is restored, and hence we can indeed speak of such *de re* knowledge as genuine *self*-knowledge.

But now a further question arises. Suppose, as I claim, it is necessary that a self should know, of any present conscious thought or experience that is its own, that it itself is the unique subject of that thought or experience.[2] How, exactly, should we suppose such knowledge to be represented in the mind of that subject? Or, to give the question a linguistic cast, by means of what sort of sentence should we expect such knowledge to be expressed by the self, assuming it to be capable of articulating its thoughts? In particular, *under what guise* may the self make reference to those thoughts and experiences of which it necessarily knows that it itself is the unique subject? My proposal is that these thoughts and experiences are precisely the ones to which the self may make what I shall call *direct demonstrative reference*. Thus, what a self knows, when it knows of a certain present conscious experience that it itself is the subject of that experience, would typically be expressible by that self by means of a sentence like '*This* experience is *my* experi-

---

[2] It may be worried that clinical conditions such as schizophrenia and so-called multiple personality syndrome present a challenge to this claim. I think not. I cannot discuss the issue in any detail, but either such conditions involve a genuine multiplicity of selves or they do not. If they do (which I very much doubt), then they only imply a novel form of communication between selves. If they do not, then consider the nature of the delusion that the self is under. The self seems, say, to 'hear voices', not realizing that it is just receiving messages from its own subconscious. But then the self correctly identifies these 'seemings to hear' as *its own* conscious experiences, and only fails to identify as its own the unconscious thoughts which give rise to those experiences. So this is not a case of a self failing to identify as its own any of its own present *conscious* thoughts *or* experiences, and hence not a counterexample to my claim.

185

ence', where the expression '*this* experience' is used to make direct demonstrative reference to the experience in question. And my claim is that the *de re* knowledge that the self always has of the identity of its own present conscious thoughts and experiences is always expressible by the self by means of such sentences (provided, that is, that the self can articulate its knowledge at all, which I do not insist that it can).

Before proceeding, I need to explain what I mean by 'direct demonstrative reference'. By *direct* demonstrative reference, then, I mean demonstrative reference which is not *indirect*, and by *indirect* demonstrative reference I mean demonstrative reference which depends for its success upon the (perhaps only implicit) performance of one or more independent acts of reference. To illustrate: we have just left a party in a hurry after another guest has insulted you, and I remark to you '*That person* was insufferably rude'. Here I make demonstrative reference to the insulting guest: but how is the reference of the demonstrative phrase 'that person' fixed in such a case? I would urge that it is implicitly fixed (for both speaker and hearer) by the sense of a certain definite description – in this case, most plausibly by some such description as 'the person who insulted you just now'.[3] (If, in the case imagined, you were to ask me 'Whom do you mean by "that person"?', my answer would be precisely to utter that description or something like it.) But, clearly, I can only use the description 'the person who insulted you just now' to fix the reference of my use of the demonstrative phrase 'that person' because I am able to make certain *other* acts of reference – in particular, a reference to *you* by means of the second-person pronoun and a reference to *the present time* by means of the word 'now'. So I only manage to make demonstrative reference to the insulting guest because I am able to rely on one or more *independent* acts of reference: hence I describe this as a case of *indirect* demonstrative reference.

Notice, incidentally, that in such a case I don't say that the demonstrative phrase 'that person' is *synonymous* with, or possesses the *same sense* as, the reference-fixing description 'the person who insulted you just now' – that would clearly be incorrect.[4] So there is no suggestion

[3] I myself would be happy to endorse a Russellian analysis of such a definite description, rather than regard it as involving a 'referential' use in Keith Donnellan's sense: see his 'Reference and Definite Descriptions', *The Philosophical Review* 75 (1966), pp. 281-304. I borrow the phrase 'fix the reference', of course, from Saul Kripke: see his *Naming and Necessity* (Oxford: Basil Blackwell, 1980), pp. 53ff.

[4] Cf. Kripke, *Naming and Necessity*, pp. 57-8.

in my proposal that when I assert 'That person was insufferably rude' what I say is analytically equivalent to 'The person who insulted you just now was insufferably rude'.[5] This point will be seen to be of some importance later.

2. REFERENCE TO ONE'S OWN THOUGHTS AND EXPERIENCES

Now, however, I need to defend my proposal that, as far as thoughts and experiences are concerned, all and only *the self's own* present conscious thoughts and experiences are available to it as possible objects of direct demonstrative reference. Consider first, then, how one may make demonstrative reference to *another's* thoughts and experiences. Suppose, for instance, I see a rock fall one someone else's toe and exclaim '*That pain* must be excruciating'. If you ask me 'What do you mean by "that pain"?', I shall perhaps say 'The pain which that rock caused that person to feel just now', so that my act of demonstrative reference to the pain relies upon my ability to make independent reference to a rock, a person and a time. It is no accident, incidentally, that reference to a *person* is required here – for, as I have remarked already, experiences are individuated by their subjects (see chapter 2, section 2, and my further remarks below). It may be true that in practice, in answer to your question 'What do you mean by "that pain"?', I might just say 'The pain which that rock caused just now' – making no reference to the person whose pain it was. But I can only say this because I feel entitled to assume that the latter description is in fact uniquely satisfied, because I can normally assume that when a rock falls on a human toe there is just *one* person whose toe it is and who feels pain as a result. However, this latter assumption has no logical guarantee since, as I remarked earlier, it is

---

[5] Consequently, it might still be held that 'that person' here functions as a device of 'direct reference' in *David Kaplan's* sense, according to which 'The "direct" of "direct reference" means unmediated by any propositional component, not unmediated *simpliciter'* and hence that 'Whatever . . . mechanisms there are that govern the search for the referent, they are irrelevant to the propositional . . . content': see his 'Afterthoughts', in J. Almog *et al.* (eds.), *Themes from Kaplan* (New York: Oxford University Press, 1989), p. 569. It seems to me that my use of the adjective 'direct' is more natural than Kaplan's, so I shall stick to it and trust this note to dispel any possible confusion.

perfectly conceivable that two different persons or subjects of experience should share part or all of their bodies (as indeed Siamese twins
do).

It appears, then, that I can only ever make *indirect* demonstrative
reference to another person's thoughts and experiences, even when
those thoughts and experiences are presently occurring to a person
whom I can currently observe. But what about *my own* present
conscious thoughts and experiences? When I feel a sudden twinge
in my tooth and say to myself '*This pain* is awful', must my act of
demonstrative reference be likewise indirect? I should say not. (Of
course, I *can* on occasion make indirect demonstrative reference to my
own present conscious thoughts and experiences – for instance, if I see
someone in a mirror wincing, not realizing that it is in fact myself, and
hence not realizing that the pain to which I make indirect demonstrative reference as 'that pain' is in fact identical with the one which I
know myself now to be experiencing.) It seems clear, indeed, that it
simply cannot be the case that demonstrative reference to my own
present conscious thoughts and experiences must always be indirect. If
that were the case, then whenever, for instance, I refer to a present
pain of mine as 'this pain', it would have to be the case that the
reference of this demonstrative phrase is only fixed for me by the
sense of some definite description involving independent acts of reference on my part. But very often – normally, indeed – no such
description is or could be required. Thus when I remark, concerning
the sudden twinge in my tooth, '*This pain* is awful', what description
could plausibly be supposed to be required by me to fix the reference of
my use of the phrase 'this pain'? No likely candidate appears forthcoming. A description such as 'the pain which this tooth is now
causing me' can't possibly be required, for I don't need to know
which tooth is hurting me in order to make demonstrative reference
to the pain I feel. Then what about, quite simply, a description such as
'the toothache which I am now feeling'? But can it seriously be
suggested that demonstrative reference by me to my own current
toothache necessarily relies, even if only implicitly, upon an independent act of reference to *myself*? That would seem to suggest that without implicitly specifying to myself that it is *my* toothache to which I
intend to refer as 'this pain', I might mistakenly take myself to be
referring to someone else's – a suggestion which is patently absurd. In
contemplating that suggestion one is again put in mind of Mrs

Gradgrind's bizarre response when asked on her sickbed whether she was in pain: 'I think there's a pain somewhere in the room, but I couldn't positively say that I have got it.'[6] Of course, if *someone else* (overhearing my soliloquy) asks me 'What do you mean by "this pain"?', I may indeed respond by saying 'The toothache which I am now feeling': but that is only because I know that my *auditor* needs some such description to fix the reference of my use of the demonstrative phrase 'this pain', and doesn't at all imply that *I* need such a description to fix its reference for *me*.

Here it may be objected that my present claims are at odds with my previous insistence that thoughts and experiences are individuated by their subjects. For I now seem to be saying that at least *I* can individuate *my own* present conscious thoughts and experiences – sufficiently for the purpose of making identifying reference to them – *without* making reference to myself as their subject. But there is no real conflict here provided we distinguish, as we must, between two different senses of 'individuate'. In one sense, individuation is something that *we do* – it is a cognitive achievement. In another, individuation is a logico-metaphysical relationship between entities. For instance, when we say that sets are individuated by their members, we speak of 'individuation' in the second sense: we mean that what makes one individual set different from another is a difference in their membership. Of course, this is a fact which must be grasped by anyone who aspires to individuate sets in our *first* sense of 'individuation'. In this first sense, someone is capable of individuating a given set – say, the set of letters of the Roman alphabet – if and only if he or she is able to single it out uniquely in thought: that is, if and only if he or she knows *which* set it is. For this it is not enough simply to know that it is the set of letters of the Roman alphabet, however – one must additionally know *which letters those are* (be able to individuate *them*), precisely because the set in question is individuated (in our second sense) by the letters that are its members.

Now, returning to the objection that has been raised, we can indeed say that thoughts and experiences are individuated (in our second, logico-metaphysical sense) by their subjects (though not solely by their subjects), inasmuch as what makes one individual thought or

---

[6] Charles Dickens, *Hard Times* (Harmondsworth: Penguin Books, 1969), p. 224. I first mentioned this example in section 2 of chapter 1.

experience different from another is partly determined by the identity of their subjects: in particular, no two different subjects can be subjects of one and the same individual thought or experience (though of course they may perhaps have numerically distinct thoughts or experiences which have exactly the same propositional content or qualitative character). Consequently, if I am to be able to individuate a particular thought or experience (in our first, cognitive sense), I must at least know who its subject is (be able to individuate its subject). Now, an act of demonstrative reference to an object is only successful if the speaker or thinker, in performing that act, exercises individuating knowledge of that object. So when I refer to another's pain as 'that pain', I must exercise knowledge of whose pain it is, and that is why the reference of 'that pain' must be fixed for me by the sense of some definite description involving individuating reference to the pain's subject. But what, then, about the case of demonstrative reference to *my own* present pain as 'this pain'? Well, again it is true that part of what makes this pain the very individual pain it is, is the fact that it is *my* pain, so that unless I know whose pain it is – know that it is *mine* – I cannot successfully refer to it by means of the demonstrative phrase 'this pain'. However, in the case of my own present pain, I *necessarily* know that it is mine: that is the burden of the self-knowledge thesis which I announced earlier. But this being so, reference to *myself* as the pain's subject can exclude no possibility that is not already excluded by what I know, and consequently can play no genuine role of conferring determinacy of reference upon my use of the demonstrative phrase 'this pain' in such a case.

Incidentally, the question of *why* we have this special knowledge of our own present experiences – necessarily know of them that they are our own – is, of course, not one that I have yet addressed, nor shall I say much more about it in this chapter, interesting and important question though it is. But if I were pressed for an 'explanation', I would venture one along some such lines as the following: one's own present sensations – and other conscious experiences and thoughts – are necessarily presented to one's consciousness in a distinctive fashion which makes their ownership unmistakable, because it is a fashion in which the thoughts and experiences of another subject could not conceivably impress themselves on one's awareness. In short, we have 'privileged access' to our own, and only our own, present conscious thoughts and experiences (though not necessarily in a sense which precludes error concerning the precise *content* of those thoughts and experiences, as opposed to error concerning their *ownership*). It is not in fact clear, indeed, what more can usefully be said about this matter, so fundamental a datum does it appear to be. (Just this might be added: our own thoughts and experiences, when present and conscious, are not presented to us as *objects* of our awareness, but as *constituents* of it, and for that reason inalienably ours.)

3. THE METAPHYSICS AND EPISTEMOLOGY OF SELF-REFERENCE

I want next to focus on the epistemic, semantic and metaphysical status of propositions expressed by utterances of the type '*This* pain is *my* pain', where 'this pain' is used in the way I normally do use it to make demonstrative reference to one of my own present pains. As we have just seen, in such a case the reference of 'this pain' is plausibly *not* fixed by the sense of any definite description involving individuating reference to the pain's subject, myself – such as the description 'the pain (of such-and-such a qualitative character) which I am now feeling'. Now, it might be thought that evidence in support of this contention is provided by the fact (if one accepts it as a fact) that 'This pain is my pain', while it expresses a necessary truth, does not express an *analytic* truth, whereas 'The pain . . . which I am now feeling is my pain' is tautologous. But matters are not so straightforward, since (as was explained earlier) there should in any case be no suggestion that 'this pain' is *synonymous* with 'the pain . . . which I am now feeling', but at most a suggestion that the sense of the latter fixes the reference of the former on a specific occasion of use. If that is all it did, there would be no implication that 'This pain is my pain' ought to turn out to be analytic or tautologous.

Even so, there *is* support to be found for my position here. For even if all that is supposed is that the sense of the description 'the pain . . . which I am now feeling' fixes for me the reference of my use of the demonstrative phrase 'this pain' on a specific occasion (when I use it to refer to a present pain of mine), it still follows that 'This pain is my pain' acquires, on this account, an *epistemic* status for me which it arguably does not in fact have. If the account that I am opposing were true, it would still follow that 'This pain is my pain', although not analytic, would express a *trivial* item of knowledge for me: I would know it to be true simply by virtue of the way in which I had fixed the reference of my use of the demonstrative phrase 'this pain' on a given occasion, and even its status as a necessary truth would appear to be threatened. Indeed, it would constitute a prime candidate for Kripke's category of the contingent *a priori*[7] – whereas in fact this pain is surely mine of *de re* necessity. What suggests this threat is that this way of construing 'This pain is my pain' invites us to see it as analogous to an utterance like 'This location is my location', where 'this location' has its reference fixed by the description 'the location which I am now occupying'. That is to say, on the view which I am opposing, the possibility does not seem to be precluded that the very pain to which I refer as 'this pain' *might have been* referred to by a demonstrative phrase whose reference was fixed by the sense of a definite description involving reference to a subject distinct from myself – as though a pain which is in fact mine *might have been* another person's (just as a location which is in fact mine might have been another person's). And that is surely absurd.

I should remark that while I deny that 'This pain is my pain', used by me to speak about a present pain of mine, expresses an item of contingent *a priori* knowledge for me, it is the contingency, not the apriority, that I dispute. I am happy to allow, indeed to insist, that the truth that I thus express is one which I know *a priori*. But this might be felt to sit uncomfortably with my earlier suggestion that the special knowledge that we have of our own present experiences – that they are indeed inalienably our own – is grounded in the manner in which they are presented to our consciousness, in short, in the 'privileged access' that we have to them. For this suggestion might seem to make such knowledge just a peculiar species of empirical knowledge and consequently not *a priori*. My answer is that everything turns here on precisely what one understands by '*a priori* knowledge'. As I understand it, however, the *a priori* status of a knowledge claim doesn't have to do with how that knowledge was *acquired* but rather with how that claim might be *justified*. Thus, for example, mathematical knowledge that five plus seven equals twelve is *a priori*, notwithstanding the fact that such knowledge may have been acquired empirically (say, by counting sets of beads). So, knowledge which is acquired through, or with the aid of, experience – and thus for example through the

---

[7] See Kripke, *Naming and Necessity*, p. 56.

kind of 'privileged access' adverted to earlier – may none the less have an *a priori* status. The mark of an *a priori* truth, I should say, is this: that if a subject comprehends the proposition in question (and such comprehension may indeed call upon experience of an appropriate sort), then he or she need have no further recourse to experience as a source of evidence to justify a claim to know it to be a true proposition. And this, it seems to me, is precisely how matters do stand with regard to the proposition expressed by the sentence 'This pain is my pain', used by me to speak about a present pain of mine. I, the subject, could very arguably not even comprehend which proposition (if any) was expressed here in the absence of appropriate experience (namely, present consciousness of that pain): but given it, I certainly need no further recourse to experience as a source of evidence to justify my claim to know that that proposition is true.

'This pain is my pain', used by me to speak about a present pain of mine, expresses a metaphysically necessary truth which I know *a priori*: or so I have claimed. But what, if any, significance does this have for views of the nature of the self? Recall my distinction, at the outset of this chapter, between accounts of the meaning of the term 'self' and theories of the nature of the self. What I now want to say is that only a certain sort of *substantival* theory of the self can do justice to the epistemic and metaphysical status which propositions such as those expressed by 'This pain is my pain' appear to have.

In order to see this, we need to turn our scrutiny away from expressions like '*this* pain' and towards expressions like '*my* pain'. What does it mean to say that a certain pain is *mine*? That in part depends on how we see the first-person pronoun 'I' as securing its reference. Although it is not a demonstrative pronoun, we can still ask whether it achieves its reference in a 'direct' or an 'indirect' way. (*Some* uses of *some* personal pronouns clearly do involve 'indirect' reference – for instance, in our example earlier of the insulting guest, I *could* simply have remarked '*He* was insufferably rude', and again it appears that the reference of this use of 'he' is fixed by the sense of some such definite description as 'the person who insulted you just now'.) But could it seriously be supposed that 'I' is *ever* used in an 'indirect' way? Well, yes, in the sense that some philosophers have advanced theories of the self which seem to imply that this is how we should expect 'I' to function. In particular, on a 'Humean' constructivist view of the self,[8] which sees it as a 'bundle of perceptions' – a set or aggregate of causally interrelated thoughts and experiences – it appears that 'I' must have its reference fixed, on any occasion of its use, by the sense of some such definite description as 'the subject of *these* thoughts and experiences', where the demonstrative phrase singles out (presumably in a 'direct' way) a number of compresent or 'co-conscious' thoughts and experiences. For if the very identity of the self is determined by the identity of the thoughts and experiences it contains (or is comprised of), it seems that there is no way in which individuating reference can be made to a self – even by that very self – save via reference to its thoughts and experiences.

However, if the reference of 'I' *were* in general fixed by the sense of the description 'the subject of *these* thoughts and experiences', then it would seem that a proposition such as that expressed by '*This* pain is *my* pain', though not analytically true (for reasons explained earlier) would, none the less, once again fail to have the epistemic and metaphysical status it plainly appears to have. The proposition in question would again be trivial in a way in which it doesn't in fact appear to be (trivial because it is trivial that *this* pain is one of *these* experiences). So what I am claiming is that not only is demonstrative reference to one's own present conscious thoughts and experiences normally direct, but so too, always, is one's reference to oneself by means of the first-person pronoun. And, indeed, it is precisely because *both* sides of the equation in an utterance such as '*This* pain is *my* pain' involve direct reference that the *a priori* status of the proposition expressed cannot be explained as arising merely from the way in which we fix the reference of either of the referring expressions concerned. Thus its status is *not* akin to that of the proposition expressed by 'I am here now', which does not convey any substantive metaphysical truth concerning *de re* necessity but derives its *a priori* status purely from the semantic properties of the referring expressions involved.[9] The truth which '*This* pain is *my* pain' expresses is a substantive piece of self-

---

[8] It is true that explicit endorsement of such a view is rarely seen these days, but many important contemporary theorists of personal identity espouse views which are recognizably its heir and which are subject to the same line of criticism – most notably, perhaps, Derek Parfit in his *Reasons and Persons* (Oxford: Clarendon Press, 1984). I discuss and criticize such neo-Humean views in chapter 2, section 2, above.

[9] For an interesting discussion of 'I am here now' as an example of the contingent *a priori*, see Graeme Forbes, *Languages of Possibility: An Essay in Philosophical Logic* (Oxford: Basil Blackwell, 1989), ch. 6.

knowledge – knowledge which, indeed, I am privileged to come by easily, but which others would need to take considerable trouble to discover. Nothing comparable obtains in the case of 'I am here now'.

I have argued, then, that a proper grasp of the nature of the knowledge which one possesses concerning the identity of one's own present conscious thoughts and experiences is inimical to a non-substantival theory of the self such as the Humean 'bundle' theory or its modern heirs. The self must be conceived of as having the status of a substance *vis-à-vis* its thoughts and experiences – they are 'adjectival' upon it (are 'modes' of it, in an earlier terminology), rather than it being related to them rather as a set is to its members. And indeed this is precisely what we should expect in the light of our earlier remarks about the individuation of thoughts and experiences – for there we argued that *they* depend for their identity upon the identity of the subjects possessing them, rather than *vice-versa*, as the 'bundle' theory would imply (recall that sets are individuated by their members, and 'bundles' – however we precisely interpret that term – are like sets in this respect). This, too, is what we concluded in our discussion of the 'neo-Lockean' view of the self in section 2 of chapter 2.

But if the self is a substance, can we say any more about what *kind* of substance it must be? Can it, in particular, be identified with the substance that is the self's body (or indeed any bodily part of that, such as the brain)? Plainly not – for I have already pointed out that it is perfectly conceivable that different selves should share the same body (indeed, they may even share the same brain, and not merely by occupying different hemispheres, as is sometimes supposed in the brain-bisection cases). Bodies, then, are shareable between selves (as are parts of bodies) – but thoughts and experiences are not. Hence bodies (and their parts) cannot serve to individuate thoughts and experiences as selves do. That is to say, what makes one individual thought or experience different from another is not determined by the identity of the body associated with it, since two otherwise indistinguishable thoughts or experiences could be had by two selves sharing the same body. (Again see chapter 2, section 2, above.) Moreover, one and the same thought or experience could be equally closely associated with two different bodies, in the converse case of a single self enjoying simultaneous possession of two different bodies.[10] Consequently, bodies cannot themselves *be* selves, since they could not in principle satisfy the condition of self-knowledge that selfhood entails: for even if a body could in some sense 'know' that a certain thought or experience 'belonged' to it, it could not be guaranteed (as a self is) to know that it itself was the unique subject of that thought or experience, since it could not even be guaranteed to 'know' that that thought or experience 'belonged' to *it alone*. Therefore, I know *a priori* that 'I am this body' is necessarily false. (The same conclusion follows if 'bodily part' is substituted for 'body' throughout.)

This argument, it should be observed, does not employ the Cartesian method of doubt – it does not appeal to the fact that I can doubt whether this body exists (or whether I have a body at all) but cannot doubt whether I exist. Such arguments inevitably fall foul of the objection that they ignore the opacity of propositional attitude contexts. But my argument only appeals to semantic and logico-metaphysical considerations. Nor is my conclusion one that specifically favours a Cartesian conception of the self – for my conclusion is only that the self is not to be identified with its body, not that the self is a non-physical, non-extended substance capable of existing in separation from any physical body whatever – which is much too strong a conclusion to be warranted by any of the semantic and logico-metaphysical principles that I have appealed to.[11]

4. DEMONSTRATIVE REFERENCE TO PHYSICAL OBJECTS: AGAINST THE LIBERAL VIEW

I want to move on now to examine a little further the notion of 'direct demonstrative reference', in particular by inquiring into its range of application to physical objects in the environment of the speaker or thinker. How must physical objects be related to me if I am to be able to make direct demonstrative reference to them – if indeed I can do so at all? The thesis I shall argue for is that any given person may make direct demonstrative reference to certain distinguished parts of his or her own body, but not to any other physical

---

[10] For my view of what it is for a self to 'possess' a given body, see chapter 2, section 4, above.
[11] For a full account of my own positive views on the nature of the self, see chapter 2, sections 3 to 5, above.

objects – demonstrative reference to these must always be 'indirect'. *Which* distinguished parts? In brief, those over which the person has voluntary control – those which he or she can move 'at will' – and those in which he or she can localize sensations of any sort. (For many of the bodily parts concerned, both criteria will be met.) The reason for this will emerge in due course. First, though, I need to challenge the more liberal view that direct demonstrative reference can be made to *other* physical objects, and also the less liberal view that direct demonstrative reference cannot be made to *any* physical objects, at least under the description 'physical'. (I make this last qualification to accommodate those who would regard conscious thoughts and experiences, to which their subjects *can* in my view make direct demonstrative reference, as identical with certain physical items, namely, certain states of those subjects' brains and nervous systems – though I hasten to add that I myself am not an adherent of any such psychophysical identity theory, as will be clear from chapters 2 and 3.)

So let us consider first the thesis that I can make direct demonstrative reference to physical objects other than certain distinguished parts of my own body. Recalling our earlier example of the insulting guest, it may be thought that the reason why in that case my use of the demonstrative phrase 'that person' was indirect was simply that at the time of speaking the person in question was no longer observable either by me or by you, my audience – and this in turn might lead one to assume that where a physical object *is* currently observable direct demonstrative reference to it by an observer must always be possible. Thus it might seem that if a chair, say, is currently in full view, I may make direct demonstrative reference to it as 'that chair' – recalling here that what this implies is that the reference of the demonstrative phrase 'that chair' on such an occasion of use is *not* fixed for me by the sense of any definite description involving individuating reference to any further object.

But suppose, now, that *more than one* chair is currently in view: what makes it the case that my use of the demonstrative phrase 'that chair' refers to one rather than another of these chairs? Perhaps I accompany my utterance of the expression by a demonstrative gesture – I point with my finger at a particular one of the chairs. That, however, suggests that the reference of 'that chair' is fixed for me by the sense of the definite description 'the chair at which I am now pointing with this finger', so that the demonstrative reference to the chair qualifies as *indirect* by virtue of depending on my capacity to refer both to *myself* and to a particular *finger* of mine. But maybe it will be replied that such a gesture is only needed in order to render the object of my act of demonstrative reference unambiguous *for my audience* (if I have one) – that I myself need no such aids to disambiguation. However, we can still ask what determines it *for me* that I am referring to one rather than another of the chairs, even in the absence of a pointing gesture. It is no good just insisting that I *know* which one I mean: that is not in dispute – the question at issue is *in virtue of what* I know this. *How* do I manage to 'mean' one rather than another of the chairs presently observable? Perhaps indeed I have fixed my scrutiny on just one of these chairs: but that alone does not compel my use of the phrase 'that chair' to refer to the one that I am scrutinizing – I could still mean to refer to the one that I see only out of the corner of my eye, in the periphery of my field of vision. Thus I am not at all persuaded by Gareth Evans's remark that 'it is the fact that I have my gaze fixed upon the thing . . . that determines which object is the object of my thought.'[12] Consequently, it seems to me that in such a case as this the reference of my use of the demonstrative phrase 'that chair' will indeed have to be fixed for me by the sense of some definite description – it *might* be the description 'the chair on which I am now fixing my gaze', or it might be one such as 'the chair which I can see on my extreme left out of the corner of my eye' – but either way the implication must be that my reference to the chair involves 'indirectness' in my sense, if only because it relies on implicit reference to *myself*. (I might remark, by the way, that we needn't suppose a speaker or thinker to have any such definite description in the forefront of his or her mind when using a demonstrative expression like 'that chair' in this way: the sense of the description may do its job of reference-fixing at a relatively unconscious level, though one would expect the speaker or thinker to be able to recover the relevant description upon reflection.)

However, now it may be objected that the argument so far at best only establishes a relatively weak thesis, namely, that when two very similar physical objects are simultaneously in view, such as two chairs, reference to either of them as 'that chair' must be a case of indirect demonstrative reference – whereas what I need to establish is the

[12] Gareth Evans, *The Varieties of Reference* (Oxford: Clarendon Press, 1982), p. 173n.

apparently much stronger claim that demonstrative reference to any such physical object is never direct, even when it is the sole such object in view. In fact, though, it seems to me that the move from the weaker to the stronger conclusion is relatively unproblematic. Cases of actual observable multiplicity only serve to make the indirect nature of all such demonstrative reference more evident. One way to show this is to point out that in any case in which such multiplicity is lacking, it must, plausibly, be possible to introduce it without this affecting the mode of reference to the originally unaccompanied object. For there is no guarantee that a speaker or thinker will *notice* whether or not another similar object is in view, and hence if he or she refers to the originally unaccompanied object as, say, 'that chair', then the reference must be secured in a way that is insensitive to the fact of whether or not another similar object actually *is* in view, and consequently in the same way as it is in the multiple case. (Incidentally, if it is wondered why the possibility of multiplicity does not create similar difficulties for direct demonstrative reference in the case of the self's own present conscious thoughts and experiences, the answer is that no such possibility arises in the latter case: for it is impossible to experience two qualitatively indistinguishable sensations or to think two exactly similar thoughts at one and the same time, in the way that one may simultaneously see two exactly similar chairs.)

5. AGAINST THE STRICT VIEW: WHY ONE'S OWN BODY IS SPECIAL

I concede that the argument of the previous section might be challenged, though I shall not pursue the matter further here as it could easily provide the topic of another chapter as long as this one. Suppose, however, that we *do* accept the conclusion of that argument: then it may be wondered how we can resist the second and rival thesis that *all* demonstrative reference to physical objects, including all parts of one's own body, has to be indirect. If my reference to a chair which I can see as 'that chair' has to be indirect, how can it be any different in principle with a *foot* or a *hand* that I can see or feel or move, even if it happens to be my own? That would suggest that even when I seem best placed to refer directly to one of my own hands as 'this hand', the reference of this demonstrative expression is still only fixed for me by the sense of some such definite description as, perhaps, 'the hand which I see in such-and-such a portion of my visual field', or 'the hand which is the locus and/or cause of these sensations', or 'the hand which is moved by an exercise of the will such as this one' (said as I endeavour to move it). Thus my demonstrative reference to the hand would at the very least depend implicitly on reference either to *myself* (for instance, as its observer or as its owner) or else to certain of my own *thoughts or experiences*. Let us consider these two possibilities in turn, beginning with the second.

Now, my hand is a part of my body which I can move 'at will', that is, as a 'basic' action – though, of course, I *can* also move it in a non-basic way, for instance by pushing it with my foot, or by pulling with my other hand on a rope attached to it.[13] It is also a part of my body in which I can localize sensations of various kinds – for example, of pain, warmth and pressure – all of which I can feel 'in' my hand. So let us consider what these achievements imply for the thesis now under examination. When I move my hand 'at will', I must of course make *that very hand* the object of my volition – the movement must ensue as a result of my endeavouring simply to *move that hand* (in a certain envisaged way). But I can only make that hand the object of my volition if I can *individuate* it – single it out in thought – quite unambiguously. And, likewise, when I characterize the phenomenal aspect of a certain pain by saying that I feel it *in a particular hand of mine*, I must again be able to individuate my hand in order to make effective reference to *it* in characterizing the pain in that way. (Note, by the way, that I do not claim that sensations literally *are* located in bodily extremities – or indeed anywhere – merely that their phenomenal character *presents them* as localized in certain identifiable bodily parts.) But the foregoing points appear to undermine any suggestion that demonstrative reference by me to one of my own hands must at the very least rely implicitly upon reference to thoughts or experiences of mine (volitions or sensations) standing in certain special relationships (such as causation) to that hand. For if I could only individuate this hand as the hand which is the object of this or that volition or the

---

[13] The *locus classicus* for the notion of a 'basic' action is Arthur C. Danto, 'Basic Actions', *American Philosophical Quarterly* 2 (1965), pp. 141-8. I use the expression 'at will' in the way Bernard Williams does in his 'Deciding to Believe', reprinted in his *Problems of the Self* (Cambridge: Cambridge University Press, 1973): see p. 148. For a detailed account of my own views about voluntary action, including 'basic' action, see chapter 5 above.

site of this or that sensation, then since these volitions and sensations must *already* carry individuating reference to this hand by virtue of their intrinsic intentional content or phenomenal character, a vicious circularity would appear to ensue. Thus, if I describe myself as endeavouring to move *this* hand, or as feeling pain in *this* hand, and then ask myself what I mean by 'this hand' in such a context, I cannot without vacuity reply 'the hand which this endeavour is directed upon' or 'the hand in which this pain is felt'.

The other possibility that we need to examine is that demonstrative reference to parts of one's own body is always indirect by virtue of relying at the very least on implicit reference to *oneself*. The suggestion, then, would be that even when I seem best placed to refer directly to one of my own hands as 'this hand', the reference of this demonstrative phrase still has to be fixed for me by the sense of some such definite description as 'the hand which *I* see in the lower left quadrant of *my* visual field', or indeed perhaps just '*my* left hand'. Now, the former kind of description – one which relies on the *observability* by the subject of the bodily part in question – plainly *cannot* always be called upon to do the job here demanded of it, for the very simple reason that cases can arise in which a subject is able, without relying on reference to anything outside himself, to make demonstrative reference to certain of his own bodily parts despite *not* being in any sense able to 'observe' them. For instance, a blind person lacking all feeling in his hand may still move that hand 'at will' and this, as we have seen, requires the intentional content of his volition to move it to carry individuating reference to that very hand. Moreover, even when one *can* see the hand which one is endeavouring to move, thinking of it under a description like 'the hand which I see in such-and-such a portion of my visual field' may not be appropriate for the purpose of directing one's volition upon it. (This is illustrated by the parlour game in which children entwine their hands and have to say which is their own – often one can only tell by endeavouring to move one's own hand in a certain manner and seeing which of the entangled hands moves in that manner, and this requires one to individuate one's own hand in a non-observational way in endeavouring to move it.)

But what, then, of such descriptions as 'my left hand', which do not rely for their individuating power upon the observability of the bodily part described? One immediate and obvious objection to the suggestion that such descriptions are needed to fix the reference of demonstrative expressions used by the self to refer to bodily parts like its own hands is that it seems absurd to suppose that I need to specify that a hand is *mine* in order to make it an object of my volition – for the idea that I might move *another's* hand 'at will' (that is, as a basic action) is just incoherent.[14] Another consideration is that a subject may well only be able to differentiate between his left and his right precisely by relating those orientations to his two different hands: he may think of his *left* as being the side on which *this* hand is located and his *right* as being the side on which *that* hand is located, in which case he could not without circularity individuate *this* hand by the description 'my left hand'. Similar considerations apply to many other bodily descriptions: we know to which of our bodily parts they apply only because we are *already* able to individuate those parts demonstratively, exercising that ability whenever we move those parts 'at will' or register sensations 'in' them. This is brought out by the fact that when a parent teaches a child how to apply those descriptions, he or she will very often rely on the child's ability to move or feel the bodily parts in question.

If the arguments of these last two sections are correct, it emerges that we *can* – indeed, *must* be able to – make direct demonstrative reference to *some* physical objects, but *only* to those that are bodily parts of ours which we can move 'at will' or in which we can localize feelings. No other view appears to do justice to the way in which thought about those bodily parts enters into the intentional content of our volitions and the phenomenal character of our bodily sensations. Direct demonstrative reference does not, then, extend only so far as the self and its own thoughts and experiences, but also to certain parts of its own body – and indeed this semantic boundary helps to determine the metaphysical boundary between that body and the rest of the world. My body *is* that physical object to which (or to distin-

---

[14] In section 4 of chapter 2, I argued that what actually qualifies a particular body as *mine* is precisely the fact that certain parts of it are directly subject to my will and/or loci of my sensations, and this provides an additional reason for rejecting the suggestion that I can only individuate my own bodily parts as bodily parts *of mine*, since that would now engender a circularity in the proposed account of what makes a certain body and its parts 'mine'. For instance, by that account it is (partly, at least) because I can move *this* hand 'at will' that it qualifies as one of *my* hands – but then if it is suggested that by 'this hand' I have to mean something like '*my* left hand', the explanatory force of that account is completely nullified.

guished parts of which) I am privileged to be able to make direct demonstrative reference. I might have been tempted to remark here that this conclusion underlines the non-Cartesian character of the dualism of self and body that I have been defending throughout this book – but for that fact that, of course, Descartes too urges that 'I am not merely present in my body as a sailor is present in a ship, but . . . am very closely joined and, as it were, intermingled with it, so that I and the body form a unit.'[15]

---

[15] From the *Sixth Meditation*: see J. Cottingham, R. Stoothoff and D. Murdoch (eds.), *The Philosophical Writings of Descartes*, vol. 2 (Cambridge: Cambridge University Press, 1984), p. 56.

Index

Index

functional dependency, 109, 113, 114, 115, 127
functionalism, 132

general intelligence, 124, 125, 128–9, 131, 133
geometry, 111
    projective, 113, 126, 127–8, 131, 132
gestalt formation, 132n
Gibson, J. J., 125–6, 131
Ginet, C., 146n
God, 58, 59, 69
'guesses', 104, 118, 122

Hacking, I., 162n, 165n
hallucinations, 92, 94, 96, 115, 116
Heil, J., 72n 73–4, 75n, 76n
Hobbes, T., 165
holism of the mental, 29
homo sapiens, 16, 18, 19, 20
Hoyle, F., 59
Hume, D., 8, 22, 28, 52, 158, 193, 195

'I', meaning of, 7, 8, 193–4
ideas, 93, 162, 167–8, 171–7, 179
    association of words with, 177–8
    'corresponding', 176–7
ideationism, 13, 162–8, 171–2, 179–81
identity, 22–3
    diachronic, 10, 41–3
    indeterminate, 43
    personal, 23, 40
identity-conditions, 8, 22, 25
identity theory,
    token-token, 23, 53–4, 72, 73n, 197
    type-type, 23, 53, 71–3
illusion,
    'bent stick', 94, 100–1, 115
    Müller-Lyer, 94, 100–1
illusions, 94–5, 100
    cognitive, 100
    sensory, 100, 114–15
images,
    mental, 167, 168, 179–80
    retinal, 101n 105, 124–6, 130, 133
imagination, 13, 97, 162, 163–4, 167–8, 170, 171, 175, 176, 177, 178–81
individuation, 8, 9, 10, 25, 26, 27–8, 30, 31–2, 54, 155, 185, 187, 194, 195, 200–1, 202
    of events, 27–8

of experiences, 26–30, 185, 187, 189–90, 195
inference, 105, 108, 121–2, 127
infinite regress, 148, 152–3
informational states, 119, 120
innateness, 49, 126, 127, 131, 159
intelligence,
    artificial (see also *computers*), 24, 123, 124, 128
    general, 124, 125, 128–9, 131, 133
intentional
    content, 11–12, 45, 101, 116–17, 139, 140, 147–50, 157–8, 202
    objects, 68, 92–3, 94, 95, 96–7, 99, 115, 146, 147, 155–6, 179
intentionality, 68, 164
intentions, 161n
interactionism, 10, 52–3, 57–8, 59, 60, 61, 62, 63, 64
introspection, 33, 112, 156
inverted spectrum problem, 174–5, 177
inverting spectacles, 130, 159

James, W., 154, 169
judgements, 11–12, 102, 104, 105, 107–8, 113, 115, 116, 117, 118, 122, 128

Kant, I., 32, 119
Kaplan, D., 187n
kinds,
    artefactual, 3, 17
    natural, 3–4, 17, 19
    nominal, 18, 21, 22
    substantial, 3–4, 15
knowledge 'of', 97

language (see also *linguistic*), 48, 49–50, 80, 89, 162–3, 164–6, 169–70, 180–1
    learning, 176–7
    of thought, 171
laws,
    biological, 5, 17
    natural, 3–4, 17, 20
    of conservation, 10, 55, 56–60, 61, 67, 77
    of perspective, 113–14, 125, 126–8, 131, 133
    physical, 10, 60, 61
    psychological, 32, 34
learning,
    language, 176–7
    perceptual, 139
Leibniz, G. W., 36, 57–9, 69

Index

Printed in the United Kingdom
by Lightning Source UK Ltd.
9653100001B/15-21

MANIPULATION
PAST and PRESENT